SAUL OF TARSUS

SAUL OF TARSUS
THE FIRST TERRORIST

JACK MINTER

BROWN BOOKS
PUBLISHING GROUP

Saul of Tarsus: The First Terrorist

Brown Books Publishing Group
16250 Knoll Trail Drive, Suite 205
Dallas, Texas 75248
www.BrownBooks.com
(972) 381-0009

A New Era in Publishing™

ISBN 978-1-97427-582-3
Library of Congress Control Number 2015945279

Printed in the United States
10 9 8 7 6 5 4 3 2 1

For more information or to contact the author, please go to www.JackMinter.com.

To my family

CONTENTS

Preface

In writing this book, I gave it much thought and prayer, wanting to be sure it was an honest examination of our journey here on earth, realizing that no matter how smart, driven, or righteous we might think we are, we might be mistaken. All we can do is try as best we can to make sure we are truly living in accordance to the will of our Father.

If you believe while reading this book that I have taken too many liberties in describing the historical lives of Saul and Jesus, which obviously involved filling in a lot of blanks, I am sorry. My goal in writing this was to help us see through the issues of the time of Jesus Christ and Saul and get a better sense of what their daily lives were actually like, how they lived during that time in history. No one on this side of eternity knows all that happened in their respective lives, but I knew the contrast was worth exploration.

Note, too, that in the first half of the book as I describe the respective childhoods of Jesus and Saul through to their teen years, I occasionally switch back and forth between their stories from one chapter to the other. In doing so, there are a number of scenes and important events that you will see described more than once—once from the perspective of Saul's and then from Jesus's view. I have done my best to keep the narrative's early chronology on track throughout this back-and-forth segment of the book, inserting cues here and there to help guide the reader while also avoiding any such change in perspective within any single chapter.

Also, I used different versions of the Bible depending on the tone of the manuscript at the place where I inserted the scripture.

Almost everything about these two men was opposite of one another. One was born into earthly wealth and power; the other one wasn't. One was a perfect human specimen; the other one wasn't. Both were serious students of the Father, one because he was forced to be and the other because he loved to be. One was admired for his knowledge and wealth and the other for his love and humility. One would end up killing because of his convictions, but the other willingly died for his.

They did share some similarities, however. Both of them were on a mission. Both were driven, and both were incredibly smart. Both incessantly studied the same Torah although perhaps for different reasons. Both taught others at an early age. I probably would have preferred learning from Jesus versus learning from Saul; I assume Saul's classes were difficult and a bit dry.

It must have been amazing to have been one of Jesus's intimates, to have watched him grow up and eventually grasp who he truly was—the Son of God. We know that before or right at the moment at the temple when he said to his parents that he had to be about his Father's business, he realized he was God's Son. That must have been an incredible self-revelation. Obviously, he never was too secretive about it—no shame in admitting his divine lineage, right?

Many of us have heard the saying that a "freedom fighter is someone else's terrorist." I define a terrorist as someone who kills Christians or what Islamic terrorists refer to as "infidels." That definition will have to be sufficient for this book unless you just like to argue.

Let me share with you what a bad fellow Saul truly was. To put it in terms we might understand, Saul was Osama Bin Laden on steroids. Not only did Saul plan the execution of thousands of Christians, unlike Bin Laden, he wasn't a coward hiding behind folks who blow themselves up. He would go out himself and kill or capture Christians. He was a well-known person in Israel; when he started persecuting Christians, he was probably the best-known person in the region.

Some of the things I wanted to examine in this book:

- Could you honestly meet and listen to Jesus and not be his disciple? Do we read the Word and make notes and forget who and what he truly is?

- Are we the current teachers of the law?
- Do we apply "oral" rules to others on top of or even in disagreement with what the Bible teaches?

We inherit both good and bad traits from our ancestors. We have to deal with certain physical diseases or issues that are inherited. Like those physical diseases, we inherit spiritual diseases as well. Some families might pass along gluttony or gossip to their offspring, while others must contend with other issues, such as pride. In developing the character of Saul, I saw that he had to deal with a prideful family.

As with physical diseases, you can understand what those other issues are and work at not having those hereditary flaws control your life or possibly end your life prematurely. The same goes with your spiritual heredity. You first have to understand what yours is and then work to make sure it doesn't harm or even kill you spiritually.

Our inherited issues seem to be much more difficult for us to control and defeat.

Finally, we must ask ourselves: Do we pray and give to take away God's wrath or to become closer to our Father?

—Jack Minter, the author

Acknowledgments

I want to thank my family for the initial editing of the text and Mike Towle for getting this manuscript into readable form. Many thanks to the outstanding group of professionals at the Brown Books Publishing Group. You made my ideas a published reality.

SAUL OF TARSUS
THE FIRST TERRORIST

My Foreword

T his is my story, and it begins back around the time that Jesus and I, close to each other in age, were born.

Thanks to the stories and other tidbits of remembrances told me over the years by friends, family, and other acquaintances, I have for the purpose of this narrative pieced together details not only of our respective upbringings but also of many of the particulars surrounding the people, events, and places that factored into our lives. Of course, there is a fair amount of literary license involved here, necessary in order for me to connect the dots and flesh out the story.

Obviously, I have very little memory of how I was raised and could not have known anything about Jesus's early childhood or the region and circumstances in which he was raised. However, I was deeply curious as to how we both were raised for the sake of contrast and comparison, and putting together all the pieces became an obsession for me. Along the way, I kept and stored copious notes, knowing someday that I would write some sort of autobiographical tome, which is what you see here. [Publisher's note: Saul's original manuscript has been translated from Hebrew into English, to include style updates such as referring to God as God instead of Yahweh.]

I also was interested in how Jesus was raised. Obsessed even. I was always curious when it was that Jesus learned that he was God's Son, how he interacted with his friends and family knowing that.

I do remember the first time I met him. I was thirteen years old, and he was several months, maybe even a year, younger than me. My regret now is that even then I was too prideful and arrogant to not see him like others did. I was already in direct conflict with God, and I had no clue. As I grew to hate Jesus, I decided his knowledge was from Satan and that mine was from God. When

Jesus appeared to me on the road to Damascus, I discovered I had it backwards: his influence came from the Father and mine from Satan. Pride had become my idol, and it was what I worshipped until that sin had led me to kill our Messiah and his followers.

Only now, as I write this, with my life about to end, do I see that I was used to fulfill prophecy and show the world that Jesus was the prophesied Messiah. Jesus came to sacrifice himself for us, and I played a role. I was even used by Satan, blinded by his hold over me to have the Church scattered out of Jerusalem so that all of Jesus's followers would be strewn across the Roman Empire. I did this by persecuting his followers in Jerusalem, which caused them to flee the city. This shows that God can even use the "chief of sinners" to spread his Word of love and forgiveness to all men.

As you read my story, please learn from my mistakes—take them to heart—and choose Jesus to be your Savior. Do it soon, I beg of you. It took me a long time, during which I hurt and killed a lot of innocent people, including Jesus. I hope it doesn't take you as long as it did me to turn from sin and embrace Jesus Christ as my Savior and ticket to life eternal in the most heavenly place.

—Saul of Tarsus

Prologue

I have been waiting and praying for this day for thirty years. Soon I will finally get to go see my Master, Messiah, and Teacher again face to face. The jailer is coming to my cell today to take me out to the block where they will chop off my head and end my earthly life so I can go home.

My Master knows that my work is finished here. I am Paul, an Apostle of the Lord Jesus Christ. I have been a messenger of his first to the Jews and then to the Gentiles. I am overjoyed to know that I am deemed worthy by my Master to be counted as a martyr for his Church. You see, I haven't always been a believer of this Son of God known as Jesus.

I probably have just enough time before the jailer comes to tell you my story. I was born Saul of Tarsus, the Hebrew of Hebrews. According to everyone at the temple and all of my peers and students, I was the world's most knowledgeable Jew and most influential Pharisee.

My family as well as all of the world's Jews were awaiting the Messiah promised to us by God. They told me how this Messiah would defeat all of the kingdoms of the earth and we would once again rule the world from Jerusalem. We would then be able to worship God in peace, and the glory of David and Solomon would once again be ours.

As I was growing up, I kept hearing about a certain family in Nazareth, an insignificant and dirty little town in Galilee (in what is now northern Israel) that claimed to have what is referred to in the Bible as the Messiah. The scuttlebutt was that the boy was a bastard child and that his father almost didn't marry his mother because she was with child and her pregnancy was not his doing.

Sadly, because the story was retold and because it gave credence to this boy being the Messiah, a caravan of kings and wise men came to Jerusalem to see this new Jewish Messiah. The leaders of the caravan believed that King Herod would know where this new "king of kings" was. However, Herod hadn't heard about this new Messiah; when he asked his wise men, he found out that the new Messiah should be in Bethlehem.

Herod instructed the men of the caravan to proceed to Bethlehem, only asking that if and when they found him there, they would return to Jerusalem and tell him exactly where the baby king was. He continued lying by also telling them that his intent was for him to go see the baby boy to worship him. Of course, Herod was jealous and just wanted to kill this interloper.

When the kings and wise men didn't return, Herod became enraged and proceeded to kill every boy in Bethlehem who would have been around this Messiah's age. Of course, this only gave credence to this boy being the Messiah because Herod thought strongly enough that the child was the Messiah that he murdered every boy that age in Bethlehem. How absurd. Herod was always a murderous, paranoid idiot.

I didn't hear much else about this boy named Jesus Christ until I was about twelve years old. My father, Jonathan, was a staunch Hebrew man and followed the practices of Judaism to the letter of the law. He had me studying the law day and night as soon as I was able to read. Because we were a very wealthy family, my parents could afford the best teachers and tutors for me. Even though we were from Tarsus, my family moved to Jerusalem when I was very young. My father arranged it so that I was selected to train under Gamaliel, considered the greatest teacher of the law since Solomon. Gamaliel took only a few students at a time, choosing to teach only the most dedicated and the smartest and, of course, only those who came from families able to pay for his tutelage.

Every Jew who possibly could came to Jerusalem at least once a year to attend Passover, our holiest feast. I remember one time in particular when I was thirteen years old and studying the Torah in the temple. It was the day after Passover when all of the Jews who didn't live in Jerusalem were returning home. I noticed this Jewish boy who I assumed lived outside Jerusalem enter the temple and start gawking around like most out-of-town Jews would do upon their first visit, checking things out. He began following my class around Solomon's Porch, listening in to what the rabbis and teachers of the law were teaching us.

We were behind on our lessons because of the feast. The first time I heard this boy speak was when Gamaliel asked the class a difficult question that none of us could answer. As we sat there contemplating the question that Gamaliel asked us about the Messiah, the boy answered it. We all looked at him and could see by his dress that he was an ignorant boy who had only studied a small amount of the Torah and Talmud. All of us who were being taught in the temple wore special clothes so everyone could tell we were scholars. When Gamaliel told us that his answer was correct, he asked the boy his name. The boy said his name was Jesus and that he was from Nazareth.

We were surprised that Gamaliel had even said anything to this boy stranger. By asking the boy his name, Gamaliel was allowing an outsider, who we all assumed was this bastard son from Nazareth, to join us and discuss the Torah. On top of this, he was a carpenter's son, a common laborer from Nazareth. Still, I had to admit I was amazed—I'm still amazed, in fact—at the knowledge and wisdom this commoner had. He also was a good-looking boy, immediately liked by everyone. Well, maybe not everyone. Over and over, I tried to discredit him as he spoke to us and answered our questions.

Up until then, I had been the brightest student in class. Now that Jesus was able to not only answer but also ask questions that we couldn't answer, at times going so far as to banter back and forth with Gamaliel, everyone started listening to him instead of to me. Knowing that this boy's great insight couldn't have come from his studying or learning from anyone in his synagogue, I started to reason that his knowledge and insight must have come from Satan.

It was impossible that this commoner could have such insight without help from either God or Satan. Since he hadn't studied in Jerusalem under one of the teachers such as Gamaliel or Nicodemus, the only conclusion I could come up with was that his insight and wisdom must have come from Satan—that he must be demonic. I had just known this boy Jesus a couple of hours, and already my hatred toward him was leading me down the wrong path—although I surely didn't know it at the time.

His good looks and sturdy physique made me abhor him even more since I had always been small. I'd also had a problem with my eyes; I had a difficult time seeing clearly, and my eyes tended to water a lot as I strained them. I was convinced that the issues with my eyes kept people from liking me as I much as I thought they should.

As we sat there that day, I stewed inside knowing that I would never be satisfied until I was able to best Jesus in knowledge or otherwise prove that his knowledge and wisdom were not from God but from the devil.

Once that day was over, I assumed, or at least hoped, that we had seen the last of him, that he would go about his business, or that his parents or someone else from his family would come and get him out of there for good. The next morning, however, he was back again and would keep coming back.

By the end of that first week, on the final day he was there, I heard him speak the first blasphemous words I had heard from him, saying that he was the Son of God. My first thought, which I said out loud, was that we should take him out and stone him, but no one else wanted to.

Little did we know at the time that he would start a new sect of Judaism called Christianity in which all of the converts would worship him as God's Son. When his parents found Jesus in the temple, I heard him say the words that would start my life's mission of stopping this Jesus and reconverting his followers back to Judaism. He said, "Why did you seek me? Did you not know that I must be about my Father's business?"

Having heard that, I studied, prayed, and meditated harder and longer than any of my peers. This was not so much for my own learning as it was to demonstrate to God my earnestness in discrediting Jesus. To me, it seemed I was the only one there when Jesus blasphemed who could understand what he had said and was willing to follow God's law. I felt I had been called to put an end to his blasphemy. I was distressed that the others, including my teachers, weren't around at that moment to hear the blasphemous statement for themselves and to have been likewise motivated to take him out and stone him. I vowed then to spend my life focused on searching, finding, and punishing anyone who blasphemed God. It became my life's work.

It took me several years and a lot of planning and scheming for my group of Pharisees, teachers of the law, and Zealots to finally set things up to get Jesus the so-called Messiah to blaspheme God in a public place with enough witnesses to have him beaten and killed. I had hoped to be able to stone him and some of his followers, but what we needed to make it all legitimate was for the Romans to be the ones to crucify him. Although I was disappointed, "dead is dead."

We finally killed Jesus on the cross at Calvary. At last, the man I had hated almost my entire life was dead and his followers had scattered. Judas, the one we manipulated into betraying Jesus, had killed himself as well.

I hated Jesus of Nazareth. I hated him since we had met at the temple the first time. I then focused on converting his followers back to Judaism or, if that failed, to kill them for their blasphemy. Since we executed Jesus, we thought his followers, these so-called Christians, would know he wasn't the Messiah and therefore would repent of their foolishness. I mean, how could he be the Messiah if he was dead? They should know he wasn't the one who was to reign like David and throw the Romans out of our promised land. However, I swore that even if there was only one of these Christians left after all this, I would go to the ends of the earth to have him or her brought back in chains to the high priest to be stoned to death for blasphemy.

When I stood below the cross where they had hung the blasphemous traitor to watch him die, I could have sworn with one of his final breaths, he looked straight into my eyes and gave me a little smile and a wink. I must have been dreaming.

1

In the most exquisite room in Tarsus and quite possibly in the Roman Empire, servants busily prepared for a wonderful event, my birth. The room had been added to my family's mansion when my mother, Sarah, had finally conceived me. The servants were finishing preparations for what would be the coming of the heir of their master, Jonathan, my father.

They were carefully perfuming and cleaning the room with fragrances that had been gathered from across the world. The room had been specially designed, built, and decorated for this day, and it had never been used for any other purpose or event. The floor and the large columns that ringed the room were made of alabaster. The walls were constructed of rare woods from all over the world and were inlaid with gold and gems. The ceiling had been painted by a master artist from Jerusalem; it depicted the Messiah being born and ruling the world with his army of angels and Jewish Zealots. My father had spared no costs to decorate this room. It was the perfect place for welcoming his new heir into the world.

The servants spoke in quiet yet joyful tones. They all had been waiting for this wonderful day, the day that my mother would give birth to the firstborn of this generation of both her and my father's families. Both families lived in Tarsus, and the expectant grandparents, brothers, sisters, nieces, and nephews flittered around the house offering to do whatever they could to make themselves useful; mostly they were just getting in the way. Father had thought of everything and was in complete control. His orders to the servants were clear. Even though other family members gave instructions to them, the servants knew never to deviate from my father's orders. Otherwise, they would be punished.

My parents' families were the most prominent families of Tarsus and the region, which is why it's fair to say that the whole city of Tarsus was anxiously awaiting my birth. My father's family had been very successful merchants for several generations, making them fabulously wealthy. My mother's family consisted of descendants of Aaron, and they were priests. As wealthy as my parents' families were, local citizens also respected and loved them for their generosity. Ever since my mother had been with child, everyone had waited with great anticipation because before then, she was thought to have been barren. I would be a miracle baby, an answer to many prayers, much fasting, and numerous sacrifices made by everyone in Tarsus.

For several years, my mother had prayed that she and my father would have a son. She had gone daily to the synagogue and prayed earnestly that God would grant her request. She promised God that if he would give her a child, specifically a son, she would give her son back to the Lord like Hannah had done with Samuel. Everyone in the city knew of this. The whole city and region loved Sarah because she was always generous with both her money and time.

As the time of my birth grew closer, my father paced outside the suite of rooms where Mother and her servants were working while waiting and praying for the miracle of his child to be born. My father had pleaded to God to have a son that would carry on his business, his name, and his fortune. He and his family had been merchants for many generations; their main business was making and supplying tents. They were the sole supplier for the

Roman army. They also did business with other leaders and their followers because all of them needed tents as they traveled.

My father had a wonderful business mind, and he applied it to everything he did outside of work, never missing a detail and always striving to be fully prepared. When he stopped pacing on this day, his mind just kept working in his head going over and over all the different assignments he had given the servants in order to make this birth perfect. This included being sure to cover all of the different sacrifices to be made as required under the law. As insurance, he had even doubled both the sacrifices and his donations to the synagogue to make certain he had done everything perfectly. Nothing would be left to chance. You could say he was obsessive.

Because Tarsus was a free city, everyone born there regardless of their heritage was born a Roman citizen. Still, my father was taking no chances; he had petitioned the Roman governor of the region to buy a citizenship for his soon-to-be-born child. He wanted to be certain his new son and all of his son's heirs would be free-born Roman citizens, afforded all the advantages of their wealth and Roman citizenry. Some of Jonathan's friends and many others in the Jewish community had tried to dissuade him from doing that since he was a devoted Pharisee and Zealot.

The Zealots were always praying that the Messiah would come, take God's people from the control of Romans, and reestablish us as the rulers of the world with their Messiah leading us as promised by God. The Pharisees were a sect of the Jewish religion that believed in the Torah or Scriptures, but they also believed in the "oral law" or the Talmud.

Most of the learned Jewish rabbis believed this from their studies to be true, that this awaited Messiah would be coming very soon. That's why they thought it hypocritical, even a waste of time, to become a Roman citizen, but my father paid for my citizenship anyway, wanting to make sure his descendants would be treated well by the Romans. He thought they would have an easier time in business if they were citizens.

My father had become lost in thought thinking through all this when all of a sudden, he was jolted back to reality: a young servant girl came rushing from the suite of rooms.

"What is going on?" he asked her as he grabbed her by the arm to stop her.

"It is almost time," she said breathlessly, gently pulling herself away to continue on her way.

She left in a rush and then quickly returned carrying a set of new and beautiful linens. More nervous than ever, Father resumed his pacing on expensive rugs he had just purchased on a buying trip, briefly remembering the hard bargain he had driven in buying the rugs. The seller had been in financial trouble and needed to make a sale to get some money because of an illness in his family. Jonathan figured that he bought them for half of what they were worth, and for that he allowed himself a brief smile. It always made him happy knowing he had gotten the best bargain.

Soon the door of the suite again flew open. This time the servant girl came running out to tell him that Sarah had just given birth to a healthy baby boy delivered by one of the female servants who also happened to be a midwife. Jonathan was ecstatic, joyously yelling while punching the air over his head with his fists. He had his heir to his fortune. He started walking briskly toward the door, but the servant girl told him to wait a few minutes until they had everything prepared for him to see Mother and me. My father had already decided to name me Saul because his family was from the tribe of Benjamin; the first King of Israel, who was also from the tribe of Benjamin, had been named Saul. Father kneeled on his new rugs to pray to God in thanks for the birth of his healthy baby heir:

"Father, thank you for giving me a son that will carry on the family name and will administer and grow the family's businesses. Thank you for giving this family wealth so my son will be prominent and his family will continue to be leaders like my family and I have been in going before him. Please give him wisdom so he can do well in his business dealings with everyone."

Once he had finished his prayer, my father went to the suite where he saw my mother and me, as her midwife and other servants busily cleaned me up and prepared everything for the rabbi and the doctor to come and check me out. All of the servants were as relieved as they were happy that both my mother and I were doing fine. Once my mother had recovered from the birth, she asked all the servants to kneel down while she prayed a prayer of thanksgiving to God for the safe delivery of her son and for her health:

"God, the Father of all things, thank you for blessing Jonathan and me with a son that will carry on your work in this world. Thank you for giving our family great wealth so our son, now yours, can use it to do good here on your earth. As promised, I will gladly give my son back to you to do your work. Please let him be full of your Spirit and do your work well and gratefully. Give him exceptional knowledge and wisdom to serve you faithfully."

After Mother's prayer, Father left the suite because in his revelry, he had forgotten to send out the birth announcement he had prepared. In fact, he had made up two messages, one announcing a daughter and the other a son, to be sent to a multitude of friends and business partners. When he had gotten to his study, he pulled a purple satin cord to summon a servant, who quickly came.

Father had made the builder of his house add a system of cords to be pulled so he would be able to summon a servant from anywhere in the mansion. Jonathan told the servant to send out the message announcing the birth of an heir, his son. The message was to be delivered in the city within the hour. Once that message went out, my father summoned another servant, telling him to prepare our home to receive all of the visitors he expected to come celebrate with him. He assumed that all of the prominent Jews and citizens would come to celebrate this blessed day and give gifts to the long-awaited heir.

2

One of the messengers had a long and difficult task. He had to deliver my father's message to Annas, the high priest. My father and Annas were close friends, and Annas had agreed to perform the Bris (the Jewish ritual for circumcision) if the child were a boy. The messenger was in luck, however, because instead of being in far-away Jerusalem where he lived, Annas was only a couple of days away, having temporarily moved closer to Tarsus at my father's request to be nearby because Sarah was about to give birth. Annas had agreed to embark on an "inspection" of the synagogues in the Tarsus region so he would be in the area.

Having left the room to summon and speak to his servants, my father was again approached by the servant girl to tell him to come back in and see his wife and son. The nurses had carefully washed and perfumed his new heir and then wrapped him in linen and satin. *What a beautiful sight,* my father thought, seeing me in my mother's arms. He walked over to the bed, squeezed Sarah's hand, and picked me up for a closer look, pulling back the covering and looking into my face. Years later, I would find out that when he looked into my eyes, he could see something a bit odd about them. He motioned a nurse over and asked her if she saw anything "different" about them. The nurse assured him that all babies look that way and that he was "perfect."

Right about then is when the doctor my father had commissioned to examine me upon my birth came by, asking my father to leave the suite as he examined my mother and the newborn, me. In handing me to the doctor, my father asked that he take a good look at my eyes to make sure they were fine.

After the doctor had finished checking both mother and child, Sarah asked for the nurses to return the child to her so she could feed me. She looked adoringly into my face and saw nothing wrong with the boy that God had finally given her.

As the doctor was leaving, my father asked him to join him for a glass of wine. He asked the doctor if his son was fine and if there was anything wrong with his eyes. The doctor reassured my father that I was fine, that there was nothing wrong with me. Even as the doctor politely tried to excuse himself to leave, my father poured him another drink, telling the doctor all of the things he and his son were going to do together in business. Jonathan was a proud father. Finally, as he walked the doctor to the door, the doctor reassured him that the baby boy was in perfectly good health and mentioned that my mother was doing fine as well.

While Jonathan bathed and got dressed in his suite with the assistance of servants, he reminded them to make all preparations for the invited guests who would be brought to my suite. I had been fed and clothed in exquisite clothing to look just like my namesake, the king.

Guests soon started arriving at the house, where they were greeted by lavish decorations and food brought in from all over the world placed all around the house. My father had given a list of invitees to his personal servant and told him to bring the guests in the order he had authorized from most important to the least. The servant went down into the house and started escorting the guests into my suite.

The first guest brought to my suite was the leader of the local synagogue, the rabbi, who brought me a gold and jeweled set of scrolls of the Torah and a gold-encrusted Talmud. The next guest was the leader of the Roman garrison at Tarsus, who delivered an exquisite folder made of olive wood with emeralds and other precious stones. It contained a parchment showing that I was a free-born Roman citizen. Guest after guest continued to come all day and into the evening bringing the new heir something beautiful and valuable. Another group of guests began arriving the next day, having traveled from farther away. Once again, guest after guest brought in more gifts.

After so many gifts and guests, my father was getting bored with the process. His guest of honor—the high priest from Jerusalem touring the area—hadn't even arrived yet. My father was hoping the high priest would arrive a few days ahead of the Bris so he could have plenty of time to visit with him, not only because he wanted to discuss future arrangements for Saul to go to the temple when he was ready to study the Torah but also because he wanted everyone to see that he was friends with the most powerful man in the Jewish world.

Another guest my father had hoped would come was Herod, the reigning king of the Jewish nation, who, unfortunately, was stuck in Rome dealing with politicians there to make certain he stayed in power. Jonathan knew that Herod would send someone close to him to pay tribute to his son since my father had always supported Herod in his endeavors. On the third day after I was born, three ambassadors on behalf of Herod arrived amid great flourish and ceremony. Each ambassador came with a gift, a price-less artifact of Jewish history from the great temple in Jerusalem.

On the sixth day, Annas finally arrived in Tarsus as part of his synagogue tour and to preside over my Bris. Although Annas was a Sadducee and Jonathan a Pharisee, they were both a part of the class of wealthy Jews ruling the Sanhedrin. My father sent a delegation to where he knew Annas was staying to invite him to come dine with him that evening. Once my father got word back from Annas accepting the invite, he was elated. Jonathan assembled his servants and had them get the feast prepared for Annas and his staff.

When his latest round of guests arrived for dinner, my father was delighted to see that Annas and his entourage were accompanied by Caiaphas, Annas's son-in-law, the next high priest. The dinner was as extravagant as Jonathan could make it. The group rested, dined, and discussed happenings around the Tarsus region and in Jerusalem. Once the group had eaten and relaxed, my father discussed the Bris and what needed to be prepared. To make sure that the high priest's delegation would be well fed while they were in Tarsus, my father had told his servants to take plenty of food to the synagogue where they were staying while in Tarsus. My father had also agreed to a large charitable gift that would be given at the Bris for the high priest to take back to Jerusalem. Before Annas left for the evening, my father asked him to come back the following day for a short meeting to discuss my future.

When Annas arrived the next day, he and my father retired to the study. Although it was somewhat premature to discuss my future, Jonathan wanted to make sure that Annas was prepared and agreeable to taking me into his special classes in the temple in Jerusalem to teach me the Torah and the Talmud. There would be some studying in Tarsus, but my father wanted me to have the best teacher: Gamaliel the Elder. After some discussion and a promise from my father of continued donations to the coffers in Jerusalem, Annas agreed to allow my father's request to have me educated at the temple in Jerusalem. Annas, furthermore, agreed to arrange for the purchase of a home close to the temple where my servants and I would stay while I studied.

A day later, Annas officiated over my Bris and official naming ceremony. My father spent a small fortune on the ceremony, inviting only a few family members and, of course, the most important citizens of the city to come celebrate with him.

During the ceremony, even after the nurse had done everything she could to make sure I would be quiet, I started crying. The noise and strangers had startled me. My father, most likely embarrassed, became angry and demanded that the nurse quiet me, but I'm told I just wailed all the harder. After several minutes of this, my father finally grabbed me and handed me to Annas, asking him to finish the ceremony. Annas complied, after which everyone praised God. After the circumcision ceremony, Annas asked my father what his son's name would be.

"Saul, just like the first king of Israel," my father said, explaining to everyone that the king was of the tribe of Benjamin, my father's family.

3

In telling the story of Jesus's birth, I will start by pointing out that although we were about the same age, our births and how we were brought up were very different.

I will start with Jesus's earthly parents, Joseph and Mary.

"Are you ready to go, Mary?" Joseph asked.

"I suppose so, Joseph," she said. "I hope I've brought everything we need to go to Bethlehem for King Herod's census. I have packed enough for a week, which should be enough if the weather is good and the roads are safe."

Although it would be faster to go through Samaria, Joseph had heard the roads were more dangerous. He didn't want to add any stress to the trip for Mary since she was so close to giving birth. He wished he didn't have to travel with Mary right then, but he couldn't help it. He trusted that God would keep Mary and the baby safe from harm. He had even rigged up a wagon to carry Mary and their supplies, and he had made it so that their donkey could pull it.

"Alright, Mary, I have packed everything we discussed for our trip. It seems like we are taking everything we own," Joseph said. "Thankfully, God hasn't blessed us with a lot of material things, so we don't have that much to take.

"Since I know carpentry quite well, I can make some things if Jesus is born during this trip and we end up having to stay for a while. We know we won't get any help from our families. Let's get started; the caravan will be leaving in less than an hour.

"It is great that we can join a caravan. There are quite a few of the travelers that are going to their hometowns to be counted in the census; others are traveling for business."

The caravan, numbering more than fifty people, left around midday. The caravan had enough men to be able to protect itself from bandits. It was large enough to protect itself but not so large as to be too cumbersome. If it had been any larger, it would have been difficult to find places to camp where enough feed and water would be available for their stock.

Mary and Joseph knew several of the families traveling with them and settled into the journey. Most of the group consisted of merchants headed to Jerusalem, while some were destined for other towns where they would be counted for Herod's census. King Herod had decreed that everyone that he ruled needed to go back to their hometowns to be counted.

They traveled for the rest of the day without any major problems and covered at least ten of the eighty miles they needed to travel to get to Bethlehem. After the group stopped for the day in the late afternoon, Joseph and the men set up camp, which for those people who could afford it consisted of a tent that would provide some privacy and shelter from the elements. Joseph had purchased a small, used tent in which Mary would be comfortable while he stayed just outside the door. Mary, heavy with child, was not moving around too quickly. She tried to help Joseph set up camp, but he asked her to rest, as he didn't want to risk anything that might induce labor and force her to give birth out on the trail.

Mary had made some snacks for the journey so they would not have to cook every meal. Once Joseph had finished setting up the tent, they both sat down outside the tent, where Joseph had also started a small campfire. When Mary and Joseph were ready for bed, they both prayed a prayer they had been saying together for the past nine months:

"God, we do not understand why we were chosen to be your earthly parents. We accepted your command and now we are expecting you. Continue to watch over us, and let us continue to faithfully serve you."

Mary, under her breath, then added as she always did, "And please help us be great parents and understand what all of this means."

The rest of the week followed the same general routine. Everyone was up before dawn, ate their breakfast, and packed their gear, placing it on the backs of their animals or in the carts. The caravan pulled out just after sunup and traveled until midday. At that point, they would stop, water their animals, and have lunch. While the people ate, their animals foraged nearby; since it was spring, there was new growth to be found from which the animals could feed. After resting an hour or so, the caravan would resume the trek, trudging along during the afternoon and then stopping to again make camp before nightfall.

Mary rode in a cart while Joseph led the donkey and occasionally helped pull the cart when they hit rough patches in the road. It was at times difficult for Joseph; his carpentry work hadn't prepared him for such an arduous journey. As the caravan rumbled on, the bumps sometimes jostling Mary around in the cart, Joseph would periodically move the cart's bedding around to make Mary as comfortable as possible. Several other families chipped in, donating bedding to place in the cart to make Mary more at ease.

The caravan's route took them past some landmarks, such as when they followed a path along the Jordan River. At one point, they stopped and gazed at the spot where Joshua had once made a man from each tribe of Israel carry a stone to the other side of the river in commemoration of when the river had stopped flowing in front of the Ark of the Covenant, allowing the children of Israel to cross on dry land. Farther on down, they passed the site where the tribe of Reuben, Gad, and half the tribe of Manasseh had built a large altar to the Lord so that they and the other tribes of Israel would remember that they, too, were God's saved children even though they lived on the eastern side of the Jordan River.

Farther on down, while crossing the river, Joseph became an unwitting source of humor when he slipped and fell into the water and then slipped and flopped back into the river several times while trying to get back to his feet. He was soaked. Mary thought it was hilarious, unable to stifle her laughter for about a minute. She then kidded Joseph that he must have thought he was Naaman for taking such numerous baths in the river. Joseph remembered the story from Second Kings and laughed as well.

After about a week, the caravan finally approached Jerusalem. From the Jordan River crossing, where Joseph had taken his unintentional bath, it was a steady climb to the city, the City of David, which always looked majestic on the horizon. While the caravan's main contingent continued on to Jerusalem, several smaller factions bid farewell to the rest and broke off at this point so they could head to their respective towns where they would be counted for the census. Mary and Joseph were among those who split off, in their case heading south to Bethlehem, where, if they hurried, they would be able to arrive before nightfall.

"Joseph, have you thought about where we can stay?" Mary asked. "I know there aren't many places to stay in Bethlehem, but I have prayed that God will show us such a place. Our families disowned us when we told them how Jesus was conceived."

"I know," Joseph said. "I have also prayed that God will provide us a suitable place to stay or that someone in our family has repented of their lack of faith and will let us stay with them."

Mary hadn't complained during the trip, but by the time they got to Bethlehem, she was completely exhausted and also concerned about finding a place where she could give birth to their son. She had started having contractions but didn't want to alarm Joseph, instead praying silently to God that he would provide for them.

Once they arrived in Bethlehem, Joseph stopped at every inn and home where they took in travelers; he started knocking on doors, seeking a vacancy. The answer each time: "We have no more rooms."

The only other option was to approach relatives in town.

"I wonder who in the world is banging on the back door at this hour," said Simon, one of Joseph's uncles.

"Uncle Simon, please let us stay with you," Joseph said, knowing that Simon not only owned a big house but also a carriage house for visitors. "I wouldn't have bothered you, but there are no rooms anywhere in Bethlehem since everyone has to come back for the census."

Joseph also explained to Simon that Mary was about to have the baby that God had promised. They needed not just a place to stay but also a place suitable for giving birth.

"Well, Joseph, that's the problem," Simon said. "Since you and Mary told the family about this baby and how it all came about, the family has disowned you both. We all thought it prudent that you moved to Nazareth because it would save our families from embarrassment. Your parents told all of us in both families that we can have nothing to do with either of you."

Simon wasn't finished. He continued to speak to Joseph, reminding his nephew what the family had been told, as far-fetched as it sounded, that an angel had come to both Mary and Joseph before they were married and told them that Mary was with child with God's son.

"You told us," Simon continued, "that you had not laid with her and that Mary was still a virgin. According to you, Mary said the angel had told her that she had been 'overshadowed' by God and become with child. You did the right thing when you moved to Nazareth. You know that if your parents had followed the Torah, you both would have been stoned. I doubt if any of the family will take you in."

"I understand, Simon" a downcast Joseph said. "I was just hoping that you would allow us the same courtesy you would a stranger."

Simon stood in the door for a few moments and said, "There is a small cave back on the side of the hill by the north pasture where I keep some livestock this time of year. No one knows that it is mine. You and Mary can stay there if you like. At least it is warm and dry."

"Thank you, Uncle Simon," Joseph said. "This means so much to Mary and me."

Joseph went back to Mary waiting in the cart. Saying nothing, he led the donkey slowly out of town toward the north pasture to walk the mile or so to the cave where Simon had directed him. Once they had made it there, Joseph helped Mary climb out of the cart and move inside the cave.

"This is all I could find, Mary," Joseph said. "No one in Bethlehem will let us stay with them, including Uncle Simon, who directed me to this cave. I am still amazed that God allowed Satan to have both of our parents and families disown us even after we explained to them that this baby you are having is the Son of God. We even told them that the angel Gabriel explained how this would happen.

"Well, no matter. God is with us wherever we go. Now let's see if I can get some straw away from the cows and other livestock so we can get a bed made for you in case Jesus comes tonight."

"In case?" Mary said, gasping as she started having another contraction. "Joseph, I started having this Blessed Child a few hours ago. I didn't want to bother you because I know how anxious you are about being God's father. So as soon as you get our supplies and beds in here, I think Jesus's Father will let him be born."

Joseph was startled by what he had just heard. He hadn't realized that the birth was imminent. Quickly, he moved some straw over into a corner to make Mary comfortable. It so happened that Simon had been using the cave as a stable for his livestock, and ample straw was available—it wasn't exactly a warm blanket and pillow, but it would do.

Once Joseph had Mary settled in, he returned to the cart and unloaded the supplies they needed for the night. He brought in all of the bedding and food they had and cleaned an area where the animals wouldn't be able to disturb them. He helped Mary onto the makeshift bed and looked around at the nursery that God had chosen for his Son. Except for the entrance, it was made up of three dirt walls, a dirt floor, and a dirt ceiling. It wasn't suitable for people, having been used for the livestock as a place to eat, sleep, and do their business.

Looking around to see what else there might be useful, Joseph found a rake and moved all of the waste out of the stable. As best he could, he covered the floor with straw so the dust wouldn't be so bad. He also set up a couple of posts and then built a rickety, makeshift fence to keep the animals from getting too close to them. As a skilled carpenter, this was rudimentary work for Joseph, and it was the first time in days that he had felt in control as the leader of his growing family.

As Joseph was finishing preparations in the cave, Mary started having stronger contractions. She couldn't help but moan and cry, and this scared Joseph. He didn't have any idea how to help Mary; fortunately, she knew what to do. In between her contractions, she explained to him what he must do to help her.

"Joseph," she said, "the first thing you need to do is start a fire, get some water from that spring we saw on the way here, and boil the water over the fire."

Once Joseph got the water over the fire to start boiling it, he went and grabbed some rags that he had had the presence of mind to pack for the trip. Still in a state of quiet panic, he prayed to God for guidance, and quickly a sense of well-being came over him. Everything was going to be all right, and the baby was on its way.

Mary worked at delivering Jesus while Joseph helped, following her instructions as she blurted them out as best she could. All this time, Mary was praying that Jesus would be born soon. She knew he would be healthy, but she sure wanted this to be over with.

After a few more moments, Joseph saw Jesus's little head coming out as Mary, in tears and with her face beet red, continued to push him out between the gasps of her pain. Joseph was there to catch the baby, and he then reached inside Jesus's tiny mouth to remove any obstructions, followed by a mild swat on the baby's behind to get him breathing. Like all babies, now it was Jesus's turn to cry.

4

The King of Kings and the Lord of Lords, all human but all God, had just arrived into the world his Father had created. The Savior of the world had been born in Simon's stable on the side of a hill in the north pasture, a mile from Bethlehem. The "servants" were a few nearby munching cows and sheep, as well as a mildly traumatized but ecstatic Joseph and a very happy, bone-weary Mary.

Joseph tied off the umbilical cord and then cut it off past the knot. After that, he finished wiping off the baby and wrapped him in the blanket he had brought; he handed him to Mary so she could see him and then feed him. What a beautiful sight. God was suckling on his mother Mary's breasts.

After Jesus had eaten and fallen asleep, Joseph picked him up, changed him, and laid him in the manger so Mary could get up and get cleaned up herself. She needed to eat and then get some rest. About the time she had finished eating, Mary and Joseph heard some footsteps outside and someone talking. Not knowing who it was and not expecting anybody, Joseph picked up the rake and walked to the entrance shouting, "Who's out there?"

"We are some shepherds tending sheep in a nearby pasture," a timid voice responded.

"What do you want?" Joseph asked.

"We mean no harm. We have been told by angels that a baby has just been born here, that he is the long-awaited Messiah."

"Please come in," Joseph said, "and tell us how you heard this good news."

The three shepherds tentatively walked into the stable, and, upon seeing the sleeping Son of God, they bowed down and worshipped him. After several minutes of worship, the shepherds rose and turned to tell Mary and Joseph their story.

"We are shepherds who live in the area, and while we were tending our flocks this evening, all of a sudden, an angel of the Lord stood before us, and the glory of the Lord shone around him!" Abel said. "We were terrified! The angel then told us, 'Do not be afraid, for behold, I bring you good tidings of great joy, which will be to all people. For there is born to you this day in the city of David, a Savior, who is Christ the Lord. And this *will* be the sign to you: you will find a babe wrapped in swaddling clothes, lying in a manger.'"

Abel went on to say that the angel was then joined by a multitude of other angels praising God and saying, "Glory to God in the highest, And on earth peace, goodwill toward men!"

"It was the most indescribable, most beautiful thing any of us have ever seen," said Abel, who then introduced his companions as Ebon and Seth.

Abel told Mary and Joseph that after the angels had departed to return to heaven, they agreed among themselves that they needed to proceed to Bethlehem to see for themselves what the Lord had made known to them. They immediately left with haste, destined for Bethlehem, where they found exactly what had been described to them by the angel.

"This is the reason we came, and it is the reason we immediately worshipped your son," Abel said. "The angels in heaven announced the birth of our King to us. We have no gifts for our King but our worship and ourselves."

After the shepherds left the cave, they traveled throughout Bethlehem and the region telling everyone what they had seen and heard. All those who heard the shepherds' story marveled at what they were told, with the shepherds eventually departing to return to their flocks, all the time glorifying and praising God for all the things that they had heard and seen.

It wasn't long before people from and around Bethlehem came to see the child Jesus; Joseph graciously allowed the visitors to come into the cave to look and to worship their Messiah. Everyone brought a small gift of food or clothing for their new Messiah. Among the visitors who arrived a bit later was Uncle Simon, accompanied by his family, to see and worship the new King. It turns out that the shepherds who had come to see Jesus first worked for Simon and had told him all they had seen and heard.

Simon, in the meantime, had repented for his lack of faith, and he now wanted to be the first among the family members to come worship Jesus.

"Joseph and Mary, I also sent the shepherds to tell both of your parents about this miracle birth, and I expect they should be showing up fairly soon," Uncle Simon said. "Our family had wanted to believe you but found your story unbelievable."

Mary and Joseph were thrilled at what Simon had told them and that God had restored their family through the miraculous birth of his Son and through the revelation of his birth from the angels to the shepherds. God had sent Joseph to Simon's house and had Simon let Mary and Joseph stay in his stable while God was getting his "Heavenly Host" prepared to proclaim his Son's birth to the shepherds and the world.

Uncle Simon was right; the rest of the families soon arrived with both sets of parents rushing to the baby's side to see their new grandson, King, and Messiah. The stable erupted in apologies, hugging, and tears of joy. Family members knelt down and worshipped their new Messiah, exclaiming, "Joy to the world, the Lord has come. Let earth receive her King."

A while later, Mary's imah (mother) plucked Jesus from the manger and started examining him. Joseph's imah also joined in and took a look as well. Mary's imah had brought Jesus some more suitable clothes, after which they again changed his diaper and dressed him in a new gown. During all of this commotion, Jesus didn't cry until he was handed over to Mary's abba (father). He had had enough handling.

After some discussion among both families, it was decided that they would help Mary and Joseph gather up the baby Jesus and all their supplies and move Jesus's family back to Bethlehem, where they would for the time being stay with Mary's imah. As they all prepared to leave the cave, bound for Bethlehem, Mary and Joseph asked everyone to stop so that they could offer up a prayer of their own with Joseph speaking to God on their behalf:

"Father, I don't even know how to express our thankfulness for everything you have done for us and your Son. Despite our early misgiving about how this whole thing would transpire over this past nine months, Mary and I were awed by you and honored in agreeing to be your vessels to have and to raise your Son. We were so thrilled that you had selected us from all of your children. Now you have shown the rest of the world, to include our beloved families, your truth and plan regarding your Son. Thank you so much for giving us back our families and letting your Son grow up in a loving, nurturing, and caring family. Father, thank you so much."

After a good breakfast the following morning at Mary's parents' home, everyone was astounded to see several people milling about outside obviously wanting to see the new baby. The shepherds' story had gone far and wide regarding the birth of the new Messiah. Joseph opened the door for them to come in, and soon others arrived. It became an almost steady procession of visitors, many of them leaving a gift.

Mary and Joseph watched all this in amazement and then started discussing where and how Jesus would be circumcised. It was decided to have a rabbi come to the home of Joseph's parents to perform the ceremony there. On the eighth day, according to the law, Mary, Joseph, and all the family members headed over to Joseph's parents' house to celebrate the Bris together. When the rabbi asked Joseph the name to be given to his son, Joseph said it would be Jesus, which was the name the angel had given him.

After the ceremony, the family enjoyed a great meal together and praised God for everything He had done for them.

As the next couple of weeks went by and the number of visitors dwindled, Mary and Joseph decided to take Jesus to the temple in Jerusalem to present the baby to the Lord. When Mary's days of purification were finished, according to law, they would go to Jerusalem. They told their parents, and they decided to go with them for the ceremony and the sacrifice, as well as to do some shopping for the new baby. While they were at the temple, Mary and Joseph also sacrificed a pair of turtle doves, which was according to the Law of Moses.

Once they had finished the sacrifice and were about to split up to go shopping—the men to look at farm equipment and the women to look over some fabric from which to make clothes for baby Jesus—they were approached by Simeon, a just and devout man waiting for the consolation of Israel (Jesus). The Holy Ghost was upon him. Simeon explained that it had been revealed to him by the Holy Ghost that as old as he was and on the verge of death, he would not see death before he had seen the Lord's Christ.

When Simeon entered the temple that day and saw Jesus, with Mary's and Joseph's permission, he took the baby in his arms and blessed God, saying, "Lord, now you can let your servant die in peace, according to your word: for my eyes have seen your salvation, which you prepared before the face of all people; a light to lighten the Gentiles, and the glory of your people Israel."

Simeon then blessed Mary and Joseph. Turning to Mary, he said, "Behold, this child is set for the fall and rising again of many in Israel; and for a sign which shall be spoken against; Yea, a sword shall pierce through thy own soul also, that the thoughts of many hearts may be revealed."

Also present was Anna, a prophetess, an elderly woman who decades earlier had been married for seven years and then a widow for eighty-four. She never left the temple, but she served God by fasting and praying night and day. As soon as Simeon finished his blessing of Jesus, Anna also gave thanks to the Lord. Anna spoke to everyone who was looking and waiting for the Messiah to come and redeem the people.

Upon leaving the temple, everyone split up and went about the errands they had agreed on. The women all went to the market to pick the fabric and get some other items for Mary so she would be well equipped to set up household in Bethlehem. That's where Mary and Joseph had decided to stay so Jesus would grow up surrounded by family, to include all of his cousins and aunts and uncles.

The men headed to a different market and looked at the new tools that were available for farming, ranching, and carpentry. Joseph wanted to be sure he had all of the carpentry tools he needed to set up shop in Bethlehem. Later, the family met at a time and place agreed on and then headed back down to Bethlehem. They had had a full and happy day.

5

Back in Tarsus, once the guests had left and the decorations had been stored, Jonathan and our household got back into our normal routine, except now my parents and servants had to add me into the mix. My mother was still weak after giving birth, so my father took over the duties of having me tended to by my designated servants and a nurse. He had put them on a strict schedule of when and what to do with me. My mother tried to change the schedule or would just spend more time lying next to me so she could gaze upon me, but the nurse would still come in and take me and do whatever my father had scheduled for her to do.

Mother slowly became stronger and was able to go to the synagogue, where she presented me to the Lord and sacrificed a lamb to conclude her purification according to the Law of Moses. Father had an unblemished lamb brought for the burnt offering and a turtle dove for the sin offering.

As the days and then weeks went by, Father kept everyone on his strict schedule although he didn't spend much time with me. Being so young, there was nothing I could do of interest to my father, who could only bide his time waiting for me to grow up enough to start joining him for activities he enjoyed. My father would get annoyed when Mother would ask him to hold and cuddle me so that I would know I was loved. My father said he didn't like to do that, that it was the job of the servants and nurses to do that for him. He said he had more important things to do and that he would spend time with me when I got older. This saddened my mother.

During my first year of life, servants and nurses cared for me around the clock. My mother learned to be content spending some quality time with me several times a day for just a few minutes each time. As the months went by, the next big thing became preparing for my first birthday. My father planned a lavish party on my behalf, giving him cause to again send out invitations across the city for all the dignitaries of Tarsus. Once again, our home would be the place to see and be seen.

By the time my first birthday finally arrived, the house had been fully prepared and was ready for our guests. Again, they all brought exquisite gifts for me. Father had minted a gold coin for all of the guests as a small token of our appreciation. Bountiful food and wine were also available. In the middle of the party, I was brought in to blow out the candle on the cake and open a few of my gifts.

Of course, my parents had gone completely overboard with their gifts for me. The servants brought out the presents and placed me in the middle of them. I just sat there looking around; Mother had to jump in to get me started opening them. Apparently, my father became bored by this, and he eventually walked over to one of his business partners to discuss a deal they were working on. My mother motioned for him to stay because she had a surprise that she wanted to tell him and the guests.

Father either didn't see or ignored my mother's motioning to him, so she sent her personal servant over to ask Jonathan to come speak with her. When my father came over, Sarah whispered something in his ear, and his face broke into a huge smile. He grabbed a wine glass and tapped his ring against it to get everyone's attention. He started by thanking the guests for coming to my first birthday party and being so generous with their gifts. Then he said, "I have just heard some great news from my wife Sarah. She just informed me she is expecting another child." The crowd exploded in jubilation since they knew how difficult this had been for Sarah. What a great ending to my first birthday party.

After the guests had gone home, and while the servants cleaned up the day's celebration, Jonathan followed Sarah up to her suite to talk about the new baby. He was excited but concerned since my mother had had some trouble with my birth. She assured him that everything would be OK, that God had allowed her to be with child again. With that assurance, my father went ahead and made plans to offer a sacrifice of thanksgiving to show Tarsus how much he loved God. My mother thought it would be wonderful to show how much they appreciated God's gift of another child.

When the day for the sacrifice arrived, my parents and I were dressed in our finest clothes and, accompanied by our entourage of servants and nurses, made our way to the synagogue carrying unleavened cakes, wafers, and cakes of fine flour. Our group took a roundabout way through Tarsus, though, so everyone could see what my father and his household were doing in giving a sacrifice of thanksgiving. Like before, it was as important to my father that he be seen performing such a grand gesture; being seen was as important to him as the ceremony itself.

How dignified and regal our family looked moving toward the synagogue to give our sacrifice to God. Tarsus residents couldn't help but see how its leading citizens (we) were so excited, that since we were so blessed, we must be obeying God completely.

As in all families when the mother is expecting, there was a lot of chatter around the city about the coming baby and whether it would be a boy or a girl. The servants took the time to try and explain to me what was going on. They told me that my mother had another baby inside her tummy. When I was in my mother's suite, they would place one of my small hands on my mother's tummy, and, on occasion, I would be able to feel the baby move.

While everyone was excited about the new baby, they were also concerned and prayed for my mother to be healthy throughout her pregnancy and during the delivery. As the day grew closer, the whole household and most of Tarsus prayed and fasted for Sarah's safety.

Father had also been busy preparing for this new birth. It included commissioning contractors to build another suite for our new baby. It would not be quite as ornate as mine since I had been the firstborn. However, it would still be extravagant, as most things were when it came to my father.

When the day finally arrived and Mother started delivering her second child, Jonathan took up watch in the foyer near her suite praying that all would go well. Hours went by with no word. He would ask anyone coming out of the suite how she was doing. After several more hours went by, a servant girl with a smile on her face ran out and told him that Mother had given birth to a baby girl. Jonathan fell to his knees and thanked God for his new baby girl and for the baby's and Sarah's safety.

While Father waited to go in and see my mother and the new baby, the doctor arrived and went into the suite to check on the baby and Mother. He stayed in the suite longer than he had when I had been born. After the doctor came back out, he told my father it was OK to go in and see his wife and baby girl. The doctor also told my father that Sarah had had another very difficult delivery and might have suffered some internal damage.

"Please be careful not to tire her or to say anything about her possible internal injuries so as not to scare her," the doctor said.

"Thanks, but how serious are the injuries?" Father asked.

"They look to be serious, but I believe she will heal in time and be just fine," the doctor said, before departing.

Jonathan walked slowly into Sarah's room and faked a big smile as he went over to see his new baby lying in my mother's arms. The baby was beautiful. My father saw how beautiful Mother looked as well. My father held the baby for a little while before asking Sarah how she was feeling.

"Tired but happy," she said.

For several weeks after the baby's birth, my father had struggled to come up with a suitable name for his new daughter, finally deciding to call her Deborah after the prophetess in the book of Judges. He hoped she would be as strong and love God as much as her namesake.

Every morning, Jonathan would check in on Sarah first and then go see me and Deborah. During those first few weeks after Deborah's birth, my father found himself enjoying his new morning ritual instead of just letting his servants and the nurses do everything. He could also see that Sarah was getting stronger day by day. It wasn't long before she felt good enough to have visitors come by.

One morning, while Father was spending time with her, Mother asked him about some news that one of her friends had told her earlier that day.

"What have you heard about King Herod sending soldiers down to Bethlehem and having them kill every boy child under the age of two years old?" my mother asked him. "Could that be true? That would be like soldiers coming to Tarsus and killing all of the boys that are Saul's age."

Sarah realized that if this were true, there were at least thirty-five boys in Tarsus that she knew of who would be in line to be massacred including me.

"Why would Herod do that?" she continued. "If that were true, why would God allow innocent children to be massacred by that madman?"

My father admitted that he had heard the same story and through his contacts, the story had been confirmed. Jonathan then told her the whole story as it had been conveyed to him.

"About the time that Saul had been born," my father told her, "there was a poor couple that had come from Nazareth to Bethlehem for Herod's census. While in Bethlehem, their son, Jesus, had been born. There were rumors at that time that this boy had been the foretold Messiah. That rumor quickly faded since there would be no way that God would have selected a poor family from Nazareth to carry on his work. Anyway, about a month ago, a caravan of wealthy priests, kings, and wise men from the East went to Jerusalem and asked Herod where the prophesied Messiah was to be born. They told Herod that a new star had appeared, that they had consulted their manuscripts and headed west to find this new King of Kings so they could worship him. They said they had been traveling for more than a year and a half to find and worship this King."

My father went on to tell Sarah the whole story about Herod, about how he had asked the priests, kings, and wise men to find this baby Messiah and to report back to him his exact location, secretly plotting to kill the child once he knew his whereabouts. For some reason, the men of the caravan decided not to tell Herod where the child was. Instead, they returned home, choosing to return by a different route.

"When Herod heard of this treachery," Jonathan said, "he went crazy. To make sure he killed this new king, he had his soldiers kill all of the boys in Bethlehem less than two years old."

Sarah was horrified at what she had just heard. She was well aware of King Herod's reputation for cruelty, but this went well beyond anything she had heard before. This slaughter of the innocent children the same age as me was even crueler than she thought Herod could be. She, like all of the Jews, prayed for the Messiah that would come some day and run all of the corruption of the Romans and their puppets back to Rome.

6

Enough about me for a while. Let me catch you up on what was happening over in Bethlehem with Jesus.

"Joseph," Mary asked?

"Yes, Mary," Joseph answered sleepily.

"Are you a little bit concerned about what we have to do?"

"What do you mean, Mary?" Joseph said.

"Well, we have to raise God's son. We don't know the first thing about raising babies or children; it scares me that we could mess this up."

"Yes," Joseph said. "I have been thinking a lot about that ever since Gabriel said you were going to have Jesus. I just can't figure out why God chose me to be Jesus's surrogate father. I know why he picked you. You are the most beautiful, caring, and holy woman in the world. I am so glad our parents picked you for me.

"Thank the Lord that our parents have accepted us back into the family so they can help us and teach us how to raise and love a child. They sure did a great job raising you, Mary."

A few days later, Joseph set up a small carpenter shop in Bethlehem. He was trained as a carpenter, and that was how he would support his small family, one that he hoped would soon become larger. Because he had so many relatives in the area, his business started off well. He worked close to the house and got to spend time with Mary and Jesus. He enjoyed going home for lunch, holding and playing with Jesus, and spending time with Mary.

Mary was very happy there as well. She had her family around her, and they all helped in caring for Jesus. Almost every day, one of the savtas (the grandmothers), aunts, or nieces would come by to help. They spoiled Him. Mary had a sister, a brother, and three cousins that had babies close to Jesus's age. It was wonderful to have them over and watch them all get acquainted. Of all of the babies that were family and were Jesus's age, two were boys and three were girls.

Life in Bethlehem was ideal. Joseph made enough money to support his family, which is one reason why he felt that God was watching over them and his son. Joseph was so grateful that the family had finally believed the story that Mary and he had told them and brought them back into the fold. As he thought about this, he was busy making presents for Jesus's first birthday. He was almost finished with a small wooden set of farm animals and a couple of shepherds for Jesus to play with. He had been work-ing on these for a while, and they looked good. As he worked, he prayed that he would be able to show Jesus the story about his birth someday. It still was like a dream to him.

All of a sudden, he felt arms wrap around his waist, and it startled him back to reality. It was Mary. She had come out to the shop to bring him his lunch and look at the progress he was making on the gifts for Jesus. He turned around and gave her a big hug. He was always pleased to have Mary near him.

After a couple of kisses, Mary placed his lunch on his work bench. Joseph set his work down and went to the bench to eat. Before he could get there, Mary reached over and caught Joseph's hand; his first thought was that something wasn't right, so he asked her if anything was wrong. She said there wasn't, but she then told him she was expecting another child. At hearing this wonderful news, Joseph pulled Mary close to him and kissed her again. He then said a prayer of thanksgiving to God and also prayed that Mary and the new baby would be safe. He next asked if they should have the grandparents over that evening to tell them the good news. She agreed. Joseph, ecstatic, quickly finished lunch and went to ask the grandparents over.

When the grandparents arrived that evening, not having yet been told what the occasion was for, Mary and Joseph had dinner waiting for them. They said a blessing and started eating their meal. It wasn't normal to have extended-family meals like this during the week. The grandparents knew something must be up. They thought it probably had something to do with their grandson Jesus. After they had finished the meal, Joseph told them the great news, that Mary was expecting another child. Joseph's father, always a bit of a jokester, asked his son if it was his child or if God had conceived this child as well. Everyone chuckled, and Mary blushed. The whole family was elated and couldn't stop hugging Mary. Joseph said he would tell the rest of the family at Jesus's birthday party the next week.

The entire family was invited over for Jesus's first birthday party. Of course, he didn't have a grasp of what was going on, but he was excited to see all of the people he loved. Once they had arrived, they played games for the children and served them cake and candy. As everyone started to go home, Joseph said a prayer of thanksgiving to God for all of their blessings.

The next couple of months went well for the family except for Mary, who was dealing with a bad case of morning sickness as she had with Jesus. Fortunately, this time, she had her family to help with Jesus and the household work.

Since there were five other babies in Mary's extended family that were Jesus's age, they took turns having him over to play with their babies. They were getting old enough to have fun together. When they would bring Jesus home, they never ceased telling Mary how fun and energetic her son was. He was a joy to be around. And, when Joseph wasn't working on anything that could hurt a toddler, he would take Jesus to his shop so he could spend time with his son.

Joseph was a good story teller, and he would tell Jesus the stories of the Jewish people and how God had set them apart to do his work on earth. He liked to tell Jesus tales about one particular ancestor, King David, who trusted God, and about how God blessed him and made him the Jewish king. He told Jesus that he was King David's heir and that he was the chosen Son of God that was to restore the Jewish Kingdom back to world prominence. Jesus enjoyed the stories his father told him; he would sit and listen to him for hours.

After several months, Mary stopped having her bouts with morning sickness and was able to slowly resume her daily routine. One of her favorite things was to rise up early, get Jesus from his mat, and bring him into bed with them. They would all lay there half asleep and hold each other before starting their day. Before they would get up, Joseph would say a prayer for guidance for the day.

After getting up, Joseph prepared for work while Mary, with her little helper Jesus, would make breakfast. They would all sit down to eat, and then Joseph would head to the shop to work. Jesus would help Mary clean up. One morning, while they were cleaning up, Mary grabbed Jesus's hand and held it to her stomach. The baby was kicking, and Mary wanted Jesus to feel it. Jesus's face lit up as he felt the baby move.

7

We now travel over to Jerusalem, where a large caravan of dignitaries has arrived looking for Jesus.

"Who could that be?" the watchman asked. "I have been watchman over the Damascus Gate for more than twenty years, and I have never seen such a large and ornate caravan before, not even when King Herod arrives."

"I agree," his fellow watchman said. "Let's go down and greet them properly to find out who they are and what their purpose is in Jerusalem."

The two men went through the gate and out to greet the caravan. The caravan group's leader approached and dismounted from a beautiful Arabian horse. This stranger, richly and immaculately dressed, strode up to the guards and explained that the caravan had traveled from the East looking to find and worship the new King of Kings. He told them they had been following a new star that had appeared about a year and a half earlier. The guards looked around and could see that the caravan was made up of several kings and wise men. The guards, however, did not have any idea what the caravan's leader was talking about; however, common sense told them they should let them into the city to find out what this was all about.

The caravan stopped outside the city and made camp because they assumed there would not be enough accommodations for them in the city. Also, they wanted to be ready to continue their search for the new King since they thought they were very close.

The leader of the caravan and his self-appointed delegation went into the city, and, when they had arrived at Herod's Palace, they asked the royal guard to see Herod. He was the "puppet" king the Romans had set up to rule in Jerusalem. The guard then went into the palace and explained to Herod's personal guard what these men had told them. It was apparent that the men of the caravan were very wealthy and important because of their appearance. Herod's personal guard returned and explained everything to Herod. Herod decided to see them right away. Herod's personal guard then told the royal guard, who told the delegation that Herod would see them immediately. The men from the delegation left, changed their attire, and returned into Jerusalem to see Herod.

Herod greeted them warmly and magnificently. Once they announced themselves, he asked them why they had traveled so far and how he could help them. One of the Magi stood up and explained. "We are a group of kings, magi, and wise men from the East. A little over a year and a half ago, a new star appeared. We consulted our parchment scrolls and found that this star was certainly to herald of the new King of the Jews. The King of Kings. We continued to consult our records and then started on our journey to worship him. We have traveled here to give him gifts and pay homage."

Herod looked at them a bit confused and told them *he* was the king of the Jews. The Magus then explained that the king they were looking for was the *King of Kings*. Stifling his anger, Herod consulted his priests and asked where this new King of Kings was to be born. After Herod's wise men consulted the Torah, they told him this King of Kings would be born in Bethlehem. Herod told the Magus to go seek out the child and when they had found him to send back word to him so he, too, could go worship him.

They thanked Herod and went back out to their caravan. They were thrilled to know they were now only two miles from finishing their quest. They packed their goods and continued on to Bethlehem with the star they had been following showing them the way—right to Mary and Joseph's home.

Once there, they all dismounted their horses and camels and walked up to the house. They knocked on the door and heard a woman, Mary, telling them to come in. When these men entered the house, Jesus ran over and jumped into Mary's lap. He had never seen so many strangers before. Mary was a bit frightened as well. Soon Joseph came in the back door to see what all of the noise was about. The caravan was large, and there were a lot of animals and people making a racket in the street. The Magi told their story to them, and, when he finished, they all came close, knelt down, and worshipped Jesus. Mary and Joseph were speechless.

When they had finished worshipping Jesus, the men motioned to the caravan leader, and he in turn motioned for the others in the caravan to come into the house, bringing their gifts. As each man set his gift before Jesus, he bowed down and worshipped the new King. Among the different gifts were gold, frankincense, and myrrh. Everyone in the house, including other family members, was speechless; they didn't know what to say except "thank you" over and over.

After all of the visiting men had had the chance to bring Jesus a gift and worship him, the Magi came back in and said that they would go south of town and camp for the evening. They also told Mary and Joseph that Herod had asked them to return to Jerusalem and tell him where Jesus was so he could later come and pay homage as well.

Once the Magi had left, Mary and Joseph looked through all of the gifts that Jesus had received. Together, it was worth a fortune. Joseph didn't know what to do with all of the gifts except for now to move them into a corner of the house out of the way, with his father's assistance.

After everyone had left, Mary put Jesus to bed. She then joined Joseph in their bed.

"Mary," Joseph asked, "what does all of this mean?"

Mary lay there thinking, and, finally, she said, "I don't know, Joseph, but maybe God wanted all of us to remember that Jesus is truly his Son, and this outward show helps us all to remember."

"Well, Joseph said, "what are we going to do with all of these gifts? There is a fortune."

"We need to pray to God, and he will guide us to his purpose."

Joseph agreed and said a prayer for wisdom.

Early the following morning, Joseph heard a light knock on the door. He got up quickly, fearing it might be a thief because of all the expensive gifts in the house. He went up to the door and asked who it was. The Magus answered, and Joseph let him in.

"Joseph, I just wanted to tell you that I have been warned in a dream not to tell Herod where Jesus was and to return home by a different route," the Magus said. "We are going to travel to Egypt, and, from there, we will take a ship back home."

At this, the Magus quietly walked over to the sleeping Jesus and worshipped him once again. The Magus then left and returned to the caravan, which was preparing to leave. When Mary woke up, Joseph told her what had happened.

After breakfast, Joseph went to the shop to start building a strong box into which he would put all of the gifts for safekeeping. He worked diligently all day on the strong box although he wasn't finished when he decided to return home and spend the evening with Mary and Jesus. He and Mary spent much of the time discussing the last couple of days and then went to bed.

In the middle of the night, an angel appeared to Joseph in a dream and told him to take Mary and Jesus and flee to Egypt. The angel told Joseph that Herod would try to kill Jesus. The angel also said to stay in Egypt until he contacted him. Joseph got up immediately and started packing their belongings to leave Bethlehem.

8

Joseph began thinking of the trip they would have to make and the potential dangers to be encountered along the road. He was concerned for their safety while being in another country and of the thieves he had heard about on their particular route. On top of all that, there was the matter of Mary being pregnant and close to childbirth.

When Joseph had finished packing, he went over to his father's house and awakened him, telling him of what the Magus had told him about Herod and then about his own dream, and he asked his father if he could buy his wagon and team of horses so Mary and Jesus would be comfortable. With any luck, they might even catch up to the caravan that had left the day before bound for Egypt. Joseph thought the caravan would help to keep them safe. Joseph's father agreed. Joseph and his father quickly hooked up the horses to the wagon and drove the wagon over to his house.

While the two men were hooking up the wagon, Joseph asked his father to keep most of the gifts they had received. Joseph knew he shouldn't be carrying all of that, so he calculated how much they would need in order to get to Egypt and then he doubled it. He knew God would take care of them. After that, he gave the rest to his father and asked him to invest it for the family.

After he and his father finished loading the wagon, they woke up Mary and Jesus and told them what was happening. Mary's first impulse was to object at the thought of moving away from their family and friends, but she quickly set her mind on staying in obedience to God. Mary and Jesus got into the wagon, and they drove Joseph's father back to his house. He went in and told his wife what had happened; she came out and said a quick but sad good-bye to them. Joseph had walked over to Mary's parents' house and had asked them to come over and join them. Once they were all there, Joseph said a prayer for safety and courage.

They all wept for a while; then Joseph, Mary, and Jesus got into the wagon and started out toward Egypt. It was a long journey, about two hundred sixty miles. In trying to catch the caravan, Joseph pushed the horses as fast as he dared. He knew the caravan would be in a hurry to get out of Israel and would be traveling fast for the first few days as well. He figured the trip would take up to three weeks since they must rest; besides that, they could not travel on the Sabbath.

As they were leaving, they told their fathers to send any messages for them to the synagogue in Alexandria. Joseph's family had some relatives in the area, and they would probably stay there until it was safe to return. That way, they could send messages to each other while they were away. They all agreed that they had to be very careful and not tell anyone else where they were going since Egypt was also under Roman control and King Herod might try to find them there.

They would buy food and supplies on the way, a strategy that helped them make good time. During most of the day, when Jesus was awake, he would "help" Joseph drive. Joseph enjoyed having Jesus on his lap helping him drive. By now, Jesus had learned to talk some, and he kept asking Joseph to tell him more stories about God and his people. Joseph obliged, while Mary stayed in the back resting as comfortably as she could in some bedding that their mothers had turned into a small nest for her. At one of their stops, Mary pointed out to Joseph that every time she was expecting, they got to go on a traveling adventure. Joseph just chuckled.

At the end of the third day, they caught up to the caravan. When asked by one of the Magi what had happened, Joseph told him about his dream. Regardless the reasoning, the Magus was pleased to have the new King with them, and he thanked God for that. Joseph was tremendously relieved that they had caught up to the caravan. Now he wasn't nearly so concerned about their safety.

The Magus, whose name it turned out was Melchior, asked a servant to go to the other two leaders of the caravan, Caspar and Balthasar, to tell them the news. They, too, came back to join Mary, Joseph, and Jesus to hear the story for themselves. Caspar decided he would have the family stay with him in one of his extra tents so that Mary would be comfortable.

As the next day dawned, Mary and Joseph got up and were soon greeted by several servants who entered their tent bringing breakfast that consisted of fruits, meats, cheeses, and nuts they had never seen, heard of, or tasted. Jesus enjoyed the meal, and the servants spoke of his healthy appetite to his hosts. They were overjoyed they had pleased the King. Then they helped pack and prepared for the day's journey.

Jesus had taken a special liking to Melchior because the older man would sometimes play peek a boo with him. During the afternoon, Melchior asked Mary and Joseph if Jesus would like to ride with him on his camel. They said that would be great as long as Jesus wasn't scared. Melchior reached down, scooped Jesus up, and put him on the camel with him. Jesus squealed with delight. Everyone laughed.

After that, Jesus didn't spend much time in the wagon except to eat some food and take a nap. Most of the time, he rode the camels or horses with his new Persian friends. All of the Magi, wise men and kings, took turns giving the baby King a ride. Jesus was so fun to be with that everyone wanted to be near him. They all could tell that he was a special child.

Mary spent the trip trying to make herself as comfortable as she could, but she was having trouble since she was so close to her due date. Meanwhile, Joseph moved around the caravan throughout the day to help make sure that all of the wagons were in good shape. He wanted to help as much as he could, and his carpentry skills made him a handy person to have around.

After about another week or so, the caravan came over a hill and everyone saw the Nile River Valley before them. They had decided to go into Cairo to replenish their supplies before heading on to Persia. Also, they wanted to get Joseph and his family over to Alexandria because Joseph had some distant relatives he wanted to get in touch with to see if it would be safe for them there.

Caspar was leading the caravan one day when a rider from the rear of the caravan came running up and said they needed to stop, that Mary was in labor. Caspar signaled to the caravan to halt and make camp, where they again pitched the tent for Mary and started making preparations for the delivery. It pleased Mary that this time she would have other women there to help her while Joseph and the other men waited outside not knowing when they would hear the blessed cry of the newborn baby.

After a couple of hours, the cries came, and a few minutes after that, one of the servants came out with the baby in a beautiful blanket. She handed the baby to Joseph, telling him that it was a girl. Joseph was elated. All of the men bowed and prayed to God for the safety of Mary and the new baby; this made Jesus a big brother. He came over to Joseph and was shown his new sister. She was so beautiful, and he loved her immediately. He went into the tent, walked over to his bed, and picked up one of the special toys his father had made him. Jesus took it out and offered it to his new sister.

Joseph then took the baby back to Mary so she could finish getting her ready for everyone to see. Joseph put her in Mary's arms, and Jesus laid down next to them. Joseph then let all of their friends come and see the newest addition to the family. They came in and offered their congratulations. Joseph announced that Mary and he had decided that the new baby's name would be Naomi. Once they left, Mary fed Naomi, and they both fell asleep. The caravan stayed there two days and then moved on toward Cairo.

Before going into the city, Joseph and the leaders of the caravan agreed that they would not disclose that Joseph and his family were from Judea; if questioned, they would tell officials that they were from Nazareth. That way, if Herod had sent out messages to apprehend them, they wouldn't be suspected.

9

As had been the case in Jerusalem, once the caravan arrived in Alexandria, it was greeted with awe and respect. Dignitaries from the city came out and greeted them. When the Egyptians inquired about their journey, they said the journey had been fine. Once the group of Egyptians had left, the Magi gave orders to restock the caravan and start making their way home. It would take them a few days to get everything they needed and to rest the animals before they left.

Mary and Joseph had never seen such a large city. There were so many sights to see. The Nile River was a marvel to them; they would go with friends to watch the boats move up and down the river and see the cargo from all over the world get loaded and unloaded. Jesus especially enjoyed going down to watch the boats with his father. It was during this time that Joseph first started telling Jesus stories about Moses, about how as a baby Moses was saved by being placed in a small papyrus boat while his sister Miriam watched over him.

During the days that the caravan was preparing to leave, Mary and Joseph found a house where they could stay until such time that God called them back home. Joseph also started visiting carpenter shops looking for work, eventually finding a shop close to where they were staying and which would allow him to work there until they returned home.

The next day, Caspar told Joseph that they would leave the following morning. Joseph invited a few of their Persian friends from the caravan to join them that night for dinner, at which time Joseph and Mary thanked them profusely for all of the help they had given them. They lingered over their good-byes, believing they would probably never see one another again. As they were leaving, Joseph said a prayer for their safety and travel.

Over the next few weeks, Mary and Joseph settled in. They had gotten back into their routine and enjoyed the synagogue, where they would worship God. One evening, when Joseph had gone there, he received a packet addressed to him that had come from Bethlehem. He opened it and started reading, soon falling to his knees shuddering before he began to tear his robes. The packet had fallen from his hands to the ground, and the rabbi who had given it to him picked it up to see what it was that upset Joseph so much. It was from Joseph's father. The Rabbi started reading:

"Joseph, we have terrible news to tell you. About two weeks after you left, a detachment of about fifty soldiers came into Bethlehem looking for the Magi and the caravan. Herod had told the Magi to return to Jerusalem and tell him where Jesus was. He told them he wanted to come to worship him as well. Herod had heard that the Magi had left using a different route and was furious. The Magi left without telling him where Jesus was staying. Herod then sent his men to search for Jesus. The soldiers first went to the synagogue where we keep all of the birth records, grabbed them, and ordered everyone to come to the town square.

"Herod had sent his palace guard and several Romans led by a centurion. Once the villagers had assembled, the centurion started calling out the names of the families that had given birth to a son less than two years old. No one could figure out why he was doing this. As each child's name was called, either the mother or father would bring their boy forward, and the soldiers put all the boys in a line in the middle of the square. Of course, they called Mary's sister's son Michael and your cousin's son Samuel into the square. A couple of names called were of boys who had died earlier. The centurion had the death certificates brought to him to have those deaths confirmed.

"When they got to the name of Jesus, the centurion was told that you had moved away. The centurion didn't believe us and had the soldiers start questioning everyone. Everyone answered with the same answer. The centurion gave a command; they grabbed Mary's father and stripped his robe from his back and started beating him with a whip. We couldn't believe our eyes. Everyone was pleading to the soldiers and the centurion, insisting to them that what we were saying was true. A few of the parents tried to take their sons and go back to their houses, but they were ordered to stay where they were.

"All of our families tried to stop the whipping, but the centurion demanded that they tell them which of the boys in the square Jesus was. The centurion thought that the village was trying to hide Jesus by having him come up when a different name was called. Mary's father kept insisting between the lashes that you had left, but they only stopped when he passed out from the pain.

"Joseph, they hurt him terribly. We aren't sure if he will ever walk normally again.

"Since he wouldn't talk, they grabbed your Uncle Simon and started beating him, but Simon's heart was not as strong as it used to be. After several blows, he suffered a heart attack and died right there in the middle of the square. The whole village then erupted in anger and pushed toward the soldiers. This caused the centurion to call his soldiers to draw their swords and told them to kill anyone who attacked them. We all backed off. The centurion again asked us where Jesus was. He told us he would continue torturing us until he found out which one of the boys in the square was Jesus. After no one said what he wanted to hear, he ordered two of his soldiers to just pick out two of the villagers and beat them. They grabbed one of your cousins, and the soldier bashed him with his shield right in the head and knocked him senseless to the ground. The other walked up to a young woman and slapped her across the face a few times until her husband came to her rescue, and then the soldier knocked him on the ground and started kicking him until he kept still. We were in shock.

"After this, the crowd was swearing in the name of God that Jesus had left a couple of weeks before. The centurion then called over his cohort and whispered something in his ear. The cohort listened with rapt attention; he had not known what the orders were telling them to do after they had assembled the boys. We watched as he shook his head and asked the centurion to repeat his command. After he did, the cohort's face fell. He turned to twenty-three of the soldiers and asked them to all go choose and hold one of the boys and then have the parents move out with the rest of us. We had no idea what they were doing, but one of the fathers told them he would not do that. The soldier grabbed his boy and knocked the father down. All of the parents began to grab tightly onto their sons, and all of the boys started crying and screaming. One by one, the soldiers took the boys by force while other soldiers physically removed the parents from the area. Your cousin Ethan tried to go in and help his wife, but he was slammed to the ground.

"The centurion was watching all of this with a look of boredom on his face. All of the villagers were begging and pleading for their sons' safety. After all of the parents had been removed, the centurion looked back over to his cohort and gave him a signal. The cohort walked up to one of the soldiers and asked him to hold the boy out in front of him. The boy was squirming, screaming, and slobbering all over. It was terrible to see. The centurion then told all of us that if we didn't tell him which one of these boys was Jesus, he would start with the one being held out in front of them and kill all of the boys one by one until he learned the truth. The whole village fell to their knees, tore their clothes, and started praying to God to save the sons of Bethlehem. When no one told the centurion what he wanted to hear, he signaled the cohort to kill the boy. The cohort raised his sword, but he couldn't do it. He looked back at the centurion; the centurion signaled again. Again, the cohort raised his sword, took a deep breath, and stopped. He could not do it. He turned slowly to the centurion, who had moved up behind him. The centurion stabbed the cohort through his throat with his sword for disobeying his order. The centurion then went up to the boy and slit his throat. We couldn't believe what we were seeing.

"After that, the centurion signaled to the next soldier to step forward with his boy, looked over at another cohort, and signaled that he should kill that one. The cohort's face went white, but he did as ordered and stabbed the young boy through. Each time the centurion asked for another boy to be brought forward, he would ask us if this one was Jesus. After we wouldn't answer, he would have someone kill the boy or he would do it himself. When he had gone through about a dozen of the boys, he ordered all of them to be killed. The village again erupted with screams and wails. Several more villagers got hurt, and three were killed trying to get their beloved child from the carnage. Joseph, all twenty-three boys were killed, Mary's father was still unconscious, and your Uncle Simon and three other villagers were dead. The centurion had even killed one of his own cohorts.

"The centurion then signaled his men to mount their horses. Once they were mounted, they rode back up to Jerusalem, leaving the bloody massacre all over the square. No one moved for the longest while. Finally, a man went over and picked up his deceased son, holding him while he wept bitterly. One by one, the parents of the boys all went to them and held them. Finally, the families of the three men who had been killed came to them and mourned over them. I went over to see what I could do for Mary's father. The square had turned into a place of the dead and its mourners. I will never forget that terrible sound of crying and gnashing of teeth. It was Hades.

"I'm not sure if anyone but a couple of us who attended to Mary's father left the square the whole day. No one would eat or drink. Finally, our rabbi asked for silence and prayed for all of the slain and for all of us who had to go on with our lives. After the prayer, he told them that the following day, the Sabbath, would start at dusk and that we needed to have all of the dead buried before then. He asked for a show of hands to see if everyone had a place to lay their sons; there were only four from the entire village who needed assistance getting a tomb. He asked that the villagers who didn't have a death in their family go home and get herbs and spices for burial. He also asked that someone in the immediate family that had had a son killed go to their home and get clothing prepared for their burial. Slowly and solemnly, the village did as the rabbi instructed.

"The only body that didn't have any mourners was the cohort who wouldn't kill one of the boys. The rabbi walked slowly over to him and started preparing him for burial. While he did so, he said a special prayer for the Roman so he might also go up into Paradise with the slain of Bethlehem.

"We then had a mass funeral for all of the slain and went from tomb to tomb placing the boys where they would spend eternity. As the rabbi was walking back to the synagogue before dusk, he was reminded of a prophecy in Jeremiah that now had been fulfilled: 'A voice was heard in Ramah, weeping and great mourning, Rachel weeping for her children; and she refused to be comforted, because they were no more.'

"We also put the Roman cohort in a tomb and prayed for him.

"Joseph, the whole village will bear witness to this slaughter. Everyone is still sitting with torn robes in ashes mourning for their families. They can't understand how something like this could happen. I can't answer it, either. Why would God let his own Son escape and put so many innocent children and their families through so much pain? We will never know on this earth."

When the rabbi had finished reading the letter, he fainted and collapsed to the ground. After a few minutes, the rabbi stumbled back to his feet, helped Joseph get back up, and then returned the letter to Joseph. After a few more minutes, the rabbi took Joseph by the arm and led him to his house so he could be with him to help comfort Mary when Joseph explained what had happened. They hadn't realized it, but a small group had gathered around as the rabbi had read the letter, and they all followed in silence.

As the group moved closer to Joseph's home, they could hear Mary singing quietly. As they went through the door, they could see that Mary was feeding Naomi with Jesus playing contentedly at her feet. When she looked up and saw Joseph, her face went ashen. She saw that Joseph was in shock and that he had torn his robes in despair. She quickly got up and ran to him asking what had happened. Not saying anything, Joseph took her into his arms and started crying. When Jesus came over to Joseph, his father reached down and held him as Jesus started crying. They stood there holding each other for a few moments. When Joseph had composed himself, he started to tell Mary the gruesome tale.

Mary commenced grieving and crying for her father and their family. She couldn't believe something like this could happen. As she fell to her knees to pray and mourn, one of the women from the synagogue who had followed Joseph and the rabbi took Naomi and Jesus to comfort them.

Mary was distraught, but she knew she couldn't go back to Bethlehem to mourn and comfort her family. She blamed herself for all of the misfortune that had happened in Bethlehem because of her son. She didn't know what to do. So she did as she always did: she prayed to God for him to grant her the ability to forgive her enemies and have her family forgive her. She and Joseph prayed the prayer every evening together as long as they lived.

The news of Herod's profound cruelty quickly spread throughout the world. Even before the caravan got back home, the Magi had heard the story. Mournful over what had happened to the boys and their families in Bethlehem, the Magi were still able to marvel at how God had saved his Son and were thankful that He had used them to aid in getting his family to a safe haven.

10

Life at Jonathan's household in Tarsus conformed to its master's regimented personality. Everything was done for a purpose, and it was done when and how he wanted. In one sense, it was an easy way to live since there was only black and white; the tradeoff was that most of the joy and peace was drained from our home.

As my mother's strength gradually returned after giving birth to Deborah, she started working on her charitable foundations and entertaining Father's friends and clients. She continued her morning routine of spending time with Deborah and me.

As my sister got older, I found myself more interested in spending time with her, being the dutiful brother looking out for his little sister. I would help the nurses bathe her and get her dressed, something that the servants took notice of and told my mother about. Her wish to have the children be close to one another was becoming a reality. My father, however, had his own set of standards. Once, when he happened to see me carrying a doll and blanket to Deborah in her room, he grabbed a servant by the arm and asked, "Why are you allowing Saul to do the work of a servant?"

My mother came to the servant's rescue, explaining that she had thought it nice to have me help with Deborah. My father was not swayed. He told Mother that his firstborn son would not do the work of a servant, ever. He also made it clear to all the staff that if anything else like this was going on, involving me as a helper, it was to cease immediately. What shocked my mother more than what my father said was how he said it—with a stern intensity she had not seen before and over such a trivial issue. Sometimes, Father went off on a tangent and she couldn't figure out why.

After Father had swept out of the room, Mother took me in her arms—I was crying because they had taken Deborah's doll and blanket from me, and Deborah was crying because the intensity and tone of the conversation had scared her. She held both of us close trying to comfort us. She was sad because of the way the morning had ended. It would have been nice for all four of us to have spent some time together. Mother held us until Deborah and I settled down. Her servant came up and mentioned to Mother that she would need to hurry to get ready for one of her meetings. Sarah handed us babies to our nurses and had her servants prepare her for the day.

Day after day and week after week, this is how our life went with two children in the house. The thing I enjoyed the most was the Sabbath; it was the one day of the week when I could spend ample time with my entire family, and that was important to me. Besides, it was fun seeing all of the different decorations and variety of foods we ate on the Sabbath. Every Friday evening, before sundown, the whole family and all of the nurses and servants would be at the house, clean and dressed. About twenty minutes before sunset, my mother would light two candles while Father recited a blessing.

We were always focused and serious when it was time to worship God. After the meal, my father would insist that we all listen to him tell stories about God and how he had selected the Jews to be his people. He told us there would come a Messiah who would cast out the Romans and once that happened, the Jews would again rule like in the days when David was king. Although he would go on and on with the same stories, I never got tired of hearing them. It was the only time my father spent any time with our entire family.

Other than the Sabbath, some holidays, and the occasional birthday celebration, the days just sort of blurred together for me. One day, when Deborah was about a year and a half old, I noticed that my mother was in a particularly good mood, and I wasn't sure why. When the nurses and servants brought Deborah and me into her room, she was humming, and then she snatched us up into her arms for a nice hug. She hadn't hugged us that well for a long time. When the servants came to take us back to our rooms before my father came in, my mother asked them to leave us with her. She told them she had some news for all of us.

When Father came into Sarah's room, he looked surprised to see both of us in there with her. The two of us got immediately quiet because my father didn't like a lot of noise. Just when it looked like my father was about to speak, most likely to question Deborah's and my presence there, my mother blurted out to everyone that she was expecting again. She was so happy because she had thought that she wouldn't be able to have any more children since she had had so much trouble with Deborah.

My father quickly put on a smile and hugged both of us before asking the servants to take us back to our rooms. Once we had left, Jonathan came over and sat next to Sarah. He took her hand and squeezed it before speaking, telling her how blessed by God they must be for her to be able to conceive another child. He said that he would pray for her and the baby's health continuously because he was very concerned. In his prayers, he would ask God to help them through this.

11

The next months went by quickly with everyone in eager antic-ipation of another impending birth, but as with her previous two pregnancies, Mother had an extremely tough time dealing with morning sickness. She would stay in her room most of the morning until she felt better. After a while, she discontinued her outside meetings and focused on staying healthy by spending much of her time at home. Both Deborah and I wanted to be a good sister and big brother, and so we "helped" as best we could, being careful not to violate our father's decree by doing the work of servants. In the morning, he would spend a few minutes with the family and then leave for work. Sometimes, he could work at the house, but with Deborah and me wanting to spend more time with him, he started working more at his office in the center of Tarsus.

Father also commenced going on trips to negotiate to buy and sell his goods. It seemed like he was spending more time traveling than he used to. When my mother would ask him why he was traveling so much, he would get defensive and tell her that he had to because of a slowdown in the economy. He had to make certain that he was getting the best deals possible. She said that she understood and hoped that business would get better so they could see him more often.

As the time approached for my mother to have her third child, Father, being concerned about his wife's health, reduced his travel schedule to make sure he would be home when the new baby arrived. He was becoming worrisome because Sarah seemed to be getting tired more than she had with her other pregnancies, with a couple of months left before the baby was supposed to be born.

This explains why my father asked the doctor to start coming more often to check on Sarah. One time after the doctor had examined her, he explained to Father that she had started having light contractions, which could intensify if not treated properly. He immediately put her into bed and told her she had to stay there until the baby was born. The doctor told my father that as long as she stayed in bed and avoided anything that would make her anxious or otherwise cause her stress, she would be fine.

Father assured the doctor he would make certain that she was attended to and would have no stressful situations.

"My concern, Jonathan, is that because Sarah's last two deliveries were so difficult, chances are the third will also be difficult," the doctor told my father. "Everyone needs to be fully prepared to help her from the very beginning. She might not be strong enough to have the baby without help."

Jonathan got up and started pacing the floor, going back and forth for a full five minutes. The doctor stayed quiet until Jonathan spoke.

"Doctor," Father said, "do you think that the baby and Sarah are at risk for their lives? When Deborah was born, it drained her, and it took her a long time to recover."

"All you can do right now is pray for a good delivery," the doctor said, as Jonathan nodded his head in agreement.

After the doctor left, Father slowly walked up the stairs toward my mother's suite of rooms contemplating what he would say to her. Most of all, he focused on being in a good mood so Mother would stay relaxed. There were times she could easily be stressed out because of his moods. Once he was outside her door, he took a few deep breaths and knocked. Sarah's nurse came out, and he asked if his wife was awake. The nurse said she was, and Jonathan went in.

Mother was sitting up in bed making some stockings for us. She put the stockings down when she saw my father enter, smiling and holding out her arms for him. Jonathan smiled back and sat down on the bed next to her, taking her hands in his.

"How do you feel?" he asked.

"I'm fine but tired," she answered. "I'm somewhat worried that the baby might be in danger, according to what the doctor told me. He was truthful with me. What did the doctor say to you?"

"He said you would be fine as long as you stayed rested during the remainder of the pregnancy," my father said.

They chatted for a while about the household and us until Mother got tired. At that point, Jonathan bent over to kiss her and said he would leave her to her handwork, reminding her once more to get some rest.

Father left the room and headed downstairs, where he summoned for his steward by pulling a cord. Father asked the steward to come into his study and motioned for him to sit down, which surprised the steward because he had never been asked to sit down with his master. My father then explained the circumstances of Sarah's condition and gave the steward new orders for the household to follow to ensure rest and comfort for my mother.

"Make sure that Sarah's suite is kept quiet and that there are always fresh flowers and her favorite treats in the room," Father said to the steward. "Also, make sure that when Saul and Deborah go to see her, they not be allowed to get up on her bed and definitely not be held by her."

Father wanted to have the steward prevent anything that could cause Sarah to lose the baby and endanger her life.

"I understand completely, my master, and I will also make sure that all of the household staff will understand these new orders and that they are followed completely," the steward said.

Every morning and every evening, Deborah and I would go into our mother's room and spend as much time there as the nurse would allow us. We loved being with our mother. Usually, just before the children came into the room in the morning, Father would arrive and spend time with Mother. He was anxious about her and the baby. He would also have the doctor come in at least twice a week to check on her to make sure everything was going as well as possible.

After a couple of weeks of this, Jonathan caught the doctor leaving and asked him for an update. The doctor was still upbeat but was concerned that Sarah was getting weaker. "She is having some instances of light contractions, which could cause her to lose the baby," he said. He stressed that she continue to stay in bed and be kept calm. Jonathan told him he was doing everything he could to follow the doctor's instructions.

One morning the following week, Father went into Mother's room and told her he was leaving on a one-day business trip; he told her that it was something he needed to do. He said, however, that he wouldn't go if she objected to it. Sarah laughed and said that everything was fine, that she had plenty of help if she needed anything.

Father was relieved and told her that he would leave that morning, complete the business he needed to do, and return the following day by dusk. With that, he gave her a quick kiss, went to his suite, and had his servants prepare him for the trip, to include packing his carriage. Within the hour, my father and the carriage were headed to the coast. He needed to check on some goods he had purchased that were being shipped into the port. Usually, he would make the roundtrip in a day, but he also needed to give detailed instructions to the ship's captain and take the captain and first mate to dinner.

After Jonathan left, the nurse brought us children in to see Mother. She hugged us both and then told us she had a surprise for us. She motioned for the servant to come over, who handed each of us a present. We each opened our present and held up the stockings that Mother had made for us while confined to bed. I promptly dropped down on the rug and, after pulling off my sandals, slipped on my stockings. I jumped up and showed

Mother how well they looked and fit. Meanwhile, the nurse was trying to help Deborah put hers on. She wasn't doing so well and was getting very frustrated. Mother tried to tell her how to do it, and then the nurse got pushed aside by Deborah, who kept saying, "I do it, I do it." I decided to give my sister a hand, but she started crying. Finally, Deborah got one of her stockings on, and, when she looked up and saw everyone laughing, she started laughing, too. Mother then reached under the covers of her bed and brought out some very small stockings. There were two pairs, one blue and the other pink. Both of us thought they were precious.

"Mother, why did you make two pair of stockings?" I asked.

"I don't know if the new baby will be a boy like you or a girl like Deborah," Mother said. "I wanted to make sure whatever it was that it would have stockings like its big brother or sister."

By this time, Mother was becoming tired, so the nurse started getting Deborah and me ready to leave. Usually, at this time, we would put our hands on our mother's tummy to feel the baby move, but the baby wasn't moving right then. Mother said it must be taking a nap. We kissed our mother good night and went to have dinner before going to bed.

12

Mother hadn't felt this happy and content in a long time. She loved her family. After Mother said her nightly prayers, her servant came in and prepared her for bed, asking her how she felt. Mother said she felt fine but that she was very tired. This concerned the nurse, who asked if she should go get the doctor to check on her.

"That's not necessary," Mother said. "I'm just tired; that's all."

Several hours later, though, around midnight, Mother woke up in incredible pain. She was having contractions that shook her whole body. Her gasping and moaning woke up her nurse, who rushed in to see what was happening. She lit the lamp and held it over Sarah. What she saw startled her. Mother was having contractions, and she was bleeding. The nurse ran to the hallway and screamed for the servant on watch to run and get the doctor. Several other servants, hearing the commotion, came running toward the room. Sarah's nurse told the male servant in the group to go get Jonathan. The servant ran down the stairs and headed for the port.

The nurse and the servants entered Mother's suite, bringing water and linens to help with the delivery. Seeing blood still oozing from Sarah, they all prayed the doctor would get there quickly.

It wasn't long before the doctor came trotting through the door, at which the servants and the nurse stepped back to allow him easy access to the bed for his examination of Mother. He gave Sarah a drink of wine laced with frankincense and myrrh to help her with the pain. He told the nurse after he had finished that they needed to get the baby delivered as soon as possible so that he could try to stop Sarah's bleeding.

The remainder of the night was horrible as everyone watched Sarah grow weaker and weaker from the loss of blood and fatigue. She was distraught about the baby and told the doctor to do whatever was necessary to save it. They were having trouble helping her deliver the baby. This would take time, and he was being very careful so as not to risk anything further with her.

Just before dawn, the baby was born. It was a girl. The nurse held Mother's hand as the servants cleaned and dressed the baby. Sarah kept pointing to her night stand, wanting the nurse to get the small pink stockings she had made for our new arrival. After a few minutes, they laid the baby on mother's breast so she could see her baby for the first time. After a few minutes, the doctor told the nurse to have everyone leave the room except her so they could see what needed to be done for Sarah. He was extremely concerned.

After everyone had left, he gave Sarah some more of the painkiller and reexamined her to see if there was any way to stop the bleeding. By this time, Mother was even weaker. Soon there was another commotion in the house with someone sprinting up the stairs. The door flew open; it was Jonathan. He ran up to the bed, knelt by his wife's side, and took her hand. Sarah smiled a weary smile at her husband and softly told him she had given him another baby daughter. Jonathan smiled back at her, squeezed her hand gently, and told her he loved her. He laid his head on her and started to cry. Mother put her hand on his head and told him she would be fine, and soon she was asleep. Jonathan lay there a few minutes and composed himself then stood up and walked over to the doctor and asked if he could speak with him out in the hall.

"Tell me, Doctor, honestly; what is my wife's condition?" Father asked.

"Sarah has been bleeding internally during some of the night, and it was a miracle she had the strength to have the baby," the doctor said. "I don't know what else to do in order to stop the bleeding. I've tried everything I know. Maybe now that the baby has been born, the bleeding will stop. My suggestion is that you start praying, fasting, and pleading for God to save her."

Jonathan was in shock. How could this happen to him? He had done everything right by the law. He couldn't believe that God would allow his beloved Sarah to die.

Jonathan stayed there for a while kneeling before her, standing up, and walking slowly into the room of his newborn baby girl, who was asleep. He looked down at her, and he reached out and rubbed her small back as he started praying.

"Jehovah, please don't let our beloved Sarah die. She has done so much good for your people here and for the family you gave me. Father, I followed all of your commandments perfectly. I do not understand. Show me what I can do to save her."

He stepped back, slumped to the floor, and continued to pray.

In Sarah's room, the nurse and the servants were all praying, as was the doctor, who kept watch over our mother. Even though she was asleep, he could see that she was getting weaker.

Father soon came over to see Deborah and me. We were overjoyed to see him back home. We usually didn't see him in the mornings but loved it when we did. He picked us up, held us for a moment, and then told us that Mother was resting right now. Still holding us, he walked back into the hall and over to the new baby's nursery so we could see our new sister. We took turns touching her. I then asked my father if I could see the baby's feet. Father thought that was an odd request, but he had the nurse unwrap the sleeping baby. Deborah and I were so excited at what we saw—on her feet were the same pink stockings Mother had shown us last night.

The news of my mother's condition had gone out from the household, and now the whole city of Tarsus was praying and fasting, too. Toward evening, Mother opened her eyes and looked around her room. She saw Jonathan sitting next to her and tried to squeeze his hand. He looked down at her as she smiled a slight smile at him while asking how the baby and the other children were doing.

"The baby is beautiful, just like you, Sarah, and Deborah and Saul are fine, but they are pestering me to see you," Father said.

"I would love to see them as well," she said.

The doctor nodded his approval, and a servant left to go bring the children back to see their mother. Deborah and I ran into the room, but Father caught us before we could jump onto the bed. He told us how Mother was very tired and that we needed to be careful not to hurt her by jumping on her. Deborah and I had both made gifts for our new baby sister. I showed Mother a blanket I had colored on for her to sleep with; Deborah showed her one of her dolls that she was going to give the baby. Mother told us how proud she was of us. After a few more minutes, Jonathan could see that Sarah was getting tired and had us taken out to go get our dinner.

Father and all of the servants resumed praying. Mother would sleep a few minutes and then open her eyes and look around the room. The rabbi had come into the room a bit earlier, and Father asked him to hold her hand while speaking a prayer for them. As the rabbi prayed, Jonathan felt Sarah suddenly grip his hand hard and then go limp. He knew at that moment that God had taken his beloved Sarah. He reached up to his robe and tore it down the right side. As the others saw what he had done, they also tore their robes and started crying and mourning. Father couldn't believe she had died. What had he done wrong?

Father was numb with grief. After staying there next to her and weeping for some time, he summoned Sarah's servant to the room. Father got up and asked her to prepare Sarah for burial. He then walked out of her room in a daze.

It wasn't long before there were hundreds of people outside our house. It seems practically all of Tarsus had come to pay their final respects to Mother. Several women from the synagogue asked to come and help prepare her for burial, which they did by washing her body and wrapping her in fine linens while anointing her body with spices and oil. After they had finished, they went back outside and continued their vigil with the other people of Tarsus.

The next morning, Father went to Mother's room to see her for the last time on earth. He was pleased with the care that had been taken to prepare Mother for burial. After the rabbi arrived, father said they were now ready to take Mother to the family's tomb. Several women came in and finished wrapping Sarah for burial. Some of them then carried her body down the steps and out into the street, where the crowd parted to let them through. They slowly walked out to where the tomb was and laid her there with her ancestors. The burial party then went back to our house to begin the seven-day period of mourning.

Still despondent and grief stricken after the burial, Father came to our rooms and tried to explain to Deborah and me that our mother had gone to Paradise and that someday we would see her again. All we knew was that we already missed Mother deeply and wanted only to be with her again.

On the first Sabbath after our mother's death, Father took all of his household to the synagogue to worship and name our new baby. After the rabbi had finished with the service, Father asked that he be allowed to name his new baby, and, with the rabbi's permission, Father took the baby into his arms and told everyone that her name would be Mara, which in Hebrew means "bitter." He explained he wanted to have her so named to remind him of the bitter way God had treated him and his family. Naomi, the mother-in-law of Ruth, had claimed the same name as an expression of grief after her husband and sons had died.

As Father sat back down, the rabbi and the congregation wore stunned looks because of the name Jonathan had chosen for the baby. She would always know that she was the cause of her mother's death: she had a life sentence.

After we got home from the synagogue, we were taken up to our rooms to go to bed. Father also retired to his suite for the evening. He could not sleep, going over and over in his mind how this could have happened to him. He thought back through his life, wondering what he had done wrong to merit this. He prayed that he would understand because he was afraid that the sin he had committed would affect us as well. He remembered the Scripture in Numbers that says, "The Lord is slow to anger, abounding in love and forgiving sin and rebellion. Yet he does not leave the guilty unpunished; he punishes the children for the sin of the fathers to the third and fourth generation."

Father did not want us punished as Sarah apparently had been for his sin. As he paced his suite, he wandered down the hall into Sarah's room, having told the servants to leave everything untouched. He walked into her closet several times so he could smell her scent that was still on her clothes. Then he would sit on her bed and think of the times they had been together. He still loved her very, very much.

After staying in her room a while, he went into our rooms and watched us while we slept, wondering how he could tell us about our mother when we were old enough to understand. He tried hard to pray during these times but felt that he just could not connect with God. Sometimes, he would fall asleep trying to pray. The next day, the servants would find him on a pallet in one of the children's rooms. Every morning, he would summon just enough energy to get bathed and clothed, at times hoping God would take him to Paradise so he could once again be with his precious Sarah. But he also was concerned about what would happen to his children if they were to lose both of their parents at such a young age.

Every day, the rabbi would come by to see Jonathan, and every day, Jonathan would tell the servants he did not want to see anyone. Instead of the normal thirty days for mourning, Father continued not to see anyone for sixty days. He thought that if he wanted to save his children, he would need to obey God twice as long as he commanded. He hoped that would atone for the sin he had committed that had caused Sarah's death.

13

During one of his contemplative bouts with his conscience, Father decided that he might not have given the correct amount of sacrifices. So he summoned a servant and told him to go out and get his business manager even though it was three in the morning. Knowing the time, the servant hesitated a few moments, only for Father to tell him to go then or he would be sold the next day.

The servant went and rustled the business manager out of bed. Father met him when he arrived at our front door and took him into his study.

"I need for you to show me all the books of accounting starting with the past year and going back at least five years to see what my income has been and what the cost of my sacrifices were," Father told the business manager. "I must have this information available for me to look at by noon."

"Yes, sir, b-but I don't know if I can pull together all the . . ." the manager started to say before he knew by the look on Jonathan's face that there would be no excuses. He must comply. He immediately left the study and hurried to his office to start pulling together all of the information that Jonathan required.

By noon, the business manager was back with the information Jonathan requested for the past two years, while associates of the manager were in his office pulling the information for the other three years. Once he came to our door, Father again guided him into the study, reiterating that the only numbers he was interested in were the net income of his businesses and the cost of the sacrifices he had made. Luckily, by this time, the business associates had arrived with the remainder of the information. Jonathan looked these over as well and, after some quick calculations, decided that he had "sacrificed" at least enough to cover the requirements of the law. He then told the business manager and his associates to leave, that he needed time to think.

As Father sat there, he started pondering how maybe the law required different percentages of his income, that instead of using his net income as the basis for determining the amount of sacrifices to be made, maybe he should be basing all of the calculations on gross income. He calculated the difference of the percentages owed on the net versus the gross income for the past five years, and, even though he had given a higher percentage than required of his net income, he was way too low on his sacrifices based on the gross income.

Deeply disturbed by what he had calculated, Jonathan again summoned a servant and told him to go and get his business manager back over to the house immediately. Father had quickly figured that the difference between his net income and his gross income over the past five years was more than twelve million denarii. Before he made any rash decisions, he wanted his business manager to confirm his calculations. Once the business manager had arrived and returned to his study, Father explained to him the calculations he had made and asked the business manager to confirm his numbers. The business manager took the books and looked them over; after a time, he concurred that Father's new calculations were correct.

Jonathan was stunned at what he had discovered. How could he have been so negligent? After a few moments of silence, he instructed his business manager to start liquidating whatever he needed until he had two million denarii, which he had calculated to be the amount by which he needed to increase his sacrifice to get back to where he needed to be although there was nothing he could do at this point to bring Sarah back.

The manager asked into what venture Father wanted to invest this fortune. Father looked at him and told him that the money would be a sacrifice to God, which shocked the manager. He had never heard of such a large sacrifice.

"Maybe this sacrifice will atone for whatever sin I have committed that God has punished me for," Father said, speaking more to himself than the manager. Turning to the other man, he added, "Once you have gathered the money, bring it to me."

Jonathan dismissed the manager and then summoned a servant.

"Prepare everyone in the household for an extended stay in Jerusalem," Father told the servant, "and have them ready to depart within the week. Once you get the word out, take this letter I am holding and deliver it to Annas in Jerusalem as soon as you can."

Jonathan spent the remainder of the week getting his businesses in order. He spent long hours at his office with his business manager and associates going over what he wanted them to do in his absence. As the week was ending, the business manager he had told to liquidate some of his holdings came to him and said that he had the two million denarii Father had requested. Additionally, Father's other servant came and told him that the household would be ready to leave for Jerusalem at Jonathan's requested time.

The trip would be a long and arduous journey of almost four hundred miles, which equated to about a month of travel. Since he was a merchant, he knew of a caravan they could travel with for their safety. Although he had sworn his business manager to secrecy, he was concerned that since he had liquidated so much into gold, someone might think he would be carrying it with them on the journey to Jerusalem. He rang for a servant and told him to ask the centurion over Tarsus to see him the following day.

When Father went over to the garrison to see the centurion, the guards showed Jonathan in immediately. Once he was alone with the centurion, Jonathan explained what he was doing. Hearing what Father told him, the centurion asked Father if this was necessary. Father said it was.

The centurion reached over, pulled a piece of paper toward him, and started writing a note that he handed Father when finished. It stated that Jonathan was in the protection of the Roman army and that he was to have safe passage to Jerusalem. The centurion then walked to the door and instructed the soldier to have ten soldiers report to him at once. The centurion told Jonathan that he would send these men along with him to assure him of safe passage. Grateful for this, Jonathan told the centurion he would be leaving the following morning with the caravan that was camped near the city. The centurion said the men would be available at his house at dawn. He also said that he would have a couple of men watch over his property while he was away. Jonathan thanked him as they shook hands.

As Father left the garrison, he felt that God had started helping him again by having the centurion's men protect his household on their journey and also guarding his property while he was away. Since he was now sacrificing properly, he felt like he was back in God's good graces.

14

The journey from Tarsus to Jerusalem was grueling. It seems I was the only one of the family not affected. In fact, I enjoyed the travel. Even as a five-year-old, I was prepared to help oversee the packing and planning for the day ahead. I wanted to be involved, but my father held his ground, telling me and the servants that I was not to be allowed to perform any of the work assigned to a servant or a slave.

During the long trip, my fellow travelers were often seeking me out. I enjoyed being around them, and they appeared to like my company. I loved hearing all the stories they told me, including details of my birth and early years that I have touched on here. Besides, I was blessed with a great memory. During the trip, I also learned a lot of Jewish and Roman history.

Once we had camped for the day, Father would tell everyone stories about our family. I never got tired of hearing about my namesake Saul and the battles he had fought and won for God and his people. Sometimes, during the day, I would grab a stick and brandish it like a sword, reenacting some of the stories I had been told. Everyone was amazed at how I could remember all of the details of the battles, but that was just how I thought; to me it was no great feat. I heard some adults say how bright a child I was, and

I guess I wouldn't argue with that. But there were still times that the child in me came out, especially at night when I cried myself to sleep because I missed Mother so much. I know that my father missed her as well, and a part of me was crying for him, too.

As our caravan approached Jerusalem, a small group of riders came toward us. They were envoys representing Annas the high priest, the Roman commander, and King Herod. They wanted to welcome Jonathan to Jerusalem. Also, my father was handed three dinner invitations, one each from the three dignitaries and scheduled for a week hence so my father would have time first to rest up from the long journey. He graciously accepted all of the invitations, and the envoys stayed with the caravan the remainder of the day.

We arrived in Jerusalem the following day, and the servants unpacked and finished preparing the house that Annas had purchased for my father. Jonathan went on a tour of the place and found that Annas had purchased a house exactly like the one he required. Father added a few things here and there then sent a thank-you note to Annas.

Life in my father's household was hectic, starting with his incessant need to have strict order in his house. That much hadn't changed. Even while finishing the remodeling of the house, my father kept his appointments with Annas, Herod, and the Roman commander, all of them offering their condolences to Father for the death of Sarah but saying they believed he would love living in Jerusalem.

During the day of my father's dinner with Annas, he spent a lot of time thinking about what was the best thing he could do for us as a family. He had ignored the three us since we had arrived, having kept himself busy getting everything in order.

As he thought through his issues, Father remembered how Mother had so much wanted a child and had promised God that the child would serve him like Samuel. Although it was later in my life than Samuel's, Father wanted to discuss this arrangement with Annas, who had already agreed to take me on as a student when I turned twelve. Perhaps he would take me even earlier after hearing Father's opinion of me that I was very bright and responsible. Father, then, could focus on getting a nurse and tutors for my sisters.

When the evening arrived for Father to dine with Annas, he made his way to Annas's villa, where a servant received him and took him into Annas's study for a drink. Father was impressed with the high priest's home, telling him so as he entered the room. As Annas and my father relaxed in the study, Annas began telling him how sad he was about Sarah.

"Thank you, Annas, although I'm not sure why God took Sarah from us," Jonathan said. "I am having trouble reconciling why he would do this to me. I have always been a righteous man. My family and I have continuously followed the letter of the law. Because of this, we have always been blessed.

"I have looked back on my life, searching for the sin that has caused this and cannot see what it was. Since I am sinless, I can only think that it was a sin of my father's that has caused this. I have decided to try to make amends for that sin by making an offering of two million denarii to the temple. I hope that God will then forgive our family of whatever the sin was that caused Sarah's death."

Annas was shocked upon hearing Jonathan's revelation, but he was elated about the money he would receive from Father. Annas needed money to pay the Romans, always more and more it seemed, to keep them pacified so he could keep his high priest's position.

"I would like to set up a time, Annas, where my household and I could come to the temple and give the sacrifice," Father said. "I want you to lead the procession and the celebration."

"Jonathan, I will honor that request and will set up the celebration for next week," Annas answered.

"Annas," Jonathan continued, "we had discussed Saul coming to the temple to study when he was twelve. I am asking that Saul be taken into the temple to begin his studies now. As you remember, Sarah had pleaded with God to have a child, and Saul was the answer to her prayers.

"Sarah promised God that Saul would be given to him for answering her prayers like Hannah had done with Samuel. Saul is a remarkably smart and focused child, and he will have the benefit of any tutors or help needed from me. I know that he will be able to be a great benefit to you and your priests."

Hearing this, Annas sat there for a moment weighing the decision he must make. If he accepted me into the temple, he would be able to ask and receive additional offerings from my father. If he didn't, then he was sure that Jonathan would enroll him in another school and that school would get the benefit of my father's gifts. Although Annas didn't need another pupil, especially one just five years old, he accepted.

"During next week's celebration of your most generous gift, Jonathan, we will also make the announcement that Saul has been accepted into the temple as a student of the Torah and Talmud," Annas said.

With that settled, both men went into dinner and enjoyed the remainder of the evening.

The following morning, while Jonathan was discussing business with his business manager, he told him to convert all of the two million denarii that hadn't been changed into gold coins. He wanted everyone at the celebration to see the large sacks of gold he was giving to God. The manager promised the gift would be ready in a couple of days.

Father then summoned both my nurse and my servant to tell them of his decision regarding me and my upcoming tutelage in the temple. This came as a complete shock to them. It was evident my father had changed since Mother's passing. It now seemed he wouldn't solicit anyone else's thoughts on his decisions. He told them to begin packing my clothes, while making sure I had everything I needed to move to the temple by the following week.

My father then called for the household steward to tell him to prepare the household to go to the temple the following week. He wanted everyone to look splendid when he gave his gift to God. With that, Father believed, he would have completed both Sarah's and his obligations to God. He looked up to heaven and said, "Sarah, I hope you can see how I have sacrificed to make sure that God will continue to bless our family."

Father didn't tell us his plans until the day before the celebration. He did this so he wouldn't have to listen to any whining or complaining until then. He hated listening to anyone or anything that went contrary to what he had decided. He alone had vetted this decision, and that was enough.

15

As the day of the celebration of his sacrifice drew closer, Jonathan couldn't sleep. He was worried about how the people and the Jewish elite would view his sacrifice. He had a big, solemn celebration planned with a lot of animal sacrifices, accompanied, of course, by the main event of putting the gold into the hands of Annas the high priest. He hoped that all of Israel would hear of, appreciate, and applaud his fabulous gift.

That morning, it was time to get everyone up and bustling. Jonathan pulled every servant's cord he could find, and as they came to him and gathered around, he told them to finish all of the preparations he had given them and to report in when they were ready but no later than 9:45 a.m. His plans were to start the procession around 10:00. He figured it would take about an hour to make their way to the temple and then another hour to sacrifice all of the different animals he had selected to give as a sacrifice.

Once the sacrifices were completed, the procession would then move into the temple, where Jonathan would say a few things regarding the gift, to include the amount and why it was being given. He would then hand Annas one gold coin as a symbol of the whole gift, at which time Annas would move over to the contribution box and solemnly drop it in, saying that the coin was a token of the gift Jonathan was giving. Annas would next walk over to the carts that were being used to move all of the bags of gold coins, where he would thank Jonathan for his fabulous sacrifice and gift. Jonathan had sent some notes over to Annas for his speech. The entire ceremony was planned and scripted to perfection.

The servants noticed that without Sarah's soft touch to help keep Jonathan's aggressiveness in check, Father was turning into a legalistic tyrant. He was getting more and more critical not only of himself but of all his servants, as if they all were to blame for my mother's untimely death.

Until 9:45 a.m., the entire household was in chaos. Everyone was rushing around making sure the list that Father had given them was being completed exactly as specified. Everyone was dressing in the garments they had chosen, and we were getting bathed and dressed.

At 10:00 on the dot, the procession began, starting out from our home in the upper city close to the home of Caiaphas. Since it wasn't too long of a walk to the temple, we chose a roundabout way that took us past King Herod's palace. Herod had heard about Jonathan's gift and came out on the balcony to acknowledge Jonathan and his household as our procession went by.

Soon they entered the temple grounds and walked solemnly through Solomon's Porch. That's where they met Annas and several guards that would accompany the procession the remainder of the way. The Roman guards who had guarded them up to this point departed because they were not Jews and therefore could not go through the Beautiful Gate into the Court of Women. As the procession passed through the Court of Women, the women stayed there while the men continued on through the Gate of Nicanor, where they would make the animal sacrifices requested by Jonathan.

As the priests brought out the animals to be sacrificed, Annas blessed each one, after which Jonathan placed his hands on each and the priests slaughtered the animal. I was watching all of this, and it didn't take me long to start feeling faint and sick to my stomach. My father and Annas immediately noticed my condition. Father looked down at me and whispered, "Don't you get sick in front of all of us. You have to quit acting like a baby, take your place among the men of Jerusalem, and make your family proud. I won't have you embarrassing me in front of everyone."

When they brought up the next animal to sacrifice, Father forced me to put my hands on the sacrifice and stand close by while the priests slaughtered it. It was a young lamb that screamed repeatedly before it died. As revolted as I was by this scene, I was more afraid of what my father would do to me if I didn't stand there and take it in. Since there was a long line of sacrifices, I finally started getting accustomed to the stench of blood and the screams of the sacrifices, leaving me more uncomfortable than actually sickened.

When the sacrifices of the animals were finished, everyone moved back to the Court of Women and completed the ceremony that my father had scripted with the giving of the gold and Annas's speech. Jonathan looked out over the people as Annas spoke and saw with great satisfaction that the people were truly impressed. He knew God would look upon and bless his family again. He quietly spoke to his Sarah and told her that he had shown the people and God his love for God.

In the ensuing days, my life became even more regimented and strict. For all practical purposes, my boyhood was over. Father had enrolled me in the temple school, where I was taught by several rabbis focusing on different sections of the Torah. Every morning, the priests would wake me and I would be required to read the Scriptures and pray for an hour. Once that was finished, I would go to breakfast and then spend two hours apiece with the different rabbis. This was my daily routine. Before the day was finished, I would join a small group of students and listen to and answer questions from Gamaliel.

Gamaliel would ask questions about what we were studying. He would try to get us to comprehend what we were studying instead of just going through the rote memorization encouraged by many teachers. Most students disliked working with the other rabbis, preferring instead the style of Gamaliel whereby he allowed time for questions and answers of what we were studying. I, on the other hand, didn't mind the memorization and the discipline required by the other rabbis in studying God's Word.

While most of the other students, much older than me, grumbled and complained about the rigorous academic schedule, I loved it. It offered a chance for me to show everyone that I was as smart as or smarter than everyone else in the school. I was quickly able to become the best student at the school. While others took part in other activities outside school, I only studied.

As my father and our household settled in to our new life in a new city, Father started traveling for business and wasn't in Jerusalem that often. When he did come home, he would spend most of his time on business or politicking with King Herod or the priests. At the house, he would just stick his head in for a few minutes to see his daughters and me when he could. In talking to the teachers, he would hear from them about how gifted a student I was.

As I grew older, I found myself focusing only on my academics; I had a thirst for knowledge and academic advancement, and I felt I was being held back by others who weren't as committed to their studies as I was. The other students usually wouldn't talk with me, and so I started gravitating to older acquaintances. Occasionally, I would be befriended by someone closer in age to me, but eventually they, too, would give up on me because I was such a legalistic know-it-all. I know this now in retrospect.

While I saw myself as the smartest, most reverent Jew who has ever lived—and nothing Father said or did discouraged me from being this way—the one thing other boys could do to knock me down a peg or two was ridicule me for my small size and my bad eyesight. They would "accidentally" bump into me and knock me down, or they would hide my glasses so I couldn't see anything. This angered me, and I swore to myself that I would get even.

As I was getting close to being thirteen years old so I could be a son of the commandment—some Jews call this their bar mitzvah—I sent a letter to Father reminding him to be at the ceremony. With his busy schedule, he might forget. I knew he would be at Passover because that's when he would always have several families over and sacrifice plenty of animals for all of his guests to see. Admittedly, I now enjoyed going through the temple with him and laying my hands on the animal sacrifices just before they were to be slaughtered.

On the morning of my ceremony, Father came by to pick me up, and we headed over to the temple. As we got closer, we started running into other worshippers, which just slowed us down, angering my father in the process. He asked one of the temple guards to clear a path for us. At that moment, we saw Caiaphas, who was the son-in law of Annas the high priest, moving toward us. The guard grabbed a couple more guards and escorted Caiaphas, my father, and me past everyone else right into the Court of Men. We just pushed and shoved our way through other boys and their fathers who were waiting patiently for the ceremony. Father was always annoyed at all of the uncivilized, country Jews who came to Jerusalem and the temple during Passover, as they served only to disrupt his routine. One of the boys caught my attention. He was a bit taller than the others, and I was struck by how he handled the jostling with calm serenity.

Once Passover was over and the crowds had departed, I was hoping to get back into my routine, to include using Solomon's Porch to study. It was springtime, a nice time of year to sit and study outside. As I was listening to one of my teachers, I happened to notice another boy who was listening to the different teachers around the porch. He looked familiar, but I couldn't put my finger on where I had seen him. As I moved from one teacher to another during the day, I kept noticing that same boy moving around and listening. This bothered me because he was hearing the same instruction I was but for free.

Toward the end of the day, when it was time to be with Gamaliel, this intrusive boy moved in closer. Obviously, he wasn't going away, which was my wish, so I decided to show this other boy who was boss in terms of students in the class. When Gamaliel would ask a question, I would quickly answer. Even when Gamaliel asked students other than me to answer, I would butt in and answer anyway. Each time I did this, I would then glance over at this other boy so I could see his amazement at my academic prowess. To my dismay, though, he wasn't even looking at me. Instead, he was looking around at the other students and Gamaliel, ignoring me.

This continued the next day as well. As Gamaliel was teaching, he asked a question regarding the Messiah. Gamaliel had asked the question in such a way that no one, including me, could answer it. While everyone just sat there, I heard a voice from behind me answering the question. I then looked at Gamaliel to see if it was the correct answer, which it was. Once the boy had finishing answering the question, he in turn asked a question of Gamaliel.

"Master Gamaliel, if I may ask you something, what kind of kingdom will this Messiah rule?" the boy asked.

Not to be outdone, I blurted out an answer before Gamaliel could speak, saying, "The awaited Messiah will rule over the world from Jerusalem, and his kingdom will reign forever."

This boy, Jesus, then asked another question: "If that was the case, wouldn't that kingdom include both Jews and Gentiles?"

"Of course it would not," I said, "because the Jews are the chosen people of God."

Then this intrusive boy asked, "Why, then, did God tell Abram *all* of the kingdoms of the earth would be blessed? And since that is true, why should we the Jews be excluding the Gentiles from worshipping in God's temple now?" No one answered.

Gamaliel was incredibly impressed and, secretly, very pleased that this other boy had stumped everyone in the class, especially me. Although Gamaliel thought I was destined to do great things for the Jewish people, he also knew I needed some practice in humility. Gamaliel then asked this boy his name and where he was from, to which the boy replied, "My name is Jesus, and I am from Nazareth." Upon hearing this, Gamaliel remembered that one of the rabbis had mentioned this boy's name and that he had wanted him for a student.

I also knew the story of how this boy was rumored at one time to be the Messiah, but my understanding was this was just a story his parents told everyone to cover up the fact that his mother had gotten pregnant before she had married. Technically, the boy was a bastard and his parents should have been stoned. They ran away from Bethlehem in shame to Nazareth. No matter; I was still miffed that this Jesus could have stumped me—after all, I was easily the smartest student in class.

This continued the following day, and my annoyance at Jesus's superior intelligence just kept growing. Soon I started asking questions myself. Gamaliel allowed it because he was curious to see how these two scholars would interact. For every question I would ask, Jesus had a very good answer and then would come back with a question that no one could answer although they tried. This went on for a while until I got exasperated and stormed off. Gamaliel was amazed at Jesus's knowledge of the Scriptures and the wisdom of which he applied his answers. He seemed to ooze God's thoughts and love. He had so much insight.

Word of this boy's brilliance got around, and a small crowd would form where they heard the lessons were being taught. They hoped that Gamaliel would again be teaching and that Jesus would be there so they could listen to his thoughts. Gamaliel decided to change up the order for the day and had his students all come over to him that morning. Father was in Jerusalem, and Gamaliel was surprised to see that I had brought him with me to the class. By this time, I had started a rumor with my father that the reason Jesus was so smart and wise was because he was a devil worshipper.

As they got started with class that morning, everyone, not just me, tried to be the one that stumped the new student. I tried it then; even my father did as well. Gamaliel also jumped in with a couple of thoughts directed at Jesus, which he calmly and sincerely answered before asking follow-up questions to help make his points.

As Jesus was finishing one of his comments, I spotted a man and a woman coming up; the woman said, "Jesus, why have you treated Joseph and me this way? Didn't you know we were frantically looking for you?"

Then I watched as Jesus looked at her with love in his eyes and said, "Why were you searching for me? Didn't you know that I would be in my Father's house?"

I couldn't believe what I was hearing. This upstart bastard from Nazareth had just said that he was the Son of God. I jumped up in anger and shouted that Jesus had blasphemed and should be stoned! I looked around and saw some shocked faces: no one else had thought of this. Father just put his hand on my shoulder and walked me away from the group. Father didn't want me to make a scene in public, and it took him a long time to calm me down.

That night, alone, I prayed and made a vow that I would get back at Jesus for his blasphemy.

16

In getting caught up in what had been going on in Jesus's life as well, I will start back where we left him and his family several years earlier, telling his story parallel to mine from his and his family's perspective.

Life for Jesus and his family in Alexandria had settled into a predictable routine. Joseph found a nice place to work close to home, and they still had plenty of money left over from all of the gifts they had received upon Jesus's birth. Joseph always thanked God for all of the physical blessings they had. Since they were still concerned about King Herod, they kept Jesus's identity quiet. They relied on God's promise of being safe in Egypt but thought it wise to also be discreet just in case.

During his family's stay in Alexandria, Jesus continued to do normal childlike things growing up, such as playing with his little sister and helping Mary around the home. One of his favorite things to do was to help Mary grind the grain to make bread. During these times, Mary told him stories of his forefathers Jesse, David, and Solomon. She told him that he would someday be a king like David and would rule his people forever. Jesus enjoyed all of the stories and wanted to be just like David. He wanted to be a man after God's own heart, a mighty warrior, and a good shepherd.

Sometimes, when Joseph wasn't doing anything that could be construed as dangerous to a young child at the carpentry shop, he would take Jesus there to help him with simple chores. While they worked together, Joseph would tell his attentive son about Abraham and the prophets and how he would be King not only of the Jews but also of the Gentiles. In explaining all of this to his son, Joseph would tell him the biblical prophecies about the Messiah and how he would redeem all of mankind. He told Jesus he would rule a spiritual kingdom that would never end.

Jesus always loved the Sabbath: he knew when the day was at hand because his whole family got so happy. They would get cleaned up and set out the items they needed for worship and to prepare the meal. The family would then spend the Sabbath together remembering what God had done for them and for their people. Many times, they would have other families over so they could celebrate together. Mary and Joseph took notice of how contented Jesus would be on the Sabbath and how happy he was.

After a few months in Egypt, Mary and Joseph started discussing where they would live once they were able to go back home. Joseph thought that they should return to Nazareth in Galilee, which would be away from Herod's son, Herod Archelaus. He would rule Judea, where Bethlehem was located, once Herod the Great passed. Herod Archelaus was almost as cruel and paranoid as his father. Herod Antipas, Herod the Great's other son who was to rule in Galilee upon the father's death, wasn't known to be either. Joseph thought that no one would think of Jesus as the boy that Herod the Great had tried to kill if he was in Nazareth. Joseph was concerned that someone in Bethlehem might accidentally say something and put Jesus and the family in jeopardy.

Mary, on the other hand, wanted them to go back to Bethlehem so they would be around family that loved them and would help raise all of their children. She was sure that Jesus was supposed to be brought up in the town where David had been raised. Since Mary and Joseph couldn't agree, they decided to pray, asking God to help them with this decision.

Jesus and Naomi enjoyed being together as brother and sister, and Jesus loved helping Mary take care of her. Joseph frequently encouraged Jesus to help his mother all he could. Joseph knew that desiring to and knowing how to care for others was something God wanted them to teach his Son.

One afternoon, while Joseph was finishing some final touches on a cabinet, the priest from his synagogue rushed in and told him King Herod had died. Joseph's first thought upon hearing the news was that now he and his family could return home. He rushed to the house and told Mary, who had just heard the news herself from a woman they knew from the synagogue. As excited as they both were, he reminded her that God would send them a message when he was ready for them to move back home.

A few weeks later, Joseph had a dream in which he was told that it was now safe for them to go home. He was also shown that they should go to Nazareth and raise their family there. When Joseph awoke that morning, he started making preparations to start home. When Mary woke up a bit later, she saw what Joseph was doing and she knew in her heart that her husband had received word from God. When she asked him what God had shown him, he told her. Although not going back and living in Bethlehem saddened her, she knew God had his reasons and that she would do his will regardless.

Over the next week, the family packed and made preparations to go home. Mary was in charge of packing the household while Joseph finished whatever carpentry jobs he had promised to customers; he started asking around for a caravan with which they could travel for added safety. It wasn't until just a few days before they wanted to leave that he found out about such a caravan. Once again, God was at work in their lives. One of the caravans that came through was being led by one of the men with whom they had traveled to Egypt. Learning of Joseph's interest in joining a caravan, the caravan leader was elated over the opportunity to be traveling with them and the King of Kings. The caravan would re-provision and start back to Bethlehem in a couple of days. Joseph went home and told Mary the great news.

Everyone from the synagogue heard that Joseph had found a caravan with which to travel, and they all came by to say their good-byes. On the evening before their departure, several leaders from their synagogue came by their house to present them a gift. Once the door had been shut, the priest opened a beautiful scroll of the Scriptures and presented them to Jesus. Then they bowed down and worshipped Jesus, the Messiah. They had always wanted to worship him but knew it could risk his life.

The trip back to Bethlehem was, happily, uneventful. As before, Jesus was very comfortable with everyone in the caravan although his parents were mildly apprehensive because of his outgoing personality with everyone. After a couple of days, they grew comfortable with Jesus being separated from them much of the day riding and conversing with the other members of the caravan.

Jesus's typical day would begin with him alongside Mary and Joseph; then one of their fellow travelers would come by and ask if Jesus could spend time with them. The others in the caravan never got tired of being with Jesus and answering his questions about nature, what they did to earn money, and where they had traveled. He was one large question!

Mary and Joseph used the time during the day to be with Naomi and to discuss the decision to move to Nazareth, among other topics. Joseph's brother was staying in the house where they had lived before journeying to Bethlehem for the census. Joseph sent a letter to him asking him to help them find another place to live once they returned. The letter said that they were headed back from Egypt and that they would go by way of Bethlehem to visit family before continuing on their way to Nazareth.

As the caravan was getting close to Bethlehem, Mary and Joseph started saying their good-byes since the caravan was actually going toward Nazareth. When the people of the caravan heard they were leaving them to go to Bethlehem, all of the travelers came by to say their good-byes to the young family. They all knew who Jesus was but promised they would be careful not to say anything to anyone later that would put him in danger. They had all fallen in love with the young King.

As Mary and Joseph approached Bethlehem, they could see a group of shepherds coming toward them. After a few minutes, they recognized them as the same shepherds who had come to worship Jesus when he was born. When they, in turn, saw it was Mary, Joseph, and Jesus, they rejoiced because he had been saved and was now safe. One of them decided to run ahead into Bethlehem to tell their parents that they were on their way. Since the family was expecting them, as soon as the shepherd was gone for only a short time, Mary's and Joseph's fathers came riding up. They jumped off their horses, ran, and hugged their children and grandchildren. They were so happy to see them safe and sound.

Once in Bethlehem, Mary and Joseph realized that it might upset their unsuspecting families and friends to see them, especially since Jesus had been saved and their baby boys had been murdered. Although they had planned to be in Bethlehem only a couple of days, they stayed over a week visiting with family. Mary and Joseph apologized over and over to their kinsmen about their boys being slain by Herod. After a lot of tears and prayers, everyone trusted God and his plan and they all felt close to him once again. Everyone in Bethlehem knew Jesus was back, and all swore an oath to keep his true identity a secret so he wouldn't be in danger. They did not want their sacrifice to be in vain. Mary and Joseph told all of them that they were going to live in Nazareth because that's what God had instructed them to do. The night before they left, the whole village prayed for their safety and for the deliverance that Jesus, their Messiah, would bring.

Early the next morning, the family left Bethlehem. There was a tearful farewell as the parents, brothers, and sisters said their good-byes. Because they thought there might be some danger traveling to Nazareth by themselves, both Mary's and Joseph's brothers and brothers-in-law had decided to accompany them.

On their way to Nazareth, they traveled through Lydda and Scythopolis. The entire trip took four days. As they got closer to Nazareth, those of Joseph's family who lived in Nazareth came out to meet them. It had been a long time, and they all wanted to see Jesus the young Messiah as well as Naomi. They took them up to their house and helped them get settled in. Mary and Joseph were happy to be where they hoped God would let them stay and raise their family.

In speaking to their family, Mary and Joseph asked them to keep Jesus's identity secret so he would be safe from Herod's son and could have a "normal" life until such time that God decided he wanted him known for who he was. They all agreed.

After a day of unpacking and getting moved in, Jesus started exploring his new surroundings, starting with their house. It was a typical Jewish house in Nazareth with one large room where the family lived and slept at night. It also had stairs that went up to the roof, where they could go when it was hot and they wanted to feel some breezes. Jesus liked going up there and looking out at the village and the hills. The house was located in the northerly outskirts of town, and he saw that there was a hill nearby where he could hike and climb.

Mary had told the family earlier that she was again with child, who would turn out to be Jesus's first brother, James, born a few months later.

17

Once the family was settled, Joseph decided to build a wood shop large enough to expand his business. He had had a small carpenter shop before he had left to go to Bethlehem, which his brother had continued to run. He liked working with his hands, and now he had a brother nearby with whom to go into business.

With some of the money they still had from the Magi, they decided to buy a piece of property out near the tarrying lot where caravans would gather on their travels through the area. There were always things that needed mending or fixing in a caravan passing by.

At first, Mary was concerned about Jesus accompanying them to the shop, but after some time, she consented and let him go, trusting God would watch out for his Son. Joseph and his brother were always extra careful when Jesus came to the shop. One day, Jesus met another boy his age named Jacob, the stone mason's son. They quickly became close friends.

Mary and Joseph were very pleased with their new life in large part because their family from Bethlehem could easily come over once in a while to visit and check in on them. It was always great to see them. Mary and Joseph were very much in love and were expecting yet another baby. About a year after James was born, another daughter was born and they named her Miriam. She was healthy and loved. Jesus and Naomi enjoyed helping Mary with her as well as the one-year-old James. Joseph again felt God was a strong presence in their lives, and he always wanted to do his will.

In our culture, the boys in the family were the responsibility of the mother until they were around five years old. At that time, the fathers were handed the responsibility to start with their training in the Scriptures and in whatever work they would eventually do to earn their livings.

One day, when Jesus was out at the wood shop visiting with his father, he started asking questions that were getting harder for Joseph to answer. Jesus thought it was interesting that when a baby was born, he or she was a completely separate person. He wondered how that happened not only with his brothers and sisters but with animals and birds as well. Joseph hedged like most parents on trying to answer that question, and he told Jesus that God made them that way. He tried to explain it better once he remembered that his young son actually was God's Son. He thought he needed to do a better job, so he prayed to God to give him the wisdom to explain these things to Jesus. Joseph knew it was going to be a difficult task as Jesus grew and God's Spirit became stronger in him.

Jesus started spending more time at the shop talking and working with Joseph when his father was working on a "safe" project where the distractions of conversation would not be an accident risk. He liked going there and talking with and asking questions of the travelers in the caravans passing through town. He was a happy, healthy, and inquisitive child.

During the year, there was a stomach epidemic that came from the travelers, and Mary, exercising caution for the health of her oldest child, sent Jesus to her brother's summer farm in Megiddo. Jesus loved it there and stayed for several weeks.

"Joseph, are you asleep?" Mary asked

"No," Joseph said.

"Joseph, have you listened to Jesus pray? He has started talking to God as he does to me. I have never heard anyone do that, and it bothers me."

"Me, too," Joseph said. "I don't know what or if we should say anything to him about it, do you? I always thought there would be an incredible bond between them, so I don't want to stop it, but I also don't want Jesus to be ridiculed or teased by others who don't understand their relationship."

"While we're on the subject," Mary continued, "I had left the scrolls that the Alexandrian synagogue gave us out and saw Jesus looking through them. I thought he might just be curious, but when I asked him what he was reading, he told me he was reading about God creating the earth and all of the living things.

"I was shocked, Joseph. I had no idea he could read that well or have that much understanding. When I asked him about what else he had read, he explained that he had read the writings of Moses and liked the stories the most about all of his forefathers."

The following morning, Joseph wanted to see for himself what was going on with Jesus. Once they were up and out of bed, Joseph got out the scroll and started reading it to the family. After a few minutes, he asked if Jesus wanted to read as well. Jesus happily obliged; he loved to read the scroll out loud. After he had read it for a while, Jesus stopped and asked Joseph several questions about the different feasts and sacrifices God wanted them to observe. When Joseph answered one question, Jesus would ask a deeper question on why God wanted them to do that. After a few more questions, Joseph finally had to tell him that he didn't know and that Jesus would have to talk to God, his heavenly Father, to get the answer. Jesus said he would do what Joseph suggested.

One day, as Jesus was walking on the hill near his house looking at nature, he saw some travelers going to his house. He was curious about who they were, but he wanted to finish looking at a new flower he had never seen. He always loved nature, so much so that his family teased him a bit about looking at the stars and the flowers and asking so many questions about nature. After a few minutes, he saw Naomi coming to get him, and he started back to the house.

Once he got to where Naomi met him, she said that their cousin John and their aunt and uncle had come to visit. Jesus always loved seeing his family. He had heard about his cousin John and how he had been promised to his aunt because she had prayed to have him. His mother and father had told him that John was going to be a prophet of God and that he would be the one to announce the arrival of the Messiah. Jesus thought that was great.

Both sets of parents wanted to see the reaction when these two special boys of promise saw each other. Mary and Elizabeth each remembered when Mary had come to visit Elizabeth while they were both pregnant. When Mary walked in, and, when Elizabeth heard Mary's greeting, the baby, John, leaped in her womb and Elizabeth was filled with the Holy Spirit. In a loud voice, she exclaimed: "Blessed are you among women, and blessed is the child you will bear. But why am I so favored, that the mother of my Lord should come to me? As soon as the sound of your greeting reached my ears, the baby in my womb leapt for joy. Blessed is she who has believed that the Lord would fulfill his promises to her."

When Jesus walked into the room and saw John, he felt as if he had known him or had at least met him before. He asked Mary if they had ever met each other, and Mary said that they had not. John was a bit older and thought along the same lines as Jesus did. Joseph and Zacharias figured they might have talked so much about one boy to the other that perhaps it seemed like they had already met one another.

After the boys went running out the door and headed for the hill to play, Joseph told Zacharias that his wood shop was doing well and that his brother was going to take charge of it while he started building a contracting business to get jobs away from Nazareth. He thought it would be good for Jesus to travel with him whenever it was practical. It would introduce him to the different towns in Galilee, and he would learn more about his people. Joseph explained to Zacharias that Jesus just seemed to absorb everything he saw and heard. Zacharias told Joseph he believed that God had started influencing the boy and that they would see Jesus do great things.

Joseph contemplated what Zacharias had said to him for a moment and then remembered the things God had told him through the Scriptures and dreams about Jesus. Joseph became more and more convinced that Jesus was to rule over a spiritual kingdom instead of a worldly kingdom. He thought that if God wanted a worldly kingdom, he would have already had one. Joseph figured that God would redeem his creation and make it a sin-free kingdom. He couldn't get past the prophecies that the Messiah would save both the Jews and Gentiles. If that were the case, the Jews would no longer have anyone over whom they could rule.

18

As busy and committed to learning as he was, Jesus also liked to have fun playing with his younger siblings and his friends, even when the weather dealt an unexpected turn. That included the time early in his childhood—when he was seven years old—that Nazareth was the recipient of a rare snowstorm. Nazareth had never seen this much snow in a long time. The resident elders told everybody about the last time it had snowed more, and that was fifty or so years earlier.

Like all children who hadn't seen two feet of snow before, Jesus and his three siblings dressed as warmly as they could after waking up and headed outside to play in the snow. After helping his brother and sister get dressed, Jesus ran out to find Jacob. He wanted to build men out of snow. Joseph had told him how to build one the night before.

Outside, he found Jacob running to find him; they had the same idea. Jacob and Jesus headed back over to Jesus's house and got started rolling some snowballs out of which to make their snowmen. They were having a lot of fun. Jesus's brother and sister came over and helped them decorate the men that Jesus and Jacob made.

Jesus thought it would also be fun to make a big snowman up on the roof of the house. That way, everyone could enjoy seeing it. So, he and Jacob ran upstairs and started rolling the snow. After they had made a couple of large balls of snow, they started running out of snow. Jacob and Jesus ran back downstairs and rolled up a big ball that would be the base of the snowman on the roof.

While they were carrying the ball of snow up the stairs, Jesus tripped and fell. Jacob couldn't hold the snowball by himself and dropped it, which sent it rolling down the steps. About the time Jesus was getting up, the ball smashed into him and knocked him down again. Once Jacob saw that Jesus was OK, he started laughing. Naomi and James started laughing as well, and then Jesus joined in. Mary heard the noise and came out to see what the commotion was. When she was told that Jesus had fallen down the stairs, she checked him over for any broken bones and didn't find any. After the good laugh, Jacob and Jesus rerolled the ball and finished the snow man on the roof.

Later that year, Jesus and Jacob started going to the synagogue school. They began by learning to speak and write Aramaic, Greek, and Hebrew. The people of northern Israel all spoke at least Aramaic and Hebrew but most couldn't write it. The school's teacher was called the *chazen*; he would sit on the floor with the students sitting around him in a semicircle. They didn't use textbooks; the chazen would recite the Scriptures and the law, and the students would imitate him.

At home, Jesus continued to grow tall and strong. Joseph taught him his trade centered around carpentry and business while Mary started showing her son how to use the loom. At the same time, both Mary and Joseph taught Jesus to love and obey God and strive to do God's will, demonstrating this as much by their actions as by their words. As they watched and listened to him, Joseph became more and more convinced of Jesus's mission of a spiritual kingdom, while Mary continued believing more in his mission to be an earthly king with an earthly kingdom. Mary's family had several very strong Zealots in her family. Also that year, Mary had another son, Joseph.

Since Jesus was such a good student, he had devoted himself to studying the scrolls that the Alexandrian synagogue had given them at home. His extra studies were putting him well ahead of his fellow students in terms of learning and classroom performance. The chazen spoke to Mary and Joseph, and they agreed that Jesus would be able to take a week off per month from school. The first week he got off, he went to his Uncle Boaz's farm and helped them sow the seeds for the crop.

Jesus woke up early every day at the farm and went to the big room for breakfast before he and his cousins and uncles went to work in the fields. Jesus loved working on the farm planting seeds, feeding the animals, and spending time just watching God's handiwork as the plants and animals grew.

After a few days of letting Jesus get started planting seeds in the field, Boaz came over to talk about how to properly sow the seeds. Jesus would reach into his sack and get a handful of seeds and throw them with his fingers loose to let the seeds trickle through. While Jesus was doing this, Boaz stopped him and explained: "Jesus, when a sower sows seeds, there are different outcomes for the different seeds depending on which part of the soil they fall on. We try to get as many of the seeds into the good soil where we have plowed and prepared it to be sown, so the seed will germinate, grow, and render a harvest of one hundred fold. If the seed falls on the path, the birds will quickly come and eat it. If the seed falls onto rocky soil, it might germinate, but it will not have enough moisture to survive and will probably die. Also, take care to avoid patches of weeds because even if the seeds do germinate and grow there, the weeds will choke them out and prevent them from producing a harvest."

Jesus asked Boaz a lot of questions. Everyone kidded Jesus about his propensity for asking so many questions because they were so different from the types of questions being asked by other children his age. One day, Jesus was working at the farm when he walked over to Boaz and asked how it was that he would sow a seed and then the seed would transform, or kind of die, and, then after it did, it would turn into a plant and have a lot of seeds.

Boaz was amazed at the question in part because he didn't know the answer, telling Jesus, "You will need to ask God."

On another of his weeks off, Jesus went down to the Sea of Galilee to visit Joshua, another uncle, who was a fisherman. Jesus loved the sea. He was up very early in the morning every day to watch the sun come up. When Joshua asked him what he was doing up so early, he would tell them he was watching God's creation waking up while telling his Father thanks.

At first, Joshua had Jesus help around the docks getting the nets ready, mending them, and using his skills as a carpenter to fix the boat and the docks as needed. Jesus was happy that he could use his skills to help. After a couple of days, when the sea was calm, Joshua and his sons Isaiah and Jeremiah took him out into the boat onto the sea to fish. He loved it. He watched and learned how and when to cast the nets to catch the most fish. He learned how to pull in the nets so they wouldn't be torn.

One morning, when Jesus was watching the men fish close to shore, he noticed that one of the boats had one of its nets full of fish. As he stood there, those in the boat slowly moved their boat toward the shore. One of the men then stepped out of the boat, and the crew handed him the net. While he held it, the rest of the crew anchored the boat, stepped out, and started hauling the net full of fish to the shore. Once they had it all ashore, they started sorting the fish from the net. The fish they wanted to keep were put into boxes, while the ones they didn't want were thrown on the beach for the cats and birds to eat.

On one of Jesus's trips to the farm, Boaz pulled out a harp when he and Jesus were going out to the pasture to watch the sheep. Boaz said that playing the harp calmed the sheep and they would stay near them while they grazed. While Boaz played, Jesus remembered the stories about David the King of Israel, his forefather. He remembered that David loved to play the harp, and Jesus eventually asked his uncle to teach him how to play. Boaz agreed, and Jesus started learning the harp right then. Like he did with everything he undertook, he learned quickly and easily. By the end of the day, Jesus was able to play several simple melodies. By the end of the week, he had added several more to his repertoire. Every time he went to the farm after that, he would take out the harp and practice and play whenever he could.

One week, when he came home, he found that Mary had again given birth and that he had another brother, Simon. As with all of his siblings, he helped take care of them and loved all of them dearly.

Toward the end of the year, a rabbi from Jerusalem came to observe Jesus in response to a letter that the chazen in Nazareth had sent him about this remarkable student Jesus. The rabbi tested Jesus for a few days and, impressed by what he saw, wanted to take him to Jerusalem to continue his studies. The rabbi explained to the chazen and Joseph that they had many classes and students where he could learn at an accelerated pace. The rabbi thought that someone with Jesus's intelligence and insight would be a great student of Gamaliel. Although Jesus's family lived very modestly with scant material possessions, they had saved many of the gifts that had been presented to Joseph and Mary upon Jesus's birth—gifts that could easily have been exchanged for the money to pay for his schooling, had they so chosen.

The rabbi told the chazen and Joseph that there was a student named Saul studying with Gamaliel that was close to the same age and learning level Jesus was and it would be great for them to study together. Joseph said he would think and pray about it and that he would discuss it with Mary and Jesus. He said he would get back to the chazen and the rabbi with their answer.

Joseph went home and talked to his wife and oldest son about what the rabbi had told him, and then they prayed to seek out what God wanted them to do. Mary wanted Jesus to go learn in Jerusalem; Joseph did not. Jesus went out and climbed the hill and stayed there until dark. Once he came back inside the house, he told Mary and Joseph that he wanted to stay and learn in Nazareth. He said that he was learning the Scriptures from the chazen, he was learning about love and responsibility from them, and he was learning about his fellow man from his interactions with all of the people in the various caravans passing through

Nazareth. He didn't think he would learn all of those things in Jerusalem.

After the family had decided that Jesus would stay and study in Nazareth, Jesus continued learning at school, spent time with his family, and, on his monthly off-week from school, he continued to learn how to farm and fish.

Since his son was becoming a very capable carpenter, Joseph called a meeting with the family and discussed with them about having Jesus travel and work with him on the weeks he had off from school. Joseph wanted to continue developing Jesus's skills as a carpenter. Once it was decided that Jesus would go with him, Joseph went for a walk with James and explained that he would need to start helping Mary with the family chores while he and Jesus were away. James had already shown he was a responsible boy and had been helping out whenever Jesus went to spend time at the farm or the sea.

Because Jesus loved nature so much, he started sketching various scenes of what he observed although he wouldn't show his depictions to anyone. He just liked to see if he could draw what he saw. Of course, like everything else he did, the drawings were very good.

One day, when the weather was bad and everyone had to stay in, Naomi happened to discover the drawings; since they were so good, she wanted to show them to everyone. She carried the drawings into the main room where everyone was relaxing. She then announced that she had the best pictures of the birds and animals around Nazareth that she had ever seen. All of the family gathered around to look at them.

When Mary and Joseph saw the drawings, they asked who had drawn them. Jesus said that he had. While the other children looked at the drawings, Joseph motioned for Jesus to come with him. After Joseph and Jesus were out of the room, Joseph sat Jesus down and explained what the Jewish oral law, or Talmud, taught about drawing pictures. Joseph explained that they thought God had prohibited them from drawing them since it went against the second commandment which states, "Thou shalt not make unto thee any graven image."

Jesus was confused: How did his drawings of nature have anything to do with the second commandment? Joseph stood there several minutes before finally looking at Jesus and saying, "Jesus, you have insights into God's laws that no one else your age or possibly any age has. We know that you are the promised Messiah of God for the world. Mary and I have seen the incredible talent you have with everything spiritual and everything you choose to do physically.

"While you are probably correct with your application of the commandment, your neighbors and teachers have interpreted the second commandment as saying that you cannot draw or sculpt any images that might cause you to worship anything but God."

Jesus looked at his earthly father for a moment and said, "While I do not think that our Father meant that we shouldn't enjoy his creation and look upon it in reverence, I understand that some may have worshipped these images. I will stop drawing them so that no one will look at them and delight in the drawing more than in the creator.

"I hope these same people won't worship the real things, either."

Once the children had all gone to sleep, Jesus destroyed the drawings and never drew another picture again.

19

The following week was one of Jesus's weeks off from school, and Joseph had decided that his son should come with him to a job he was working on near Cana. Although Mount Tabor was out of the way, he wanted to take Jesus there and tell him all of the things God had done for his people around the Mount.

Jesus had always wanted to go there ever since he had read all of the stories that happened there. Mount Tabor was only about five miles away. They could go by there early in the morning and still have plenty of time to make it to the job by noon.

On the way to the mount, Joseph and Jesus talked about the battles that had been fought, won, and lost on the mount. The one they liked the best was the one spoken of in the book of Judges. It was when Deborah judged Israel and summoned Barak, telling him to march to Mount Tabor, promising Barak that God would deliver the Canaanites to him.

Barak was afraid and asked Deborah to come with them. She accompanied Barak, and, just as she had said, God delivered the army of the Canaanites to Israel. The head of the Canaanite army, the mercenary Sisera, had run from the battle. When he arrived at the tent of Yael, the wife of Heber the Kentia, he asked to be hidden; when he fell asleep, Yael drove a tent peg through Sisera's skull.

Once they started the climb to the top of the mount, Jesus ran ahead on his way to the top. In earlier trips there, Joseph had been up to the top a few times, and he had told Jesus of the grand view offered from the summit. As Joseph was finally getting to the top, he saw Jesus standing on the peak and watched him slowly turn in a circle to see everything surrounding them. Once Joseph joined his son at the top, Jesus looked at him and said, "From here you can see all the kingdoms of the world."

After spending a few more minutes looking around the summit, they hurried back down and continued on to Cana, where they spent the week working together.

On the way home from Cana, Joseph decided he would add a room onto his wood shop and get Jesus some tools of his own so he could have his own carpentry enterprise. Jesus was delighted. During the remainder of the year, they worked on the room and finished it in the fall.

Also that year, Jesus started having a group of boys over to the house to study the Scriptures. Since the family had their own scrolls, they were able to read them whenever they wanted. No one else in Nazareth had their own scrolls except those at the synagogue. While Jesus had each of the boys from the study group lead the study each week, he was the acknowledged leader of the group. He would always help them better understand the words of the scroll and how God wanted them to act because of them.

That was the year that Martha was born to Joseph and Mary. She was a beautiful little girl that was the happiest baby they had ever seen.

By this time, Jesus had three brothers—James, Joseph, and Simon, as well as two sisters. There was another boy that their mother had given birth to, but he passed away very young. His name was Amos.

During the winter that year, they didn't get much snow, but it got freezing cold a couple of times. Jesus was amazed as he studied the water at how many different forms it could take. It could be ice, liquid, or steam. He thought it interesting that when water turned into ice, it expanded, whereas all other things would shrink when they froze.

The next couple of years in Jesus's life were typical of a boy going through puberty and becoming a man. He also was truly starting to feel the presence of his Father. As with all of us, we begin sensing and feeling his presence and act upon that. Sometimes, we make the wrong decision, and sometimes, we don't. Because Jesus didn't inherit a sinful nature from an earthly father, his connection to the presence of his Father in heaven came upon him in a much stronger fashion. He felt drawn more and more to spend time alone reading and listening to him.

Mary and Joseph were aware of what was occurring. When Jesus spoke to them about it, they would say that they understood. Jesus would also speak to them about his mission and how he was trying to understand exactly what it would involve.

He started attending the advanced school at the synagogue. There was a new boy named Micah, whose family had just moved into Nazareth, and he was starting there as a new student as well. Jesus greeted Micah in a friendly manner, but he didn't want any part of Jesus. One day, after school, though, Micah went up to Jesus and tried to start an argument with him about a scripture they had disagreed on in class. As Jesus started to walk away to avoid a confrontation, Micah pushed him. This surprised Jesus because no one had ever done that to him before. Jacob, Jesus's friend, quickly intervened, grabbing Micah and telling him to not be pushing anyone around in Nazareth, especially Jesus.

This was something Jacob and Jesus had spoken about many times, Jesus's apparent unwillingness to defend himself. The truth was that Jesus and Jacob liked to roughhouse and wrestle, and Jesus could pin Jacob every time when he wanted. However, Jesus was unwilling to stand up for himself out in public. Since Jacob knew Jesus wouldn't fight, he decided he would be his protector.

Jesus continued traveling and working with Joseph. He was learning how to not only work on the projects they were hired to do but also how to price them and organize the work and the workers for the projects. He became aware that the workers they hired needed to be paid their wages the day they worked so they could buy food for their families. Some of the other contractors wouldn't pay them their wages until after the job was finished, and it would cause problems dealing with the day laborers.

20

One day, the widow woman who lived across the street, Sarah, ran over to the house early in the morning before Jesus left for school. She had been a widow for many years. She made the best bread and always gave Jesus a bit of honeycomb that he would roll up in the bread. They were good friends.

This time, though, Sarah was distraught, telling Jesus that she had lost one of her coins. Jesus knew she was on a tight budget, and he immediately went to her house and helped her start moving furniture around, sweeping out underneath, and looking for the coin. After about thirty minutes, Jesus moved a cabinet, spotted the coin, and gave it to a visibly relieved Sarah. She grabbed Jesus and gave him a hug. She then went and got him an extra-sized piece of bread with a double-sized piece of honeycomb.

Each day after school, Jesus would go to the woodshop and work on different projects. It also got to where leaders of the caravan familiar with his handiwork would start dropping off projects for him to do when they came through Nazareth, knowing he did such good work.

This is how Jesus started getting to know a lot of the people of the caravans; they, in turn, kept him informed about what was happening in other areas where they traveled. Jesus found it very interesting to listen to the different politics and events outside of Nazareth. He would always ask them if they worshipped God and if the people they saw worshipped him as well. He was continually amazed when he was told that some people worshipped other or even multiple gods.

The leaders of the caravan were always asking Jesus to go with them since he was such a good carpenter and he could make different things out of wood and sell them. Besides, he was such great company to have around. Jesus would usually have something he would sell them that they would then trade on their trips.

The week after the lost-coin adventure with Sarah, Jesus was headed down to the farm. It was time to help shear the sheep. When he arrived there, he went up to the house, but there wasn't anyone home. He set down his bundle and headed out to the barn to see where everyone was. They weren't there, either, but it looked like all of the sheep were there.

At this point, he looked out toward the pasture and saw his Aunt Hannah heading back to the barn, so he started out to meet her. Once they got close enough to each other to talk, Jesus asked her where everyone was. She said they were all out looking for a lost sheep. The reason Hannah was heading back in was that she had heard the rejoicing when her husband had found the sheep. It had been caught in some thorns in a gully on the back of the farm. Jesus then saw Boaz coming over the hill carrying the sheep on his shoulders with all of his cousins around him.

Meanwhile, back home, Mary once again was with child. She loved children, and it had gotten to where it seemed like she was having another child at least every other year. This year was no exception; her due date would be after Jesus returned home from the farm. Right on schedule, Jude was born. Now that there were other siblings grown up enough to help out with the new baby, Joseph stayed in town only a couple of weeks after Jude was born before he headed back out to work, accompanied by Jesus.

Joseph had a job he was working on in Scythopolis, one of the chief cities of the area and once known as the ancient Hebrew city of Beth-shean. Joseph reminded Jesus of how King David had conquered the Philistines and pushed them out of Israel and that it had happened right in this part of the country. Jesus remembered there were a lot of different battles and history in that area.

The city had been rebuilt to include a beautiful outdoor theatre and a gorgeous pagan temple. Jesus noticed how clean and well kept the city was, and he could only think that the citizens of the city must be proud of their city. Jesus remembered seeing the city from Mount Tabor, but now he was seeing it close up. When Jesus mentioned how beautiful the city was, Joseph said that he couldn't wait to take Jesus to Jerusalem to see that city and God's temple.

After work, Jesus watched the men of the city practice to compete in track and field games. He watched them practice for several different events. The ones Jesus liked the best were the foot races and the javelin and discus throws. When Jesus mentioned this to Joseph, he was surprised and spoke to Jesus sharply about the sin of vainglory. Jesus wasn't thinking about the games that way but as a way to show glory to God and to keep the body in shape.

This had been the only time that Joseph had yelled at Jesus, and it would be the last. Taking note of what Joseph had just done, Jesus started to understand that to complete his mission and obey his parents, he would need to be very careful so as not to disobey or shame his parents and family. Jesus knew he would need to focus on this as he spent time with his Father meditating and praying for guidance. He had to carry out his obligations and his mission. Seeing the Gentiles in the cities where he traveled made him realize that his mission was to both the Jews and the Gentiles.

After the trip, when Jesus was praying and reading the Scriptures, he started understanding even better that he had a much stronger connection to God than anyone else he knew. He felt his presence all of the time. This included when he was working or studying, or while playing the harp or traveling. Soon he asked Mary and Joseph about this, and they retold him the story of his conception and birth. Although Jesus had heard it many times, it was always good to hear it again.

As the year progressed, he started realizing that he was God's Son and that he had an earthly mission that God had given him. Yet, he was having trouble accepting this role. He didn't want to be different from other men, but he understood as the Spirit helped him finally get comfortable with who he was. He prayed and prayed to only do God's will whatever that might be. Along with that, he continued to pray about his mission and his dual nature.

As time went on, those who knew him best would see Jesus spending more and more time out on the hill. His brothers and sisters would tease him about it some, but Jesus took the teasing well, and they finally gave up. Jesus always got along with his siblings, but Joseph and Jude seemed a bit more annoying than the others, and their personalities were more aggressive. Jesus tried to spend more time with them, especially Jude.

Mary and Joseph watched Jesus closely, seeing him grow in knowledge and wisdom almost by the day. He not only understood everything he read in the Scriptures but had already exhibited more wisdom than many people who were much older and experienced. His outlook was so different, and he never worried about things that others did. The only time he showed concern and would say something was when the behavior he saw could cause physical damage or was against God's Word.

One of the things that bothered him was the differences his parents had regarding his mission. He had prayed and asked for his Father's guidance and knew his Kingdom was a spiritual kingdom for all races of people not just the Jews. He explained this to his parents so they would understand, but Mary still hoped he would be a king like David and reign on earth as well. He also prayed to God about the best way to stay obedient to his parents with their knowledge of the Scriptures and the oral laws, as well as his own thoughts.

The following year, Jesus would complete his schooling at the synagogue and become a son of the commandment. Jesus also was in that awkward stage of puberty with his voice changing and all of the other physical changes going on. His siblings started teasing him again when he tried to sing for them, and his voice would squeak and squawk. They would all just laugh and laugh. He would laugh right along with them.

Now that he was finished with school, Jesus was going to work every day. Joseph and Jesus agreed to start bringing James to the woodshop so he could learn what they did as well with both Jesus and Joseph working alongside him. Joseph was still traveling a lot, though, and, in fact, had just bid on some work for Herod Antipas. Joseph contracted to do some remodeling in the throne room.

As Jesus was praying during this time, his earthly mission was coming stronger and stronger into focus. Since there wasn't anyone else he could talk to about this, he turned to Joseph for many discussions about his mission. The two became very close, and Jesus relied on his father's wisdom and judgment.

During the summer, Jesus would spend time with the people of the caravans like before, soaking in all their stories from around the world. Jesus also would spend time helping with the children as well as seeking solitude up "on the hill" with God. Sometimes, his brothers would sneak up on him to see what he was doing. They always found him praying and reading the scrolls.

During the final days of school and during the summer, the chazen would plead with Jesus to continue his schooling in Jerusalem. The priests in Jerusalem had heard a lot about Jesus and wanted him to come and study there. Because Jesus would be going to Passover that spring, the chazen wanted to set up some meetings for Joseph and Jesus with the priests and work on getting Jesus enrolled. Jesus and Joseph talked about this some, but neither one of them was thinking that would be something Jesus would do. When the time came, Joseph knew that Jesus would head to the hill and with God's help, he would decide what he would do.

As the winter left its grip on Nazareth, Jesus was getting more and more excited anticipating the work of his Father in front of him. First, he was going to go to Jerusalem, the City of David, during the Passover to participate in the ceremony to become a son of the commandment.

21

As Passover had gotten closer, prior to Jesus's completion of his schooling, Mary and Joseph had decided to go to Jerusalem to watch the ceremony in which Jesus became a son of the commandment. It had been a while since the family had been to Jerusalem, as it seemed they were always busy with the work, the children, or having children. So, Mary and Joseph started planning the trip. In their absence, they would have Joseph's brothers look after the woodshop, and Joseph's sister-in-law watch over the children.

When the day finally came for them to go to Jerusalem for the Passover, a group of families from Nazareth that had decided to go gathered just south of Nazareth. The idea was for them to travel together for the purpose of safety. They would all need food, clothing, and shelter for the trip. It reminded Mary and Joseph of the time they had gone to Bethlehem to be counted for the census. In fact, it was almost exactly the same date on the calendar. At least this time, Mary wasn't about to have a baby.

On the first day of the trip, they went south to Jezreel and around Mount Gilboa so as to avoid Samaria. Although it would take less time, they wanted to stay ceremonially "clean" so they could go to all of the different ceremonies and feasts at the temple. As they traveled on, one of the fathers would tell all of the various stories about the area in which they were traveling and what God had done there.

One of the stories Joseph told was about the wealthy woman of Shumen who had great faith and how Elisha, a prophet of God, had told the wealthy woman that God had heard her prayers and then she had a son. In Jezreel, Jacob's father, the stone mason, spoke of Ahab, Jezebel, and Jehu. At Mount Gilboa, Joseph told the stories of Saul, King David, and Jonathan. Toward the end of the day, the caravan reached the Jordan Valley.

On the second day, they traveled through Jabbok, where Joseph told the stories of Gideon and the Midianites. That evening, they camped near Mount Santaba, where Herod's Alexandrian fortress was. Joseph told Jesus what a cruel king Herod had been and retold him the story of Herod killing the boy babies of Bethlehem. It was at this fortress where Herod had left one of his wives in prison and buried two of his sons that he had strangled.

The third day, they traveled to Jericho, where they would stay for the night. The family walked up to ancient Jericho to view where the Israelites had followed God's plan and had made the walls fall down. One of the reasons they wanted to go to the city was to see where one of their ancestors lived—the prostitute Rahab. Joseph told Jesus the story again and then said that God never looked at the physical being but at the heart.

It was an hour-and-a half-walk up to the ancient city. They spent the day looking over the area and then went back to the present-day Jericho. They wanted to have a relaxing rest of the day and get prepared to go up to Jerusalem the next day.

The fourth day was the day Jesus had been looking forward to for a long time. He was finally going to see his Father's house and the priests who cared for it. The Nazareth group started early that morning. They would travel most of the morning and then rest once they got to Bethany, just a couple of miles from Jerusalem. The journey today would be all uphill. As they struggled up the road, at about the halfway point, Jesus saw his first glimpse of the

Mount of Olives. From where he stood, he could see the Jordan River and the Dead Sea.

As they continued up the road, Jesus caught a good glimpse of the City of David. This is what he had been most eagerly anticipating. As they continued up the road, Jesus couldn't keep his eyes on the path but kept looking up at the city and the temple. How magnificent was his Father's house.

The group decided to rest at Bethany. It was there that they met Simon, the father of Lazarus, Mary, and Martha. Lazarus was the same age as Jesus, and they immediately became good friends. They spent some time there, and, as they parted, they promised to get together again before Jesus left to return to Nazareth.

As Jesus looked around and saw all of the Jews that were coming to the feast, he wondered if they lived differently from him and his family and what they did to earn their bread. As he followed along with the crowd, he was getting more and more excited. As they passed through the gates into Jerusalem, he couldn't help but stare at the gates and the walls and see how impregnable they appeared to be.

As they entered Jerusalem, they arrived at Solomon's Porch. They took a few moments to see this magnificent site and then continued down into the Lower City, where they were going to stay at the home of one of Mary's brothers, Gideon, during the feast. Mary's family all knew about the miraculous birth of both Jesus and John his cousin.

Besides going to the feast and observing the Passover, Joseph was going to use his time in Jerusalem to attend meetings he had set up with a couple of different academies where they thought Jesus would come to study when he turned fifteen, if circumstances and finances allowed.

The next morning, Joseph, Mary, Jesus, and a couple of members of Mary's family headed out to see the sites. They started early to get around to the most popular locales before the crowds would start forming.

They went back up to the temple and began the tour at Solomon's Porch. After looking at everything on the Porch, they started into the central area of the temple. They passed a guardrail that had a sign saying only Jews could proceed past it on penalty of death. From there, they went up fourteen steps through the Beautiful Gate to an area called the Court of Women. Across the Court toward the Gate of Nicanor is where Mary and Joseph had brought Jesus when they presented him after his birth. As they continued through the gate, Mary and the women had to stop because they were going to the Court of Men.

When Mary stopped, Jesus wanted to know why she couldn't go with him. She said she was forbidden to go any farther into the temple but that he should go on in to see all of it. Jesus stood there for a minute and said, "If my mother who is as good a follower of God as any man I know isn't allowed to see the rest of God's house, I'm not allowed, either." She tried to reason with him, but he still wouldn't go in.

As he stood there, Jesus watched as all of the men dragged their offerings up the stairs to have them slaughtered by the priests. The stench of the blood as well as the excrement and the screams of the dying animals started making him sick. His uncle said that it was normal for anyone to be sick the first time they saw this spectacle, but over time you got used to it. (I know the feeling.) To the sensitive, nature-loving boy, it was a shock, and he knew he could never get used to it.

After leaving the temple, they headed into the Upper City and saw the Hasmonean Palace, Herod's Palace, and the House of Caiaphas, the next high priest.

Once they were back at the home of Gideon, they rested for a while and then ate their evening meal. They all talked about what they had seen that day and then made some more plans for the following day. Jesus usually helped lead the conversation at the table, but this evening found him quiet.

"Are you feeling OK, Jesus?" Joseph asked.

"Yes, Father, I am, but I'm feeling troubled by some of what I saw and experienced today, and I need to be alone for a while," Jesus said.

"I understand," Joseph said. "Go, and, if I can help you with anything, you know I am here."

Jesus excused himself and went out onto a balcony to talk to his Father about the day's events. Secluded on the balcony, Jesus started feeling closer to God than he ever had before. As he started speaking to his Father, he heard him say that his mission on earth was starting and that he would be more and more about his Father's business.

Jesus now identified himself as the Son of the Father. His mind could now distinguish between his earthly flesh and his spiritual mission on earth. From that moment forward, he started blending that mission with everyday life.

Starting for bed, Jesus had come to the realization that it had been the most thrilling day of his life. He thought he would have trouble going to sleep, but a feeling of comfort filled him and he slept soundly.

Joseph and Jesus were scheduled the next morning to go to the ceremony where he would become a son of the commandment. They walked back to the temple and made their way into the Court of Men. Although he was still indignant that women weren't allowed in, Jesus didn't say anything.

As all of the boys were getting lined up to be inducted, there was a commotion outside of the gate. One of the temple guards was clearing an aisle to allow a group of men and a boy into the court. At the head of the group was Caiaphas, the next high priest, leading a man and boy that were spectacularly dressed. They pushed their way into the court and then into the front of all of the other fathers and their sons. While this was going on, Jesus heard one of the other boys say that the father and son were Jonathan and Saul—my father and me. Jesus and Joseph both remembered that the rabbi who had tested Jesus in Nazareth had mentioned me as a very astute scholar. They didn't realize that Jesus and I were close in age to each other.

During the dedication ceremony, Jesus was disillusioned because of the routine and obligatory nature of the ritual. After the ceremony, Joseph and Jesus walked around the temple taking in the vastness and splendor of the temple. He had heard that almost a quarter of a million worshippers could worship there at one time. Even though he was impressed by the temple, he wanted to hear and see more of the customs and rituals of worship.

While they were finishing the ceremony and walking out of the gate, Lazarus and his father approached Joseph and Jesus and invited them and Mary to celebrate the Passover with them in Bethany. Joseph thought about it for a while, and then he agreed. He would head back to Gideon's house and tell them. Lazarus and Jesus were enjoying the moment, and they also looked forward to seeing each other later that day.

Listening to the worshippers, Jesus kept hearing that the rituals and sacrifices were all conducted to turn God's anger and wrath away from the worshippers. He was sad that the Jews believed this. He knew that his Father could not view his children on earth in such a way. He knew that his Father is filled with goodness and mercy and that he couldn't love us any less than our earthly fathers.

As he watched the procession of the animals going to slaughter for the sins of the worshippers, Jesus thought that if you could "pay" for your sins once a year no matter how sinful you were, there wasn't much motivation not to sin. Since you had to sacrifice anyway, it didn't cost anything.

When Jesus went back out to the Court of Gentiles, he was disgusted to see all of the courtesans, beggars, and prostitutes. It reminded him of the pagan temples he had seen, like the pagan temple in Sepphoris. He didn't understand why they were allowed near the temple; he was disgusted with the lack of spirituality seen at God's temple. They left and prepared for the Passover.

As the family walked to Bethany, Jesus was drawn to the serenity of the Mount of Olives. He stopped there a few moments and then caught back up to his parents.

22

After the Passover ceremony was complete, the families said their good-byes and started home. When they traveled, the women and men walked separately. When they were going to Jerusalem, Jesus traveled with the women; however, going back home, he could travel with the men. Mary thought Jesus was with Joseph, and Joseph thought he had decided to travel back with Mary and spend time with her. They didn't realize he was missing until that evening.

Curious as much as they were concerned, Mary and Joseph backtracked to Jerusalem the next morning, and as they went through the temple, they looked around some but didn't see Jesus. They went to Gideon's house and asked if they had seen him, but they hadn't seen him, either. As it was getting late, they stopped looking and discussed where they would start looking in the morning.

The next day, they went to Ain Karim in the Hebron hills, which was about eight miles from Jerusalem and where Elizabeth and Zacharias lived with John. They hadn't seen Jesus, either. They said a quick farewell, started back up to Jerusalem, and spent the remainder of the day looking around the city and in the temple. They asked everyone they knew if they had seen Jesus.

No one had. Now, they were getting distraught. They didn't know of anything else to do but go back to the temple in the morning and keep searching and asking. They mustn't have realized the bond that Jesus had made with Lazarus's family in Bethany.

Jesus had been staying at Lazarus's house where they had the Passover meal. After spending the day at the temple, the day his parents left for Nazareth, he had started walking toward the Mount of Olives. He seemed to be drawn to the serenity of the garden, which is where he stayed sorting through all of the different feelings and concerns he had from his time at the Passover. During this time, he also spoke to God about all of what he was feeling and experiencing. When it was getting late, Jesus decided to go to Lazarus's home since it was just a short walk and he enjoyed the family. They were all surprised to see Jesus when he knocked on the door. They had assumed he had gone back to Nazareth with his parents.

Once he had finished eating, Jesus excused himself and went into their garden to do some more thinking and contemplating of his mission. Early the next morning, Jesus left for the temple.

After Lazarus got dressed, he went in to where Jesus was staying and saw that he had departed. Lazarus went in to see his father and suggested they go to the temple and see what Jesus was doing. Simon said he would be available to go around midday.

Before Jesus went to the temple, he spent some more time with his Father in the garden. After that, he headed to the temple, where he listened in and then joined the discussions on Solomon's Porch. Several groups were discussing the Torah. One of the groups Jesus gravitated to was led by Gamaliel. This rabbi had a small group of students with him. Jesus was intrigued with the lessons he was teaching and stayed close. One student he recognized from the ceremony: the one who had crashed into the ceremony late with Jonathan. He remembered hearing his name was Saul. Me.

As Gamaliel taught, he asked a question regarding the Messiah. When none of his students would answer, Jesus spoke up and answered the question, and then to help make his point, he asked Gamaliel and the students what type of kingdom the Messiah would rule over. I immediately jumped in and told everyone that the awaited Messiah would rule over the world from Jerusalem and that his Kingdom would reign forever.

After I said it, I looked around to make sure everyone agreed. Jesus then asked a question: "If that was the case, wouldn't that kingdom include both Jews and Gentiles? And, if so, why would the Jews exclude the Gentiles from worshipping in God's temple now?" No one answered.

Gamaliel then asked the boy his name and where he was from.

"I am Jesus from Nazareth," he said.

Gamaliel remembered that one of the rabbis had mentioned something about this boy and said that he wanted him to learn from him. I remembered the story and thought he was the backwater boy from Nazareth that could easily be a bastard since someone had mentioned his mother was pregnant before she was married.

Anyway, I was annoyed because I couldn't answer Jesus's question and also because he started asking questions. This was not common, but Gamaliel allowed it to see how these two scholars would interact. For every question I would ask, Jesus had a very good answer and then responded with a question that no one could answer although they tried, me included. This went on for a while until I got exasperated and stormed off. Gamaliel was amazed at Jesus's knowledge of the Scriptures and the wisdom of his answers. He seemed to ooze God's thoughts and love.

Gamaliel thought Jesus spoke like one who had authority or had been there when the things they discussed happened. He had so much insight.

Lazarus and Simon came by and listened to them discussing the Scriptures and were also amazed by what they saw and heard. As Mary and Joseph walked through Solomon's Porch, they saw the crowd of people, but they kept moving, continuing to look for Jesus. By day's end, still no luck.

That evening, during a casual conversation at Gideon's home, Gideon mentioned that he had heard from a friend about some amazing boy who had been at the temple the last couple of days. He heard that he was debating with the teachers and rabbis of the temple about the Scriptures. Joseph looked over at Mary and said, "That sounds like Jesus. We will go there tomorrow and see."

After it started getting late, Jesus returned to Bethany to stay with Lazarus and his family. He enjoyed the whole family, including Mary and Martha. They got along well. On the way there, he stopped and talked to his Father for some time and prayed that he would be able to show the people his *loving* Father instead of the one supposedly full of wrath that they talked about.

The following morning, after his time in the Garden, Jesus returned to the temple. As he was walking out onto the Porch, he saw that a large group of people had gathered who, he correctly surmised, were waiting for him to arrive. They all wanted to hear his thoughts and interpretations of the Scriptures. Gamaliel and his students were there, and with them was Jonathan, my father.

I had mentioned this boy to Father, and he wanted to see for himself. Yes, I was angry that I was being pushed aside in the discussions with the teachers and bystanders intent on hearing Jesus's thoughts on every point. I used to be the one everyone thought was the most knowledgeable, and now I was a second-class citizen, practically anonymous. I told my father that Jesus must get his knowledge from the devil since there was no way he could be that knowledgeable just going to the schools he went to in Nazareth.

As the class got underway, everyone was trying to be the one that stumped the new student. I tried it; then Father did as well. Gamaliel also jumped in with a couple of thoughts. Jesus calmly and sincerely answered the questions and would ask his own to help make his point. He was already a skillful teacher.

As he was finishing one of his comments, Mary and Joseph came running up to him, and Mary said, "Jesus, why have you treated Joseph and me this way? Didn't you know we were frantically looking for you?"

Jesus looked at her with his loving eyes and said, "Why were you searching for me? Didn't you know that I would be in my Father's House?" Jesus then said good-bye to Gamaliel and his students and started home with Mary and Joseph.

While Jesus was leaving, I started whispering in Jonathan's ear very intently. I wanted to make sure he had heard what I thought I had heard, but Father wasn't sure. As I said earlier, in recalling this occasion, I believed that Jesus had committed the atrocity of blasphemy and should be stoned to death. Jesus basically told everyone that he was God's Son.

As Jesus left the city and looked back at the temple, he vowed to free his people from their spiritual bondage.

Both of us boys had started our respective life's missions.

23

During the following week, I continued to confront the priests about doing something regarding the blasphemy Jesus had uttered. I told them that Jesus should be brought back to Jerusalem to be tried, convicted, and stoned.

When I couldn't get the priests to do anything, I started asking my father Jonathan to go to Caiaphas or Annas to have them look into it. But Jonathan had other things on his mind and told me to stop obsessing about this Jesus. He said my pleas made me look like a weakling and that others were saying the reason I was so incensed was because Jesus had shown he was smarter than me and had more insight into the Torah than I did. Even though I was told to forget it, I went around my father and contacted Annas myself; I told him about the incident and what Jesus had said. Annas thanked me and said he would look into it.

Another week went by and still nothing: no response from Annas, and no one else seemed to care. I soon realized that I was the only one smart enough to understand the implications of what Jesus had said. I knew then, because of my far superior intellect and insight when compared to the other students and the priests, that I would have to figure out a way to trick Jesus into saying something blasphemous in public. Only then would everyone else finally hear and grasp what I was talking about. Next time Jesus came to Jerusalem to study or to Passover, I would be ready for him.

Since I couldn't rely on anyone but myself to figure this out, I was determined to be the most knowledgeable Jew who ever lived. I wanted to show that God was with me by allowing me to become the most knowledgeable Jew since Solomon. I had heard that all of the priests, rabbis, and scribes had said that they had never been around anyone so smart and as driven as me. Since no one else could see through this Jesus but me and wouldn't do anything about the blasphemous words he had spoken, I swore an oath to God to prove that Jesus's knowledge was from Satan.

Considering my brilliance, I knew that next time I confronted Jesus, I would be able to prove him wrong, answer any question he could throw at me, and then ask him questions he wouldn't be able to answer. As I studied, God would give me the knowledge and ability to do this so I would be able to show everyone that my knowledge was from God and that Jesus's was from the devil. As I prayed and meditated, I felt chosen by God to prove that Jesus was a fraud. I got up early, went to the temple, and studied as long as they let me stay; then I would go home and study some more.

Gamaliel assumed that my focus and hatred for Jesus would soon wane and that I would revert back to my old way of studying, which, considering my old class schedule, was almost as stringent as the schedule I was working now except with the hate focusing me more. Gamaliel could see that I was proud of myself as I continued to master different parts of the Torah.

One afternoon, Gamaliel took me aside and asked, "Saul, why are you so consumed with learning?"

"I am compelled to learn and serve God with the gifts I have been given," I said.

"What are those gifts?" he said.

"My family wealth, my drive, and my intellect. God gave me those three gifts, and I am obligated to use them to his glory."

I also told Gamaliel that I was embarrassed because Jesus had shown knowledge and insight that I didn't have. I swore to Gamaliel that that would never happen again.

Gamaliel was astonished at the passion of my remark.

"Saul, there is no doubt that you should use the gifts that God has given you for his glory," Gamaliel said. "That alone should be your reason for developing those skills. Make sure that part of the reason isn't hate. God can take care of himself."

As Gamaliel walked away, I thought about what he had said and reminded myself that God would need someone on earth to carry out his mission in regard to Jesus. I looked up to heaven and swore to God that I would be ready when God was.

I continued my stringent study schedule for a few more months, and I advanced well beyond my fellow students. It got to where Gamaliel just gave me an outline of the different lessons I should complete on my own. I was so far ahead of my fellow students and most of the teachers that I couldn't stand sitting in their classes anymore, and they felt the same about me. Knowing they were inferior to me, they didn't want me around.

Other students were starting to complain to teachers because I knew all of the answers. They felt disinclined to answer questions because if they were right, I would chime in with a comment; if they were wrong, I would answer and make fun of how stupid they all were. As I continued on my schedule, Gamaliel seldom saw or answered questions from me. He would have to search for me to see what I was studying and ask if I needed any help. Of course, I didn't.

Eventually, I just ignored the other students, even the ones I had studied with outside of class. Or if I did see them and they tried to engage me in conversation, I would make fun of them. Like most boys that age, they in turn started making fun of me and calling me different things. Their favorite was "Who do you think you are, the Hebrew of Hebrews?" Then it was shortened to "H-squared."

The name-calling got to me. When I asked them to stop, they just laughed at me. When I tried to grab one of the boys, he punched me in the stomach. I doubled over and for a while couldn't catch my breath. Most of the boys laughed and walked away. One stayed and tried to help me, but I yelled at him and told him to go away. As I slowly caught my breath, I decided that would be the last time I would try anything physical. As it was, I was small and weak because I didn't do anything but study. I also knew that I would someday make each of those boys pay for how they had humiliated me. Further, I would find out what each of the boy's parents did for a living and see to it that my father would make them pay.

One Friday afternoon, when Father was in town, he came by the temple to talk with me. He wanted me to come by the house and spend time with the family. I usually worked every day and never spent much time with my family. Even on the Sabbath, I would do what was required and then go back to my studies. I was happy that my studies, or "work" as defined in the Talmud, included meditating on the Torah. I could obey the Sabbath and still do my work.

I didn't want to see my sisters, either. As we had grown older, we had grown apart. They were silly, and I had nothing in common with them. Although I didn't want to go and spend time with them, I agreed to go there. Jonathan wasn't asking; he was just telling me to come nicely.

On my way to the house that evening, I thought back to when my sisters and I had been close years earlier. After our mother passed and Jonathan became distant and commanding, we had helped each other work through all of the different emotions and issues associated with death, especially our mother's death.

After we moved to Jerusalem and Jonathan placed me in school, I wasn't around very much. At times, I missed the relationships I had with them and having friends my own age. One time, I had tried to discuss my mission with Deborah. While she listened to me, I could see she didn't understand the aggression and hate that oozed out of me when I told her about the blasphemous Jesus. She never gave any indication that she understood me, only asking why I had so much hate. So, I just stopped talking to her about it.

As I continued meditating, studying, and praying, I felt more and more that I was doing what God wanted me to do. Although

I was isolated and friendless, I knew that it was a small price to pay to be one of God's chosen.

One evening, after I had gone home, I went up to the roof where I liked to pray. I had felt especially close to God the past week and wanted to keep in intimate communication with him. As I meditated and prayed, I kept thanking God for giving me such great gifts with which to serve him. I was proud that I had been chosen and swore to stay focused on my mission. I prayed, "Thank you, God, that I am not like everyone else."

24

When I was around fifteen years old, I remember most of my fellow students getting betrothed to be married. Their parents were arranging marriages for them. Father had spoken to me about this, and I kept telling him I wasn't getting married. But he had other plans for me.

Father came to me and said we were going to discuss the plans he had made regarding the wife he had chosen for me. I was able to deflect this conversation for a few months, but Jonathan finally told me to come by the house one evening so we could discuss the girl he had selected for me. I pleaded with him not to make me marry because I had sworn an oath to focus on the mission God had given me, which, in his annoyance, Jonathan called "Saul's silly mission."

Jonathan insisted his plans for me were at least as important as mine if not more so, that his plans were a part of God's will for our family. He told me that God had blessed our family with wealth and he was focused on making sure that would continue, to include adding more political allies and power to our family. Jonathan cared less if my wife and I would be happy as long as we produced an heir and the match connected our family with the "right" families. It was part of my sacrifice to be powerful and wealthy.

My father sat me down and told me he had worked out a match for me with a girl who was a niece to King Herod and from the tribe of Levite. This arranged marriage would permit our family to have familial relationships with the rulers of the Jews and allow our children to be priests. Jonathan said he couldn't think of a better match for me. He said it had been approved and that we would meet each other when the father of the girl decided it was time. As much as I objected, telling him that my mission would consume 100 percent of my time and focus, Jonathan told me to shut up. He said the marriage was happening no matter what. Then he stood up and walked out of the room.

After a couple of weeks, I forgot about the arranged match and continued focusing on my studies. One day, when I was at home, Deborah sat down and wanted to talk about the girl and the marriage. She was very excited and said she knew the girl our father had matched me with. The girl's name was Miriam. She was beautiful and kind and would be a great wife for me, my sister said. They went to the same school and were good friends.

"She's been over to our house, Saul, but I don't remember if you were ever there when she came over," Deborah said. "I've been to their house in Jerusalem and have also been to their family farm near Nazareth. They're great people."

Deborah mentioned that when they were there, Miriam's uncle Boaz, who owned a farm near her family's farm, had introduced them to a young man about my age named Jesus. Boaz said he was a great scholar and was also his nephew. The uncle introduced him as Jesus from Nazareth. Now Deborah had my attention.

"Deborah, please repeat for me that last part about this other boy," I said.

"Sure, Saul," she said. "One time when I was visiting Miriam at her family's farm near Nazareth, we met this boy about your age about whom everyone was raving because he was such an amazing scholar."

I exploded.

"Deborah, I know full well who this Jesus is, and I assure you that he is from the devil," I yelled. "I know this because I have met him and have heard him speak blasphemy, saying he is the Son of God.

"Don't ever say his name around me again. *Please.*"

Deborah was shocked by my response. Stunned for a few seconds, she finally asked me to talk about it. That only made me angrier, and I told her to leave me alone.

Before I stormed out of the room, I told her to tell Miriam that I didn't want to marry her and that if I did, it was only because Jonathan made me.

"I don't have time for a wife and family," I said, my voice still angry. "I would never ever have any sort of family relationship with Jesus of Nazareth."

Deborah sat there a few more minutes and then slowly got up and walked away, going up the stairs and to her suite. Much later, I would find out that Deborah had resolved then and there she would never try to talk to me again, that every time she did I only hurt her.

A few months later, Father summoned me to tell me I was to meet my betrothed the next day. The servants would lay out my clothes and then we would leave to go to her home for dinner. When I objected, Jonathan ignored me.

"Father, I have heard that Jesus is part of the family you are forcing me to marry into," I said.

He again ignored me. Although I did not want to go, I went home and got dressed as ordered. As we went to Miriam's home, Father counseled me on what I was to do and how I was to conduct myself. He wanted this meeting to go as he and Miriam's father had planned.

When we arrived, the servants showed us in, and we were seated at the table. In a few minutes, Miriam and her father entered the room. Even though Miriam was partially hidden under her veil, it was obvious something was wrong. She seemed reluctant to come into the room, and her father kept whispering to her as they entered. Finally, they sat down at the table. Miriam's father motioned to the servants, and they started serving dinner. This customarily happy event had become very tense.

After the meal, Miriam quickly left the room; I wished I could have as well. I had to listen as the two fathers planned out the marriage. They agreed that the match would be great for the two families, especially in business.

When Jonathan and I left for home after the dinner, I started to plead my case not to marry. Father grabbed me and was about to hit me, only to draw back. He warned me I was to obey him without question or that I would face dire circumstances.

25

One morning, while I was studying at the temple, I heard several people calling my name. I was studying in a quiet place where I wouldn't be disturbed, and I didn't want to be bothered now. So, I let them look for me until I came to a good stopping point in the scroll I was reading. At that point, I finally called back to the searchers, who ran to where I was, a look of complete panic on their faces.

"What do you want from me?" I asked, noticing that they were servants from our house.

"Sir, we have some terrible news about your father," one of the servants said, bowing.

"What could possibly be so important to disturb me while I am studying?"

"Saul, your father was killed by a group of thieves while he was traveling to Tarsus for business," the servant said.

I couldn't believe it. While I stood there in shock, the servants all started talking at once. I screamed at them to shut up. I needed to think of what to do, of whom I needed to talk to about this. My sisters would just be clingy and crying, and the rest of my family was all in Tarsus. I then thought of the different people I knew in Jerusalem and realized I didn't have any remaining friends. The priests and students didn't like me because they were jealous of me, and I couldn't stand being around them anyway. The only one that I could think to talk to was Gamaliel although even he wasn't that close to me anymore.

Picking up my scrolls, I started to Gamaliel's office. On my way there, I kept thinking about my father. Jonathan had been traveling more and more on business, and, when he was home, he hadn't spent any time with me. We were in different worlds: he was all business, and I was all mission. Since the engagement dinner, we had grown so much apart that we rarely spoke. He had never forgiven me for not wanting to be married, which would have helped him to advance further in business and to also produce an heir. Besides, Jonathan had started getting even stricter and controlling, which I took to mean that he didn't want to deal with anything he didn't want to deal with, and that included me.

Gamaliel had already heard about Jonathan before I got there, and he had hoped to see me and help me through my loss. We spoke about other things at first, as Gamaliel knew I would turn to talking about Jonathan when I was ready.

"You know better than everyone that I am on a mission and cannot be bothered by dealing with being the head of my family," I said. "That would be too distracting. I am not exactly sure what to do about this and thought you could help me get my plans together."

"Saul," Gamaliel said, looking straight at me, "that's a strange comment to say at a time like this, even coming from you. You shouldn't make any major decisions for at least a year. Right now, we are in the time for mourning and being with family and friends so you can comfort one another."

I looked down at the floor for quite a while. When I finally looked up, I said, "Gamaliel, I have no friends, and I don't know any of either Mother's or Father's families in Tarsus. We moved here when I was young, and I have never been back there. The only family I know are my sisters, and I don't know them that well. We were put in separate schools when we moved here, and we only saw each other on Sabbath for a few minutes."

Both of us sat there thinking. It was clear that Gamaliel was praying how he could say something to comfort me and break down the emotional barriers I had built around myself. I was praying how I could remove this new familial burden so I could stay focused on my mission. I didn't want to have anything to do with raising my now-parentless sisters and administering my father's estate. I would need to get in touch with my family's attorneys, accountants, and business partners to discuss how my sisters would be cared for and the estate administered without my involvement.

When it was time for me to leave, Gamaliel stopped me and said a short prayer for me: "Father, please look down on Saul as he makes important decisions that will affect him and his family for the rest of his earthly life and even his next. Have mercy and give him discernment to be a good older brother to his sisters so he can take care of them and his father's estate. Help his business associates give him good advice."

Once I got home and plowed through the mourners both inside and outside the house, I headed toward my father's study. Both of my sisters walked up to me and tried to hold me. I stood there stiffly until they stopped. I never was an affectionate kind of person. After a few minutes, I told them I needed to go into the study and think about what I ought to do.

Once I got to the study, I reached up to pull a cord to summon a servant. I had never done it before but had seen Father do it a lot. I reached up and pulled the cord that I had seen my father pull to summon the steward of the household, Gabriel, to the study. It felt great. It gave me new power. When Gabriel appeared, he told me how sorry he was for my loss. He then started explaining to me how long he had served my father Jonathan and all of the details his duties involved. I listened for a few minutes and then cut him off, saying that I wanted to meet tomorrow morning with my father's business associates to get a full accounting of everything.

"Sir, everyone associated with your father is in mourning right now, so could this wait until the mourning period is over?" Gabriel asked.

"No." I said. "Get the men here as quickly as you can, or I will find someone else to do your job."

It was obvious to Gabriel that the apple hadn't fallen far from the tree.

Gabriel sent out messengers to all of the men he thought should be at the meeting, but all he got back were responses saying they couldn't meet, that they had other commitments. Gabriel replied to them, telling them all what I had said and how I had said it, echoing my father's demanding style to make sure they were there.

The following morning, I was in my study, having arrived there early to pray and meditate about what I wanted to do during the meeting with the business associates. I had looked at the books that night and had made some decisions about how I intended to manage the estate. Now I was ready to meet, and, like my father, I was impatient. Even though it was thirty minutes before the time I had told them to meet me, I started pacing and getting agitated. I couldn't stand waiting on anyone.

As the managers arrived, I had Gabriel seat them outside in the hallway until they were all present. A minute before the meeting was to start, two of the managers still had not arrived, but, just at the last moment, they came running through the door with their books. That's when I stepped out into the hallway and motioned for them to step inside and told them to be seated. The room had been set up per my request, such that I could sit behind my desk and have the men in a semicircle in front of me.

Once they were all seated, I stood up and said, "Gentlemen, I asked you here to discuss my father's estate and how we will be administering it going forward. I know little of what you did for my father, and I will ask each of you in turn what it was you oversaw for him. Once you have finished, you may leave. Do not go out of town for the next month, however; I want you to be available for me on short notice during that time.

"I will see that all of the decisions needed to go forward will be made and executed within this month. I know Jonathan trusted you as I will. I also know that he very much ran all of these businesses hands on, on a day-to-day basis; I will not be doing that. I will continue to focus on my life's mission and will work with this group to have the estate well maintained. I now will ask everyone to leave the room while I speak to the attorney."

I waited until everyone but the attorney had left then started discussing with him all of the legal matters that I thought needed to be discussed.

Since I was so well read, I knew a lot about the law and how the estate could be managed. I only had the lawyer there to make sure that I knew how everything was set up legally so I could put in place the structure I wanted implemented. I asked the lawyer many questions and made copious notes. After I had finished with him, I asked him to leave and send in the accountant.

As the lawyer was leaving, he went into the hallway where the other men were. After closing the door behind him, he said, "This boy is smart and understands the law well. I assume he knows about accounting and the different businesses. I started the interview thinking he only knew the Scriptures and took him too lightly. I suggest that the rest of you be ready for a very in-depth interview."

The lawyer then told the accountant it was his turn to see me before he headed out the door and to his office to gather the information I had demanded of him. I wanted the documents in my hands by ten o'clock the following morning.

When the accountant entered my study, I gave him the same sort of inquisition I had given the attorney. I asked him many probing questions. At the end of the meeting, I told him to bring documentation of everything I had asked for and to be back at nine o'clock the following morning.

Next to see me was the business manager, Ezekiel. Once he was seated, I asked him questions about the different businesses and why they had been organized in their current structure. Were they all profitable, and, if they were, was it because of Jonathan's presence, or were the businesses all stable enough to continue without Jonathan's constant involvement? As the manager struggled to answer my questions, I told him I didn't need immediate answers. He looked relieved until I told him to be back at eight o'clock the following morning with the answers.

After Ezekiel's interview was finished, I pulled the cord, and Gabriel came back in. I asked him to go and find my sisters and bring them to me. I wanted to discuss with my sisters what I was going to do about them.

While waiting for my two sisters to arrive, I looked over some legal documents regarding my sisters' future that I had prepared before contemplating how I was going to explain what I was planning to do with them. I wanted them to know that I was prepared to care for them from the estate and that I had no reason to change any of the arrangements Jonathan had made for their lives and marriages. I wanted them to know that Jonathan had documented what their dowries were to be and that I had no inclination to change anything he had decided. The one thing I would tell them that I would change was that I had decided to cancel the marriage arrangement that Jonathan and Miriam's father had planned for Miriam and me. I wanted them both to know before I told Miriam and her father, mostly out of respect for Deborah's love for Miriam.

Both girls came into my study still in mourning and wearing their mourning garments. They were nervous because they never knew what mood I would be in. Father, although aloof, had always treated them with love and respect.

As they entered my study, I asked them to be seated. I then explained to them as concisely as I could what my plans were for them. Both said they understood; then they thanked me. Both were sad, however, that I wouldn't be marrying Miriam.

"Saul, if you aren't marrying Miriam, who will you be marrying?" Deborah asked me.

"I don't have time for marriage because of my absolute focus on my mission," I said.

"How will you be able to carry on our family name, and how will you be administering the estate?" Deborah said.

"There's nothing I wouldn't give up to complete my mission," I said. "I will be hiring professionals to administer the estate.

I have sworn an oath to God, and everything else in my life is subservient to that oath."

After a few moments, I asked the girls to leave the study because I needed to finish preparing for my morning meetings. I was disgusted that I had to deal with family issues when I should be studying, meditating, and praying.

The following morning, right at eight o'clock, I called for Gabriel and told him to have Ezekiel come into my study. When he got there, I motioned for him to sit down and then asked him to start answering the questions I had posed to him the day before, beginning with the tent-making companies.

"Please don't dawdle through this, either, because we have only an hour," I told him.

After the hour had finished, I asked him to go out and get the accountant for the next meeting, but not to leave—to stay there until I called him back into my study. I went through the same process with the accountant and then with the lawyer, starting at nine o'clock and ten o'clock respectively just as I had scheduled it the day before.

After all three had been in their separate meetings with me, they sat out in the hall for about thirty minutes. After a while, they asked the servant what was going on, but he didn't know. A few minutes later, there was knocking at the front door. The servant went to open the door, and in walked a group of men headed toward the study, passing by the three men seated in the hallway. When the newly arriving group of men came around the corner, the three seated men could see that it was Annas the high priest, Gamaliel, and their entourage.

Once the new arrivals got to the door of my study, Gabriel showed them in before asking the three men out in the hall to come back inside the study, where we would all meet seated in chairs assigned to them. Once they were seated, I began speaking:

"Gentlemen, I have asked you here to tell you how we are going to administer my father's estate. I have spent an hour each with my lawyer, accountant, and business manager this morning following a brief meeting I had with each of them yesterday. I now know enough to be able to make all of the decisions needed. I want to get this behind me so I can focus on my mission. Additionally, I have spoken to my sisters, and they now know what it was they needed to know as well."

Everyone looked at each other, and I knew what they must have been thinking about how arrogant and ridiculous I was to believe I knew everything there was to know about the estate after just one day. The one exception probably was Gamaliel because he knew what I was capable of when I was focused. I stood up and started telling everyone my decision.

"First, I want everything that is in my father's estate transferred to and administered by the priests," I announced. "Second, all of the estate will transfer to the priests either upon my death or if the Sanhedrin votes with 75 percent approval to transfer the titles of the estate before I pass. That way, if they determined I'm not following the Torah and the Talmud, they can take away my rights to the estate."

Everyone in the room was stunned. The estate was an enormous fortune.

"The next order of business is to declare that my marriage to Miriam is cancelled," I continued. "I asked Annas to be the one to inform Miriam and her father since they were in his family. I also told Annas to deliver what he determined to be the proper amount of money to them for their trouble. Annas wasn't very happy with my decision since he was one of the men who had helped negotiate the match. He foresaw no problem with Miriam and her father, but he was a bit concerned about Herod Archelaus's reaction. After he thought about it some more, he knew he could buy them off. He now had unlimited funds to make sure that his family would always be the high priests."

I then talked about the different businesses and how they should be structured and either rolled into other businesses where it makes the most sense or sold. I told my lawyer, accountant, and business manager to report to the priests to be selected by Annas for the purpose of administering the estate. They would report to me until everything was settled but would then work with the priests going forward, provided those priests decided to hire them. The three men all looked at one another in shock. They had been working for the wealthiest and most powerful man in the Jewish nation, and now they were to report to a priest? As one of them started to speak, I told them all to leave except for Annas, Gamaliel, and another priest that I knew named Nicodemus.

Now with just the four of us there, I thanked the other three for agreeing to oversee the estate so I could focus on my mission. I also brought up that I had heard that Annas might know who had been involved with the gang of thieves who had robbed and killed my father. Annas said that they hadn't caught the group yet but that the authorities thought it was led by a man named Barabbas. Annas said they were combing the hills trying to find them.

26

With the administration of the estate and the team in place to oversee the businesses and finances, I re-focused on my mission.

My life returned to a very disciplined and stringent routine. I would get up early then go to my roof to meditate and pray. After that, I would have my breakfast then leave to study and worship at the temple. There, I would focus on certain parts of the Torah and cross-reference that with the Talmud to better understand what God meant for the normal Jews. I needed to completely understand how the rabbis had interpreted the Scriptures in the Talmud. Once I completely understood and memorized everything I needed to know, I would then be able to use the scriptures to trap Jesus. I couldn't imagine Jesus being able to understand them as completely as I would.

As I gained in knowledge, the priests and rabbis asked me if I would teach some students, some of whom were much older than me. I reluctantly agreed. My stipulation was that I would take only the top 5 percent of the students. My reasoning was that by teaching them, I would learn more and that by plying my knowledge with a larger group, I would in turn learn where normal men encountered difficulties in understanding the material; ultimately, I could use that knowledge to trap Jesus. My students would unwittingly be a test group for me to prepare for my encounter with Jesus.

First of all, though, there was the issue of the students and their lack of regard for me. When the priests told the students I would begin teaching them certain portions of the Torah, they complained, telling Gamaliel that I was too knowledgeable, too disciplined, and too arrogant to be a good teacher of men. They told him that they thought my classes would be too demanding. They told him that although I was a great student, I would be a terrible teacher.

One day, after I had finished teaching my first class of the day, Gamaliel asked me how things were going. I told him I thought things were going well but felt that the students couldn't keep up with the lessons. They were complaining to me that with all of the homework I was making them do to prepare for their lessons, they weren't able to prepare for their other lessons and have any free time to spend with their families and friends. I always told them, "To be worthy of God, one must sacrifice everything else in this life."

Gamaliel looked at me for a moment then took my arm and asked me to walk with him. As we strolled through the court, Gamaliel talked with me about teaching and the reason for it. He told me that he knew I had a high degree of knowledge and drive and that he hoped I could take a small part of that and impart it to the students. As we continued to walk, he said that both the students and other teachers were complaining about my intolerance for the other classes and lessons and that the time needed to prepare for them was hurting the students' learning and their morale. He continued by saying that it seemed I had an ulterior motive for teaching other than just teaching the students a part of what I knew. He was certainly right about that last part.

We continued in silence for a few steps, Finally, I said, "Gamaliel, you know of my mission and my personality. You have been my teacher for many years. I respect you and what you are saying. You are right about one thing: I am teaching for a different reason than most. I am teaching to see where the brightest students here have trouble understanding the Torah so I might be able to prove that Jesus is a fraud."

After a few more steps, Gamaliel looked at me and said, "Saul, I had hoped that by teaching these students, you would shift your focus just a little bit away from your mission and help these students understand God better. It seems that instead of that happening, it has caused a rift between the other teachers and the students. That's not right. I have decided that it might be best to suspend your teaching and ask you to travel around Israel speaking and teaching at the synagogues. We think that spending a week at each one will let them all see a man that is focused on God and witness what great gifts he has given you."

Gamaliel continued, "Saul, we also want to add you to the Sanhedrin council. Your father served the nation and the elders in this respect. The high priest Annas has selected you to be on the council because of your family's status and your great knowledge. You will be the youngest member of the council of the seventy of Israel's top leaders."

Hearing this pleased me greatly. By being asked to be on the council, my quest and mission were fortified. I had validation. All of Israel would now know that I had been chosen of God since I had been chosen to be a part of the Sanhedrin.

It didn't take me long to get prepared to be a traveling rabbi. By going to the different towns with the same message and lessons, I didn't have to prepare each day for classes as I had been doing while teaching at the temple. I could refocus on my learning with plenty of time left over to meditate and pray.

Because Jonathan had been murdered while traveling, I planned on having plenty of guards with me. I had hired several retired Roman legionnaires to accompany me on my travels. The evening before I started my first trip, Annas came by my house unannounced. When I went to my study to meet him, he looked at me proudly and said, "Saul, if I had a son, I would pray he would be just like you. You are everything our people need to see in a man of God."

As we looked at each other, Annas waved to his servant, who held up a magnificent linen robe with embellishments showing that I was a Sanhedrin council member and listing all of my achievements in scholarship. I had never seen anything like it. Annas asked me to put it on. Once I did, I walked up to a mirror, and we both looked proudly and approvingly at the robe. I knew that this robe with its adornments and embellishments would show all of the people that I was chosen by God.

I looked over at Annas respectfully and thanked him for such a splendid gift.

"Saul, there is no one that is more deserving than you are of that robe," Annas said. "I want everyone to know what a great sacrifice you have turned yourself into for our nation."

Annas then wished me good luck and God's safety on my travels.

My first stop wasn't very far, just to Bethlehem. The priests and I had discussed this, and we figured that starting off close would help make certain I had all of my supplies with me; if I was missing anything, I could send someone back to pick it up. The week before, the local leader of the synagogue in Bethlehem had announced that the greatest student of our time, Saul of Tarsus, would be reading from the Torah and interpreting it for those at the synagogue the following week. Everyone in Bethlehem had heard of me, and they were anxious to hear me and have their sons learn from me.

As I entered the synagogue, everyone stood up and moved toward me to meet me. They were all very amazed and impressed with the robe that Annas had given me displaying all of my achievements. They assumed I must have been chosen of God to have been so knowledgeable at such a young age.

Calmly, I made my way to the front of the assembly and sat down. The synagogue was packed. Just before the service was to start, I heard a commotion outside. Suddenly, the crowd parted and in walked Annas and Gamaliel with all of my students. They wanted to be present to hear my first reading of the Torah. The leader of the synagogue asked several people occupying the seats in front to move back to allow these prominent and important visitors to sit in these most honored seats. I was elated. This was a moment to remember for the rest of my life.

After my week in Bethlehem, I moved from town to town reading at the synagogues and teaching the Torah and the Talmud. With the help of the priests, I had simplified my teachings so "the people" could understand my thoughts and interpretations of the Torah.

The one village where I wanted to teach was Nazareth, the home of the blasphemous Jesus. I had heard that he read at that synagogue almost every week, and I wanted the villagers there to now hear my *true* message from God. After three months on the road teaching in the villages, my message and teachings were perfect. I couldn't wait to teach in Nazareth.

Upon our arrival in Nazareth the next Friday morning, I had my servants set up our tents near where the caravans staged. I then started asking about where Jesus lived and where he was. One of my servants told me that Jesus lived right down the street but that Jesus's family's wood shop was across the street from where we had set up camp. I couldn't help but walk by the shop, look into the windows and the door, and see the men working there. I peered inside but didn't see Jesus.

When I went back to where the tents had been set up, I told my servants to prepare me for the Sabbath. Then we began our slow walk through Nazareth en route to the synagogue. We always paraded through the town I was speaking in just prior to the service so everyone would see we had arrived and that it was time for them to head to the synagogue. While we were walking, one of my servants came up to me and whispered in my ear. I had to stop. My servant had just confirmed that Jesus wasn't in Nazareth; he was out at his uncle's farm. I fought back my anger and then prayed to God, asking him to help me with the lesson so these poor misguided Jews would listen to the real truth. After my stay in Nazareth, I was scheduled to go back up to Jerusalem.

After I had traveled around Israel teaching for half of the year, enjoying it immensely, I decided that this was something I needed to do for the rest of my life. I needed to be a light to all of the people in Israel and teach them the truth of God's law. Each time I returned to a village that I had been to before, I had a new and different lesson for them. I could tell that everyone always listened sincerely to my every word.

Over the next several years, I continued with my mission and schedule, all the time growing in knowledge and prestige. I was asked to serve in every position that was available although I only accepted one if it would further my mission. There were many additional things I wanted to do for God, but I wasn't able to do it all because of my busy schedule.

Every Passover prepared me with questions to have ready to trick Jesus if he came around the temple. I studied and prayed to show everyone that my knowledge was directly from God. Over the years, I would see Jesus or hear he was at Passover, usually bringing one of his brothers for the ceremony of becoming a son of the commandment, but I never had the chance of being able to question Jesus while anyone was around. It seemed like Jesus was afraid of confronting me; his absences had to be more than just coincidence. I assumed Jesus didn't want to confront me now because the devil's spirit kept him away from me. I, on the other hand, couldn't wait to show all of Israel that I was indwelt by God.

27

When I last discussed Jesus, we had met at the temple when we were just made sons of the commandment. He had stayed in Jerusalem and listened to us study at the temple.

Once Mary, Joseph, and Jesus had returned back to Nazareth from Jerusalem, Jesus continued being the son and brother he had always been. If anything, he seemed to be more content than ever. He would spend his days working with Joseph and his brothers, but he would always either start or finish his day out on the hill with his Father in heaven. Most of the time, he and Joseph would work somewhere out of Nazareth, but it would not be so far away so as to make it difficult for him to return home every weekend. Jesus enjoyed spending the Sabbath with his family and friends. He loved to think that everyone would be able to take a full day to think about and worship God for all of the great and wondrous things he had done for all of them.

Now that Jesus was a son of the commandment, he started reading and discussing the Torah at the synagogue on the Sabbath. Everyone loved to hear Jesus read and discuss the Scriptures. Joseph overheard one of the worshippers telling another that he had never heard anyone discuss the Scriptures so clearly.

"He speaks as one who has authority or even like he was there when the events he reads happened." one worshipper said to another. "It is truly amazing."

When he got home, Joseph passed along to Mary what he had heard between the two worshippers.

A typical day started early with Jesus either going up on the roof or up the hill to pray and meditate. He would then come back inside and eat and get ready for the day, whether it would involve traveling with Joseph to work on a job or staying home and building or fixing things for people in the area as well as travelers from the caravans.

When he worked in Nazareth, he wanted James to come to the shop so he could teach him how to build and fix things as well. While they worked, Jesus would tell James about all the things he had learned, and he would tell his brother stories of God's people. James loved spending time with Jesus. By the end of the day, a few more people usually would come by the shop to spend time with Jesus. They were drawn to him.

At home, Jesus would have supper with his family and discuss the day's events. He would then help Mary get all of the children ready for bed; that's when he would tell them a story before they went to sleep. They felt safe and secure when Jesus was with them, and they loved his stories.

Jesus was truly starting to feel God's presence and was waiting for him to show him what his earthly mission would be.

All this time, Joseph was still traveling and working on large jobs. He started using multiple crews in different places and would travel to locations weekly to check on the work, bid for new work, and keep good workers on his jobs. Business was thriving, and there was a lot for him to do. Since Joseph was no longer doing the work himself, and with business at the shop picking up, Joseph and Jesus decided to divide up the work; Joseph would manage the out-of-town jobs, and Jesus would focus on the work at the shop and training James.

James was now old enough to start his training in the carpentry trade, and he quickly showed himself to be a natural. One day, as Jesus was working at the shop, his good friend Jacob came in and said that he and his father had bought the site next door and would be opening their masonry shop there. Jesus was ecstatic, thinking it was a great idea; he loved Jacob and his family, and this would allow them to see each other more often. When Jesus mentioned this to his family at dinner that night, he was looking at Naomi to see what she would do. He knew she had a crush on Jacob. When Naomi saw Jesus looking at her, she blushed, and then everyone laughed. It's hard to keep a secret in a tightknit family.

It took about a month for Jacob and his father to build the shop. All of a sudden, Naomi started showing more of an interest as to what was going on at her brother's shop, often bringing a small lunch to be shared by Jesus and the other men at the shop. Jacob took notice and usually joined them for lunch.

As James was making such great progress, Jesus started talking to Joseph more and more about his mission and his need to start focusing on it once Joseph and James were able to provide for their family. Joseph agreed and thought it would be soon because James was learning quickly. The jobs out of Nazareth were going well, and they were always getting new work. Joseph thought that within the year, Jesus would be able to start his advanced studies and begin the mission God had sent him from heaven to do.

28

One morning, while Jesus and James were fixing a wagon wheel, one of the men of the crew from Sepphoris came running up to the shop and said that Joseph had been hurt and wanted to see Mary. Jesus sent James to get Mary while he ran to the tarrying lot where the caravans stayed to ask one of the men he trusted to take Mary in one of their wagons to see Joseph. When she arrived at the shop, there was a wagon waiting to take her and the messenger from Sepphoris back to Joseph.

When asked by Mary what had happened, the messenger explained that Joseph had been traveling to Sepphoris to check some work at Herod's palace when he was attacked by thieves, robbed, and severely beaten. When asked if the identities of any of the thieves were known, the messenger said that Joseph had mentioned the name Barabbas as one of the gang. Barabbas and his gang were notorious in the area for robbing and killing travelers.

Mary, the messenger, and the man Jesus trusted to drive them departed; Jesus and his family went home and prayed for Joseph to be brought back to them safe. Through the rest of the day and well into the night, many villagers and several of the men from the caravan came by the house to pray for Joseph.

The wagon returned early the next morning with Mary. When everyone went out to see her, they could see that Joseph had passed. Everyone tore their clothes and started mourning for Joseph. Although Jesus felt the same physical loss as the rest of his family and Joseph's friends, he felt that he had also lost one of the only people on earth who he felt understood his mission. They had spent a lot of time together discussing how he was to be the spiritual Messiah for all of the nations of the earth, not just the Jews. They also discussed how his Kingdom would be a heavenly kingdom and not an earthly one.

The family made preparations for Joseph to be laid to rest, and the whole village came out to bid him a farewell. After the ceremony for Joseph, the family spent the accustomed time mourning and grieving for him.

After the family had gone through the mourning period, Jesus called a meeting of his family to discuss with everyone what they needed to do to keep the family functioning properly. He assumed his role as the head of the family but made it clear he would vet all of his decisions with the family.

Jesus said that Mary and he had discussed the plans for their family and wanted everyone to know what they were and to ask any questions or offer suggestions. Jesus told them that Mary and he had decided that he would take over as the head of the family with the responsibilities for the family. He told them that included the financial, emotional, and spiritual duties. Hearing all this, Naomi and James together asked how Jesus was going to be able to focus on his mission while being responsible for them. Jesus told them that his first responsibility was to them and that he would postpone his mission until God asked him to start.

Jude and Joseph, who were still incensed that the robbers hadn't been caught and punished, wanted to know if Jesus and Mary had heard anything about what the Romans were doing to investigate the murder case. Mary said that they hadn't heard anything. That simply confirmed what the two boys had always thought about the Romans in the first place—they didn't care.

After the meeting, Jesus went around to the different job sites outside of Nazareth and made sure they were finished properly. Afterward, he told the crews that he wouldn't be working outside of the Nazareth area for the foreseeable future. He needed to be close to home for his family.

29

With his mission work now on hold, Jesus spent almost all of his time raising his family while also working at the shop, interacting with the men from the caravans and continuing his daily retreats on the roof or on the hill. This was something he had meditated and prayed on with his Father, agreeing that one of his most important responsibilities, for now, was to help Mary at home.

Jesus was a wonderful surrogate father to his siblings, and he made sure all of them felt close to him so they would share their joy and pain with him. He made sure the boys had time to go to school and would also ask them to share the lessons they learned with their sisters in the evenings. Jesus thought everyone should know God's love and laws.

As each of his brothers became of age and had finished his studies, he would take them to Jerusalem to participate in the sons of the commandment ceremony. He thought it was important for them to go to Jerusalem not only for the ceremony but for the Passover as well. For a couple of years after Joseph passed away, Jesus didn't go to Jerusalem for the Passover. With everyone working together, it didn't take long for the family to be running smoothly. Mary and Jesus decided that he should go to

Jerusalem for the Passover to be with his people and listen to the teachers discuss the Torah.

The first time he went back to Jerusalem for the Passover was to take James. While there, he stayed with Lazarus and his family instead of with his own relatives. There was an extraordinary bond Jesus felt with Lazarus's family. He would spend many hours with them discussing the law and all of the things they had done during the year. The first time he saw them, they told him how sad they were over Joseph's death. Their own father had passed away the year before, and they knew the loss Jesus felt.

One evening, while they were having dinner, Mary, Lazarus's youngest sister, said, "Jesus, we heard from our father while he was dying that Mary and Joseph had told him that you were the Messiah we all have been looking for. Over the years, after we had first met, several of your aunts and uncles confirmed that, and we have also met John, who is positive you are the Messiah from God."

Lazarus looked disapprovingly at Mary and then at Jesus, and he asked Jesus to forgive her for bringing this up. Jesus looked at both of them and Martha, and he said, "For some reason, I have always felt very comfortable with you. I know my Father has put you in my life so I may have true friends while I am here. If you remember the Passover when we first met, you must remember how troubled I was and even stayed with you after Mary and Joseph left for Nazareth. It was during that Passover that I realized I was the Messiah and God's Son."

All of them just sat there stunned and yet overjoyed for a few minutes at what they had just heard. Lazarus finally spoke and said, "I remember those days and how distraught you were at times and how joyful you looked at others. I also remember you going to the temple to discuss the Scriptures with the priests, teachers, and scribes.

"After you left, it took months for them to quit debating and arguing the different insights you had brought up during your short stay. Jesus, we are not sure what we should do. We don't know if we should be worshipping you or what. We do believe you are the Messiah, and we want to do anything we can to help you with your mission."

Jesus looked lovingly at them, and, in so doing, he felt God's presence strongly. He said, "Your confession is not from men but from my Father. I accept your offer to help me in my mission. Like you, I am waiting on him to show me his will so I can begin."

Early the next morning, they saw him leave and go to the Mount of Olives to pray.

After he had spent several hours there, Jesus went into Jerusalem to listen to the teachers. Although some recognized him from the first time he had been there, he didn't enter into the discussions. There was one young man there, however, that he remembered from his first Passover, the same young man who had once tried to engage him in argument. When he asked one of the teachers who he was, the teacher told him his name was Saul, me.

After a few hours, Jesus went back to Lazarus's house and told them that he and James would head back to Nazareth early the next morning.

30

One evening, back in Nazareth, just as the family was finishing dinner, Mary started talking about one of their cousins who had just been betrothed. As usual on such topics, that started the girls discussing it and wondering how it would work out and when they would get married. Mary said that she didn't know but she was sure it would be wonderful. It was two families she knew well, and both were great families.

After a few more minutes of conversation, Mary turned to Jesus and asked him what he thought about it. Of course, everyone at the table looked at Jesus to see what he would say. As he looked at Mary, he asked, "Mother, is there anything you want to tell me, or anything I need to know about? Are you planning a match for Naomi or James?"

Both Naomi and James spoke up and said that it couldn't be them, but it might be time for Jesus. Jesus took the teasing well. Everyone thought he would be a great husband and father. All of them knew there was a nice family in Nazareth that had often spoken to Joseph about having their daughter marry Jesus. After the younger children had gone to bed, Jesus asked Mary to join him on the roof that evening.

Mary believed she knew why he had asked her to go out there with him. She thought it might be to ask her to go with him to meet the family Joseph had been talking to about the process of Jesus getting married. Once they were on the roof, Jesus started the conversation on that very topic, but he took it in a different direction. Jesus told her that he had spent many hours meditating and praying to his Father about his getting married and having an earthly family. He told her that they had decided it would be too distracting to his mission to have a wife and family. God and Jesus felt that helping raise his siblings would be enough training for the mission he was to complete.

Hearing this saddened Mary. She had always thought that Jesus was destined to have a wife and family. She could only imagine how good a husband and father he would be, and it got her to wondering how God would produce an heir for his Son to reign in Jerusalem forever. Mary thought through this for a while and then remembered the promises God had made to Abraham and Sarah. She also remembered how Jesus was conceived. God had a plan.

When his mother mentioned that he had to have a wife in order to have an heir, Jesus took her by the hand and explained to her again that his Kingdom was a spiritual kingdom, not an earthly one. Mary and he had discussed this many times.

Going forward, Mary never again said anything to or tried to persuade Jesus to get betrothed or married. She also had never told Jesus about a certain young lady who had hoped to be betrothed and then married to him. The young lady was named Sarah, and she was in love with him. The following day, Mary went over to Sarah's house and told both the parents and her of Jesus's decision to remain single. They were all sad. The girl said that she would never marry anyone else because she had given her heart to him.

For the rest of her days, Sarah kept her word and followed him during his ministry; she would later turn out to be one of the women at his cross on the day he died.

31

In the days and weeks to come, Jesus started spending more time either on the roof or on the hill with his Father. He very much wanted to start his mission, but he knew he had his responsibility to his family. One way he could begin his mission, he reasoned, was to continue showing God and his love to his family, the villagers of Nazareth, and the world through the men that he met who traveled with the caravans.

Jesus loved everyone, and that love was returned. He continued training his brothers, and each of them learned quickly. His brothers and sisters had normal sibling issues, but Jesus was such a good father to them and they loved him so much that every issue was resolved quickly and without lingering bitterness. Usually, he would have the warring siblings come to him. He would ask God to help them all understand each other, and each would then address his or her specific problem. Once they had truly listened to each other, they usually settled the squabble quickly. Afterward, Jesus would lead them in a prayer of thanksgiving.

One of the lessons he felt was a must for his brothers was to take responsibility for themselves and the family. Only a year after Joseph passed away, Jesus asked James to take over the responsibilities of the wood shop and the family finances. Once he and the family felt that James was capable, Jesus then could start focusing on his mission.

Now that James was leading the family, Jesus would work with him and offer him advice, and he would also help out drumming up business for the shop. As James gradually took the reins, Jesus started traveling to the farm and the sea to allow James more freedom. Also, Jesus could work at both places and send money back home to James.

One day, while Jesus was trimming fig trees at the farm with his cousins, Boaz walked up to the tree that Jesus was pruning and looked at it closely. Always curious about nature, Jesus asked him what he was looking at. Boaz explained that the fig tree was old enough to be bearing fruit but hadn't. Jesus asked him what his plans were for the tree. Boaz replied that he would dig a deeper trench around the tree so it would get more water, put some extra fertilizer around it, and make sure the surrounding weeds were pulled. The hope was that the tree would respond and bear fruit.

Jesus looked at the tree thoughtfully and then asked Boaz what would happen to the tree if it still wouldn't bear fruit. His uncle looked at him and said that the tree would be chopped down and burned. They would then be able to use the place where that tree was to plant and grow another fig tree that would produce fruit.

After he and Boaz had finished dressing the fig trees, Jesus went back to Nazareth. Mary had wanted him to be home for the Sabbath. Once he arrived there, Mary asked that he come sit with her, James, and Naomi for a few minutes.

Once they were seated, Mary said, "Jesus, James and Naomi have both been betrothed for the required time, and both want to get married. I think that we should allow that."

Jesus stood up and hugged both James and then Naomi, and he told them how great this was. As he sat back down, James said, "Jesus, we all know that you have stayed here and become our surrogate father and helped raise us even though you have to fulfill the mission God gave you to do. We appreciate and love you for this. Please don't think that with Naomi and me getting married we will shirk our responsibilities to our family. We won't; we will continue working with the family. I think it's safe to say you can now start spending more time on your mission."

Jesus thanked both of them then told them that once the marriage vows had been taken and everything was back to normal, he would start focusing more on what God was showing him to do.

As the festivities were completed for the weddings, Jesus went to meet with a couple of caravan masters he knew to plan a trip with them to Alexandria, where he would go to study. He had listened to the men from the caravan discuss their different religions and ideas about God. Now he wanted to better understand what they were thinking and how they had come to those conclusions. He didn't understand how anyone could confuse another type of god for his Father. The caravan masters gave him their approximate schedule and told him they would be honored for him to join them on the journey. Jesus told them it might be a couple of months but that he looked forward to traveling with them as well.

The next day, Jesus told James that he was going to the sea to work with the fishermen. He told them he would stay at least a week this time instead of just a few days like he used to; that was fine with James.

The next morning, Jesus found a small group of travelers and went with them to the Sea of Galilee. Once he was there, he stayed with his uncle Joshua and helped him with the fishing. He told them he would like to stay and work with him longer than usual, telling him of the arrangement he had made with James to take care of things back home. Joshua agreed with his plans, assuring Jesus that he had done the right thing.

One afternoon, after everyone had finished fishing and was on the docks making preparations for the following day, Joshua came down to see Jesus and introduced him to the other men with whom he would be working. The first man was Zebedee, who was there with his sons James and John. There were also two other men, Andrew and Peter. Joshua told him that Zebedee had a couple of fishing boats and that James, John, Andrew, and Peter, who were about Jesus's age, would fish with him. As Jesus shook their hands, the men all had some premonition that something was different about him. They told him they had heard about him and what a wonderful teacher he was. Zebedee asked Jesus if he would read the Scriptures in the synagogue the next Sabbath, to which Jesus agreed.

32

Back in Nazareth, life for Mary and her family was going well with James assuming the role of male head of the household and his siblings growing up to help him.

At first, Jesus would come home every other Sabbath as well as for the weddings of close friends and family. He loved going to weddings and celebrating with his family. Also, he always made it a point to take his brothers to Jerusalem when they had finished their requirements to become sons of the commandment. Joseph had thought it important to take him to Jerusalem, and he remembered how much that meant to him and what it would in turn mean for his brothers. Still, he was always careful to stay away from the classes being taught at the temple. He wanted the celebration to be about his brothers and their achievements and to avoid tense discussions with various groups regarding religious teachings. Jesus would show his brothers the sights and spend time with Lazarus.

As Jesus spent more and more time away from Nazareth, to include speaking at different synagogues, he was beginning to become known for his ability to speak, discuss, and read the Torah. By now, everyone knew who he was, and they always wanted him to read when he was there. Jesus would travel around

Israel working at his trade or staying with his uncles and working with them. As he traveled, he focused on showing God and his love to all people.

One day, while traveling, he heard a story about another traveler who had been robbed. Those kinds of stories usually got his attention because his father had been killed by robbers. Simeon, a fellow traveler, told Jesus a story about another traveler who was robbed, beaten up by a gang of thieves, and left for dead. Several people later came upon him, but they didn't stop to help, assuming he was dead. The passers-by who ignored the man included a priest and a Levite. Finally, along came Ephraim the Samaritan, who, when he checked on the man, found that he was still alive. Ephraim helped him as much as he could before taking him to an inn in the next town, where he asked the innkeeper to go find a doctor. He gave the innkeeper some money to help with the injured man then told the innkeeper to send him a bill for any other expenses incurred.

Jesus continued to travel around Israel. Whenever his sojourns took him close to one of his uncle's farms, he would stop in to see them; they always enjoyed having him, inviting him to stay a while. Likewise, Jesus loved being around them and getting the chance to read at their synagogue.

One afternoon, while Jesus was at the farm, he was watching the sheep in the pasture and playing his harp. Since the sun was getting hot, Jesus moved a very large rock over into the shade of a bush so he could sit in the shade and play. While he was sitting there playing and singing a song that King David wrote from the book of Psalms in the Torah, he saw Boaz walking toward him. As Boaz got closer, Jesus stood up to greet him, and then both men sat down on the rock Jesus had put under the bush.

Boaz looked up at the bush that was casting shadow they were using as shade and commented to Jesus that it was a mustard plant. Jesus said he had thought that was what it was. Boaz continued that it was an interesting plant because as large a bush as it was, it had come from a small seed. Boaz reached up and pulled a seed pod from the bush, rolled it in his hands, and showed Jesus just how small the seeds were.

Both men looked at the seeds for a minute, and then Jesus said, "It seems if you live and do the will of our Father and have faith that he will use you in his will, he can use just a small seed and turn it into something great."

That Sabbath, Jesus was going to speak at Boaz's synagogue. On Jesus's way there, one of his cousins, Jeremiah, mentioned that there had been a traveling rabbi that had been there a month earlier and that his message had been very strong and concise, much superior to what other rabbis had preached. Everyone who had listened to the rabbi said he was one of the brightest and best of all of the students at the temple and that he was already a member of the Sanhedrin. The young man's name was Saul. Jesus said he had met me a couple of times and that I was indeed quite knowledgeable.

As Jesus got up to read from the Scriptures at the synagogue, the congregation went quiet. Jesus's message was almost always about how much God loved his people and how good the Father had always been. He reminded them of God's promise to always be their God if they followed his commandments. Giving the people a type of message they rarely heard from other rabbis, he reminded them that they were already the chosen people because of their birthright but that they still had to keep all of God's laws. Just saying you were Jewish didn't make you right under the law.

Early the next day, Jesus and Thomas, a cousin of his, headed over to the sheep pens to get their sheep so they could take them to the fields to graze. As they neared the pen, Thomas started talking to the sheep. He called each of them by name and asked them to come to the gate. While they stood there, several of the sheep made their way to the gate where Jesus and Thomas had stopped.

When Jesus called a few by name, none of the sheep would even look at him; others would actually try to move away from where he was standing. When Jesus asked Thomas about this, Thomas said that every morning he or his brothers would come and call out their sheep. Sometimes, the sheep would come to them just from hearing their voices, and, other times, they would have to call the sheep by their name to get them to come. If some-one they didn't know—such as Jesus—came up and called them, they wouldn't come because the sheep didn't know him or her.

Once all of the sheep had come through the gate, Thomas shut the gate and led the sheep out to pasture, where they would spend the day grazing. Jesus stayed with Thomas that day and played the harp and read from the Scriptures. Jesus loved playing the harp just as much as he savored reading the law and discuss-ing it with his cousin.

Because it was getting close to Passover, Jesus left his cous-in's family and headed out for Jerusalem. He had found out there were several groups going there, and he joined one so he would be able to travel safely. As far as he knew, no one had ever caught any of the gang led by Barabbas that had robbed and killed Joseph. As he was coming up to the city, Jesus stopped in Bethany and visited with Lazarus, staying with his family during the Passover.

While he was at Passover, Jesus would get up early and go to the Mount of Olives and on into the Garden of Gethsemane to pray and meditate before going into the city and then the temple. He prayed to God that he could help the people know of their love for them and to prepare their hearts to see him as God's Son. He wanted the people to know that he loved them and was going to fulfill all of the prophecies regarding his coming as the Messiah. This would help them recognize him.

Whenever he went to the temple, Jesus would always be disgusted with the courtesans, the money being changed, and the buying and selling of sacrificial animals. All this took away from the worship of God. It was impossible to focus on God when people were selling not only animals but also themselves. Usually, he went through Solomon's Porch quickly to get away from all of this sinful, degrading activity. He then proceeded into the Court of Women, where the crowd was all Jewish and there was no buying or selling going on.

Jesus typically would then go and listen to different rabbis teach. Most of the time, he would just listen for a while then move on to another, never saying much. One thing that confused him about the teaching of the rabbis was their focus on the explanation of the law in the Talmud instead of focusing on the Torah. The Talmud was just an interpretation of the law, not *the law*. Also, some of the teachers were inclined to suggest that the Talmud was an extension of God's law, and, therefore, everything in the Talmud had to be obeyed like it was the law.

As Jesus got closer to one of the teachers, a student looked at him before slipping away to go looking for me, Saul. I had told everyone to be on the lookout for Jesus so I could go and ask Jesus some of the questions I had prepared for him, hoping to trip him up into more blasphemy. It was common knowledge among the students and rabbis that I was determined to debate Jesus, and they thought it would be great to see me get the best of the country rabbi.

It didn't take long for this student to find me; I was off helping to sacrifice animals in the temple, which seemed ironic because of the aversion I had once had to being around animals being so gruesomely sacrificed. The student whispered to me that he had seen Jesus. Immediately, I handed the rope of a bull that was about to be sacrificed to another man. At that, I departed alongside this other student who would take me to where he had seen Jesus.

When we got back to that spot, however, Jesus was nowhere to be found. We split up and looked around for a few minutes, but we couldn't find him. As I started to leave to return to where I had been at the animal sacrifices, this student told me he wanted to know what questions I planned to ask Jesus. I told him he would need to be there to hear them as I was asking the questions of Jesus.

It turns out that Jesus had also been seen by Nicodemus, who asked him to come and speak to one of his classes the following afternoon. Jesus agreed before departing to the Garden for a while and then on back to Lazarus's home for dinner. While they ate, Jesus told Lazarus that he had agreed to teach at one of Nicodemus's classes the following afternoon.

"That's a great idea, Jesus," Lazarus said.

"After the Passover," Jesus said, "I'm going to go to Alexandria to study and speak there. I have made arrangements with a caravan with which I can make the trip."

"That shouldn't have been difficult," Lazarus said, "since every caravan leader that travels through Israel knows you as Jesus from Nazareth."

The following morning, Jesus again left early to go to the Mount of Olives to meditate and pray. After lunch, he went into the city and then into the temple, where he found Nicodemus. This is where he had told Jesus to meet him. Nicodemus and Jesus walked over to where Nicodemus's class met, where Jesus sat on the floor with the rest of the students. Once situated, he read some law to them and then asked them questions to help them better understand what they were reading. Nicodemus was amazed how well Jesus could teach and how easily he led each student to the correct answers.

After a couple of hours of discussion, they all knew that they would need to stop for the day and prepare for Passover. As they finished the lesson, Jesus said a prayer of thanksgiving for many things, especially the Passover. Neither the students nor Nicodemus had ever heard anyone pray like Jesus. As they remembered the prayer, they remembered it being like Jesus was talking and thanking his Daddy. The prayers we were taught didn't have any of the intimacy that his did. Some thought it was interesting that he felt so close to God that he could pray that way while others thought that it was close to blasphemy.

As Jesus finished praying, one of the students, just like the day before, excused himself and ran to find me. He found me finishing my last class of the day, and, when I heard what my impromptu messenger had to say about Jesus's whereabouts, I headed over there. When I got there, though, all I saw was Nicodemus talking to some of his students. I rushed up and asked him where Jesus was. Nicodemus looked around and said that he had just been there, that I had barely missed him. Again, Jesus had left for Lazarus's home for Passover before I could question him, and, for the moment, I didn't know where he was. I was stymied again.

33

On the morning following the Sabbath of the Passover, Jesus said his good-byes to Lazarus and his sisters and headed out to find the caravan he would join for the trip to Alexandria. Alexandria had one of the most renowned libraries in the world, and he wanted to go there so he could study the different writings. He needed to understand the different ways men read, saw, experienced, and interpreted God so that he would be better equipped to teach all men about their real Father's love.

As he traveled, Jesus spoke to the caravan leaders as well as to the whole caravan about God and his love. Most of the travelers were not Jewish and had to be taught that God was separate from his creation and that you should worship the Creator and not the created. For some travelers, Jesus's teachings were very different from anything they had heard before. It's no wonder Jesus spent as much time answering questions as he did teaching, and this is how it went all the way to Alexandria. Once there, he made his way to the Alexandrian library.

Jesus stayed in Alexandria for some time and taught at the synagogues and anywhere people would listen to him about God's love. Sometimes, it was at the side of the seas, sometimes at a river bank, and at times in pagan temples. As he continued teaching, he felt closer and closer to his Father. He knew he was fulfilling his mission.

As the years went by, Jesus traveled around the Roman Empire telling everyone that there was one God; he was their Father and he had created them as well as everything else. Jesus told everyone that their God loved them and had a plan so that all of them could be his sons and daughters. He also traveled to the East proclaiming the same message to all who would listen, and there were many who did. All this time, Jesus seemed to have a knack for being in Nazareth whenever his family most needed him.

Everywhere he went, he taught. Because of his great teaching ability and his fresh teachings that loving God with all your heart and loving your fellow man were the only laws required of people, he was asked to speak and was offered teaching jobs at different universities, temples, and synagogues. His messages had a captive audience, and the numbers were growing.

34

Now that we have Jesus and his life caught up to where mine was, we can move on with the story of what I was doing.

"Gamaliel, have you heard of this man named John that is out by the Jordan River telling everyone the kingdom of God is at hand?" I asked.

"Yes," Gamaliel said, "we have known about him for quite some time. He was born from a priestly family in Hebron and took the Nazarite vow. He has been teaching in the hill country for a few years but has recently started preaching by the Jordan and baptizing his followers for repentance. He is saying that we all need to repent because 'the kingdom of God is at hand.'"

"Saul, I'm glad you brought up the subject of John. I have discussed this with a few high-ranking members of the Sanhedrin, and we would like you to go listen to John and learn exactly what it is that he is teaching. We don't need a radical teacher or his radical ideas teaching our people anything we don't want them to hear. The Romans seem to always like to put us Jews in our place."

I readily accepted the task; I suspended my classes and my travel for a few months to go out and listen to John. In Gamaliel, it seems, I had a friend who was starting to see things my way, reaffirming that what I was doing was the true way of God.

I took along my usual entourage when I went to see John. I had been speaking all around Israel and knew exactly what provisions I needed to be comfortable.

As we left Jerusalem, our mission was to go to where John had been last reported preaching and baptizing. As we got closer, we started meeting other travelers also going to listen to John. As we rounded a hill, we saw the Jordan River below. Looking closer, we could see a large number of people standing and listening, getting their first look at the man now becoming known as John the baptizer. I had heard that he wore clothes made out of camel's hair with a leather belt around his waist. Word was he just ate wild honey and locusts. I thought this had to be a joke, a form of mockery, but the man that I was looking at dressed exactly as they said he would.

John stood well out in the river with a couple of his disciples calling out for everyone to repent and to come to him to be baptized. Eventually, when there was no one else going out to John to be baptized, he and his disciples waded out of the river, and from there John walked up onto a large boulder and started announcing his message.

What John said in preaching to the people was succinct and easily understood. He covered three main points. The first was that the Messiah was coming soon and he, John, was his messenger. The second was that everyone needed to repent of their sins and be baptized. The third was that this coming Messiah would pay the price to redeem the whole world. Needless to say, I was fascinated.

I stayed and listened closely to John for the rest of the week to make sure he wasn't teaching anything that was improper or incorrect in regard to the Torah or Talmud. What he was doing was confirming the prophets and the prophecies of our Messiah.

As the Sabbath approached, I decided to return to Jerusalem and spend it at home. As we were entering the city, I happened to see Gamaliel. I spoke with him for a few minutes and told him I would come by after the Sabbath and give him a report on what we had seen and heard that week regarding John the baptizer.

I was at the temple by early morning on Sunday praying and meditating when Gamaliel and three of the Sanhedrin members came upon me, Gamaliel having known where I liked to pray. Once we had all exchanged greetings, I reported to the group that I had spent close to a week listening and studying the message John was delivering to make certain John and his disciples were not teaching anything contrary to our teachings.

The priests were grateful for the report and asked me what I was going to do next. I told them that I planned to go back and listen to John the next week. I also mentioned that a few of the elders and teachers of the law might want to go and listen to John to confirm for themselves what I had told them. Gamaliel, however, suggested instead that I go listen in on John and his disciples once more, and, if I came back with a similar report, a small group of them would come to listen. They wanted to be absolutely sure that John was truly what I said he was. Another concern the priests had was that by their going to hear John at this point, it would be viewed by others as endorsing John's message, which is something they wanted to avoid.

After collecting my servants, I started back out to where John was teaching and baptizing. As we traveled to the area around Gilgal, where we had heard John was to celebrate the Sabbath, I started thinking that it might be smart to get close to John and his disciples to show the people that I approved of his message. Once we had unpacked and were settled, I would look for John, introduce myself, and ask him a few questions. I wanted to show the people that John was a messenger from God and that I agreed with his message. I wanted the people to identify me with John's message. I couldn't decide if I would go so far as to be baptized by John, but I would keep listening closely to see if there would be any legal reasons I couldn't.

I learned from John's disciples that he typically arose very early each morning and went out to a remote place to pray and meditate. Wanting to speak with him privately, I woke up early with my servants, and we kept an eye out for John until we saw him go to where he would commune with God. I followed at a distance, and, after I thought John had enough time to be finished, I walked up to where he was and introduced myself.

I told John how powerful and truthful his message was and that I could see why such crowds of people came out to hear him and be baptized.

"Thank you, Saul," John said, "and you should know that I have heard about you as well, to include how knowledgeable you are. Your own reputation as a speaker and teacher precedes you, and I would like to hear you at some point."

I told him that I had listened to his message over the past week and was looking forward to spending another week with him.

After listening to and meeting John, I decided I would ask him some questions the next day about his message. I moved up close to where John was teaching, and, in a loud voice, I asked, "John, are you the Messiah you speak of?"

He looked at me and said, "No, I am not the Messiah. The Messiah will come, and I am not even worthy to tie his sandals."

"John, how will we know this Messiah when he comes?"

"I baptize with water, but he will baptize you with God's Spirit," John said.

John's message amazed me and affirmed for me that it would be OK for a group of priests and teachers of the law from the Sanhedrin to come down and show the people that they agreed with John's message. I summoned one of my servants and told him to take the message I had written to Gamaliel, telling him that they should make plans to come listen to John's message the following week.

I decided to stay and listen to John the rest of the week. Instead of going back to Jerusalem, I celebrated the Sabbath near where John was teaching. I sent a servant to tell the leader of the Gilgal synagogue that I would be coming there for the Sabbath. Usually, when I sent such a message, I would be invited to read from the Torah at the service, such was my reputation. A couple of hours later, the servant returned and said that they would be expecting me, that they would be honored if I read the law and interpreted it for them. The servant told me he had accepted on my behalf.

When we got to the synagogue, every chair was filled. Most of these people had already heard me speak, and they knew there was no one that had my knowledge of the law and Scriptures.

I decided to read from Isaiah 40:

> Comfort, comfort my people, says your God. Speak tenderly to Jerusalem, and proclaim to her that her hard service has been completed, that her sin has been paid for, and that she has received from the Lord's hand double for all her sins. A voice of one calling: In the wilderness prepare the way or the Lord; make straight in the desert a highway for our God. Every valley shall be raised up, every mountain and hill made low; the rough ground shall become level, the rugged places a plain. And the glory of the Lord will be revealed, and all people will see it together. For the mouth of the Lord has spoken.

After I had read this, I said that it did sound like John's message. I stopped for a moment and then looked out at the congregation and asked how many had gone to listen to John. Several hands went up. I then said, "Everyone should go listen to John's message since it is from God." A few moments later, I solemnly walked through the synagogue and then to the tent where I was staying. The people of the synagogue sat there while I left. Then they all got up and went home, saying among themselves they would go hear John the following week.

One of my servants came up to me in the tent and asked why I had told everyone to listen to John. I told him that John's message was strong, but I knew if I endorsed it, more people would go listen to him and repent. Since I was so well known, and John wasn't, the people would listen to me.

I went back out the next day to listen to John some more and was delighted to see that many of the people from the synagogue had come to hear him as well. As John spoke his message, followed by a call for repentance and baptism, he made his way out into the river with a couple of his disciples to baptize anyone who would come forward. As I stood there, I saw a few people go out to be baptized but not as many as I thought there should be. Perhaps if I were to be baptized, others would follow. I looked over at my servants and told them what I was going to do and that they should consider it as well. When I stood up and started toward the river, they followed in obedience.

As I walked slowly and solemnly to the river, I heard quiet murmurings from the people there, which is what I had hoped would happen. Once John was free, I waded over to him to be baptized. I wanted to be baptized by John not by one of his disciples although it would be all right if my servants were baptized by one of John's disciples, just not me.

As I approached John, he asked if I was repenting of my sins. Although I didn't think I needed to repent since I followed the law perfectly, I agreed and was baptized by John. I was just trying to be an example to the people. As I came out of the water, I could see my servants being baptized. As I walked out of the river, many other people started toward the water. Things were going just as I had planned with people following my lead.

Later that day, I received a message that several of the priests and teachers of the law were coming to hear John, including Gamaliel, and this pleased me greatly.

Two days after I was baptized, one of my servants, whom I had instructed to be on the lookout for the priests from Jerusalem, came and whispered to me that the priests would be arriving in about thirty minutes. At the time, I had been teaching one of John's disciples; upon hearing this good news, I excused myself and went out to meet them.

Once they were all settled inside my tent, Gamaliel said to me, "Saul, do you have anything to report to us? We have heard some interesting things from people who were down here."

"Yes, I do have something to report to you," I said. "I spoke at the synagogue this past Sabbath and asked the people there to come out here and listen to John. I think his message is from God. Also, when John wasn't getting many of the people to come forward to be baptized, my servants and I went into the water to set an example of being baptized by John. Several people followed us in and were baptized as well."

Gamaliel looked at me and then at the other priests and said, "Saul, that is what we had heard, but we couldn't believe it until we heard it from you."

I looked at all of them and could sense by their expressions they did not approve of what I had done.

"Before you judge me," I said, "you need to listen to John and his message."

"Saul, that would be the only fair way for us to judge you," Gamaliel said.

Gamaliel and the priests said they needed to get cleaned up and put on their robes before heading down to listen to John. I told them that they could use my tent and servants.

When we got to the river where John was still teaching, the priests could hear his strong voice and his earnest pleas to repent because the Kingdom of God was at hand. They all smiled and nodded at the message.

As we approached, the whole crowd that was listening to John looked up at us, taking note of all these distinguished teachers and leaders of the Sanhedrin coming down the path to hear John. I always enjoyed being seen with these men. I knew that all of the people envied my position, power, knowledge, and wisdom. As we continued to get closer, John finished one of his teaching points and then turned to look at us.

"You brood of vipers." John shouted at us, raising his fist into the air. "Who warned you to flee from the coming wrath? Produce fruit in keeping with repentance. And do not think you can say to yourselves, 'We have Abraham as our father.' I tell you that out of these stones God can raise up children for Abraham. The ax is already at the root of the trees, and every tree that does not produce good fruit will be cut down and thrown into the fire."

Everyone in the crowd was stunned into silence, including the priests and the teachers of the law. They stopped and looked around trying to see at whom John could possibly be yelling. As we stood there in utter amazement, John repeated what he had said and made sure everyone knew he was speaking to us. The other priests stood there for a few more seconds and then looked over at me, shook their grey heads, turned, and departed, heading back to Jerusalem.

After I watched them leave, I looked back at John, who had resumed teaching. He didn't seem to know or care who he had insulted and what that could mean regarding his teaching. As I slowly walked back to my tent, I realized that I could be severely punished for getting the priests to come all this way to listen to John, only for John to insult us. Likewise, they now think I had erred in helping John to get more disciples and baptize them.

As I watched my servants pack for the trip back, I reasoned that I would need to do some extra sacrificing and donate some additional money to the temple once I had returned. That usually calmed things down among the priests and other leaders.

35

After I returned to Jerusalem, I sacrificed and gave until I was back in the good graces of the priests. They still weren't pleased with what had happened with John at the river, so they put me on several local tasks where they could watch me closely for a few months. They had me working where no one could see me, hoping that everyone would forget what I had done.

However, I was livid that John had turned on me when I had everything set up for him to win the endorsement of all the ruling group of priests from the Sanhedrin. Didn't he realize how much more effective he would have been with me and the Sanhedrin endorsing his message? I swore that I would get even with John as soon as I could.

One morning, after I had finished praying and meditating, one of the students came to tell me that he had heard that John was Jesus's cousin. He said the Messiah that John was teaching about was Jesus. I couldn't believe it. I grabbed the student by the arm and asked him to repeat what he had just said. Once he did, I turned and looked up to heaven for a few moments; I couldn't believe God had let me be tricked by them. I left to go home, leaving the student standing there. I needed some time alone to process what I had just been told and to understand my latest setback.

My thoughts were in turmoil as I wondered how God could let me be set up by John to embarrass me like this. Thankfully, for that moment at least, the priests didn't share my passion about proving Jesus a fraud. Once I got home, I went to the roof and spent the morning in prayer reaffirming my mission with God. I complained to God that he had let me be taken in by this imposter John and wondered what I had done wrong so that God had allowed this to happen.

After I had finished praying, I went back to the temple and started looking for the student who had given me the message. I needed to get some more information from him. After circling around the temple, I spotted him listening to Nicodemus. I walked up to the group and asked Nicodemus to excuse the student. As we walked away, the student introduced himself to me as Samuel. He was from Migdal, close to where John was baptizing people, and he knew John's family well.

I asked Samuel if he would work with me on a project. Samuel said he would love to, but first he would need to get the requisite permissions from the priests. Because Samuel was from the area and knew John and his family, he would be able to go spend time listening to John without John and the disciples being suspicious of him. I wanted Samuel to use his access to and trust of John to make sure he wasn't teaching any false messages to the people. Samuel said he would be honored.

I spent the next few days gathering the permissions for Samuel. Considering the tongue-lashing John had given the priests, it wasn't too difficult to get those permissions. They wanted to shut John up. They didn't like people listening to him instead of them. Since it wasn't far away, Samuel could go there three or four days a week and then come back to report to me without much problem. Samuel asked if he could have one or two of the other students join him if their schedules permitted. He thought it would be good to have others listening as well, and I concurred.

Samuel left the following morning. When he got there, he was startled to see so many others present to listen to John and to answer his call to repent and be baptized. Samuel didn't remember John being that interesting; something about him had changed, and it was significant.

Samuel listened carefully and wrote down John's main points so he would have a concise report to bring back to me and the priests. One afternoon, Samuel's best friend, Joshua, came to listen to John. Neither heard anything about John's message that alarmed them. After the morning's teaching, Samuel and Joshua left and returned to Jerusalem to report to me and celebrate the Sabbath.

Once they arrived, they sought me out and delivered the notes they had taken. After I had asked them a few questions, I thanked them and told them to come by my house after the Sabbath. I had some more questions for them and also told them I would need for them to go back again to listen to John. They said they would.

After the Sabbath, Samuel came over to my house and waited for me in the study until I had finished praying and meditating on the rooftop. Once we were settled in my study, Samuel told me he was available to go listen to John for three days that week.

"Does Joshua want to go as well?" I asked Samuel.

"Yes, he does, as long as his schedule allows it," Samuel said.

"Thanks, Samuel," I said. "I appreciate what you are doing. You are providing a great service for the priests and the Sanhedrin."

The next morning, Samuel and Joshua headed back to the Jordan River Valley to hear John. Again they marveled at the great number of people who were likewise headed to hear John teach, taking down notes of some of what he was hearing from these others. Several of the men walking along near Samuel speculated as to who John truly might be. One said John was just what he said he was, a messenger telling the people to repent because the Messiah was coming soon. Another of the men said John was more than that, kind of a prophet from God. A third traveler said he thought John was Elisha risen from the dead. Still another offered the opinion that John was the Messiah that he said was coming even though John had denied that.

As they approached where John was teaching and baptizing that week—he had moved up the Jordan River to preach his message—they saw that the crowd had gathered and was listening intently to his message. John was teaching about marriage and the family and how the Messiah would be able to heal those broken relationships if those involved would listen, repent, and do what he said. As John was finishing his message, someone in the crowd asked what he thought about Herod marrying Herodias, his brother's wife. John thought for a moment and then condemned Herod and Herodias for divorcing their spouses before getting married to each other. John said, "It is not lawful for Herod to have Herodias."

Both Samuel and Joshua thought that was interesting, and, by law, John was correct. That made them believe that John was a true messenger from God if he had the ability to stand up and publicly judge Herod. Samuel looked over at Joshua and told him what he thought about John and his praise for him. Joshua agreed. As they were standing there, they saw a couple of Herod's soldiers leave the crowd and start back toward Jerusalem. They both looked at each other, knowing this was not a good sign for John, and they wondered what might happen to the baptizer.

Again the next day, Samuel and Joshua went to the Jordan. The crowds were a bit larger than before, probably because a few had heard the criticism of Herod by John, arousing interest as word spread. As they waited near the road that led to Jerusalem, a few travelers passed by them. As one group walked by, the two students heard one of the men say something to another, and somewhere in that exchange they heard the name "Jesus."

There were two men and two women in this particular group of travelers that was moving close to John, who suddenly exclaimed, "Look, the Lamb of God, who takes away the sin of the world. This is the one I meant when I said, 'A man who comes after me has surpassed me because he was before me.' I myself did not know him, but the reason I came baptizing with water was that he might be revealed to Israel."

As the man John referred to went out into the river to be baptized by him, John tried to deter him, saying, "I need to be baptized by you, and do you come to me?"

Jesus replied, "Let it be so now; it is proper for us to do this to fulfill all righteousness."

Then John consented and baptized Jesus.

According to Samuel's report, this group of people looked up toward heaven and stood transfixed for several moments. After that, the other travelers in the group were baptized. As the two women and other man from the group walked out on the bank after being baptized, I heard one of the women refer to the man that was with them as Lazarus. As Lazarus started drying off his clothes, someone walked up to him and asked, "What was the name of the man that John just baptized?"

"That is Jesus," Lazarus replied.

While Samuel was writing all of this down to give to me later, he looked around to see where Jesus had gone. He thought Jesus might start teaching or do something else worthy of being reported to me. Samuel finally looked across the river and saw Jesus climbing out of the river and walking up the hill by himself. There wasn't anything out in the direction where Jesus was headed except desert.

Although Samuel was supposed to stay another day, he figured it would be more prudent to immediately go back to see me and tell me what he had witnessed. He went to Jerusalem as fast as he could, and, once he was there, one of the priests told Samuel I was at home. When he arrived, I was with some guests and had told my servants I wasn't to be disturbed. Samuel insisted he see me, though, and he started making a commotion, knowing it would get my attention.

I came out of my study to tell the servant to take care of whatever the commotion was; when I saw it was Samuel and that he was drenched in sweat from his journey, I invited him into my study and told the servant to get him something cold to drink. Upon entering the study, Samuel saw that he had interrupted my meeting, so he politely asked to be excused, but I wanted to hear what had caused him to come back early. As we sat down, Samuel handed me the tablets upon which he had written the notes for me to see.

The first set of tablets related the incident of John criticizing Herod. After I read them, I smiled because now I had found a way to get back at John for how he had treated the priests and me. I would inform Herod as soon as I could get an appointment. I waved one of the servants over and wrote out a message for him to take to Herod immediately. Herod happened to be in Jerusalem because his birthday was coming up, and he always celebrated it in Jerusalem. After I got the chance to meet with Herod, John's problems would begin.

As I started reading the next set of Samuel's tablet notes, I saw where Jesus had gone to John to be baptized. Again, the intense anger was stirring inside me. *Jesus, here?* After a few moments to calm myself, I turned to the group of people in my study and read to them about the baptism of Jesus. Upon finishing the reading, I told them that this Jesus whom John had baptized was the same person who had blasphemed God eighteen years earlier at the temple by saying he was God's son.

The group listened closely as I outlined for them how I wanted to work with them on pursuing Jesus to see if his wisdom was from God or from Satan. We also needed to make sure he wasn't blaspheming anymore. I told them that he was becoming a very popular rabbi even though he had never even finished his schooling. The group of men in my study agreed that I should find out what I could about Jesus however I needed to do it.

The four men with me in the study? None other than Gamaliel, Nicodemus, Annas, and Caiaphas.

36

I spent the next week continuing to have John investigated. Eventually, I found out several things about him I wished I had known before getting mesmerized and baptized by him. Everyone in the region believed that he was a son of promise.

The story was that John's father, Zacharias, a priest, had been doing his duties in the temple when an angel was supposed to have come to him and foretold that his barren wife, Elizabeth, would have a son and that he would be a messenger from God and prepare Israel for the coming of their Messiah. When this baby was born, they named him John. I also learned that John was a cousin of the bastard child Jesus. It seems that John and Jesus were working together to trick the people into believing Jesus was the Messiah. Even though I wasn't just an ordinary Jew, they had even suckered me in and I had been baptized.

Herod had made time to meet with me about John the following day. I used that opportunity to warn Herod about John's criticism of him as well as the threat I perceived from the two rebels John and Jesus. Herod needed to know the truth of their mission, which was to have the people believe they were the Messiah's prophesized messenger and the Messiah himself.

"We should be careful not to allow these two men and their co-conspirators to get the people all worked up about the Messiah coming," I told Herod. "I would hate for the Romans to blame you if the people started any riots."

"I have heard the same stories, Saul, and some of my soldiers are keeping a very close eye on them," Herod said.

After meeting with Herod, I returned home and went straight up to the roof to pray and meditate, seeking God's will for me in regard to this conspiracy. Over the next few hours, my mission from God became clear. I went downstairs and sent a servant on an errand to set up a meeting for me with Gamaliel. I told the servant that I would be going over to the temple in a few minutes and would wait on Gamaliel at his office near where the Sanhedrin met.

After I arrived, I sat, waiting and plotting. I didn't have to wait long. Gamaliel always took my requests to meet seriously. Once he arrived, I started laying out the conspiracy as I saw it happening. At first, Gamaliel wasn't sure that I had interpreted all of the facts correctly, but, as I continued showing him how the conspirators were using prophecy to deceive the people, he started coming around to my point of view. After I gave him a few more illustrations of what had been reported to me by Samuel, Gamaliel was in complete agreement with me.

"Saul, I want you to take charge of this situation," Gamaliel said. "I am sorry we didn't take your earlier warnings more seriously.

"There are a few things that need to be done quickly. First, you will need a few more men to help keep track of both of these men's whereabouts and what they are saying and how the people are responding. We need to be careful and build the evidence carefully, as both of these men are popular with the people. As we have discussed many times, most of the people do not know the law and prophets well enough like you and I do to understand God's thoughts. They do not have the insight we do to be able to interpret the law or see how they are being manipulated by these conspirators.

"Saul, you have my confidence to do whatever you feel necessary to stop this threat. I will call a meeting of the ten leaders of the Sanhedrin to explain this to them and tell them of our agreement. Let's keep this just within our small group until we get the evidence we need to arrest them."

Gamaliel continued: "Saul, I am glad you told Herod about John. Herod will need to do something about John if he keeps on judging him and Herodias. Hopefully, Herod will take care of John for us."

My mission was finally getting on the right track.

Over the next two weeks, I recruited a few more men to keep track of John and his family. I then recruited a few more to start checking up on Jesus and his family. A week later, the men returned with their respective reports. The men charged with spying on John and his family came back with a detailed report about what they had seen and heard. However, while the men checking on Jesus and his family returned with a detailed report on the family, they had nothing to report on Jesus. No one seemed to know where Jesus had gone. As best as they could figure out, after Jesus was baptized, he had walked out into the desert and hadn't come back.

I thanked them and told them to reduce the reports into a concise document, which I then had one of my servants deliver to Gamaliel.

So, what could Jesus possibly be doing out in the desert by himself? That's the first thing I asked myself. Maybe he was meeting with someone out there for the sake of privacy so no one would see them meeting.

The following week, I received the updated reports from my men checking up on John and Jesus and their respective families, and I forwarded them to Gamaliel. As my scouts were leaving, I asked both teams to work together this time to focus only on where Jesus was and see what he was up to. For keeping track of John and his family, I called in my two inquisitive students Samuel and Joshua since they knew the area the best; maybe they could hear from some of John's followers and find out where Jesus might have gone.

While sitting in my study one day the next week, one of my servants came in to tell me there were two men at my door. It was one man from each team, and they said they needed to speak to me now. At first, I was annoyed because both of the men were way too early for the weekly meeting, which was scheduled for the following afternoon. All I could think, and hope for, was that maybe they had learned something important enough to come in early.

As the men came in, I noticed that it was Samuel, who was watching John, and Philip, the one on the team watching Jesus's family and searching for him. First, I addressed Samuel, asking him what was so urgent for him to come back to Jerusalem a day early. When he started talking to me, Samuel spoke slowly and acted embarrassed about his report.

"Sir, everything started out like what we had seen before, with Joshua and me taking turns listening to John while the other interviewed the people," Samuel said. "But, one time, when it was my turn to be with the people, talking to them and taking notes, I happened to look over at the river where John was baptizing people, and I saw Joshua getting baptized. I couldn't believe it."

After Joshua came back out on the bank, Samuel said he went up to Joshua and shouted, "What are you doing?" Joshua said that after listening to John and studying the Torah, he thought John was right and that he should be baptized. At that point, Samuel said, that's when he turned around and came straight to see me.

I couldn't believe it. I was about to condemn Joshua for being such a fool but then remembered I had fallen prey to John as well. I thanked Samuel for his report and asked him to find another scouting partner not so gullible that he could take with him to replace Joshua when he went back to observe John.

I looked over at Philip and said, "Hopefully, you have better news for me than Samuel did."

Philip looked at me and haltingly started his report. *Well, here we go again,* I thought. He told me that while his team was watching Jesus's family, he overheard them getting ready for a wedding of one of their close friends. He reported that the family thought Jesus would come back from wherever he was to attend that wedding. They weren't disappointed. As the festivities started, Jesus showed up and started celebrating the wedding of his close family friends. He also had a few new men with him that people were saying were his disciples.

"We didn't realize it," Philip said, "but Jesus plays the harp and sings exceedingly well. He played and sang most of the songs for the wedding. All of the wedding party loved having him there. Because Jesus came to the wedding, everyone who was invited brought several other guests with them, both to enjoy the wedding celebration and, more importantly, to meet and hear Jesus.

"Because of the extra guests, we heard that they were running out of wine. We all wondered what would happen. We were feeling sorry for the bride's father because he was going to run out of wine for his daughter's wedding."

I interrupted Philip and said, "OK, OK; you found Jesus and everyone loves him. We already knew that. Why did you think this was so urgent?"

"Well, Saul," Philip said, "after they ran out of wine, the head steward started handing out new wine. No one could figure out where he had gotten it from. Everyone said the new wine was so much better than the wine they had served earlier. The guests thought it was strange that they would save the best wine for later in the party.

"When we asked one of the servants where the new wine had come from, he said that when Jesus realized they were out of wine and the father was going to be embarrassed, Jesus asked the servants to fill some jars with water and then take them to the head steward to drink. We did what he asked, and, in the time it took us to take the jars over to be tasted by the steward, the water had turned to wine."

I jumped out of my chair in a rage. This had to be the most ridiculous thing I had ever heard. Jesus was using this family's wedding to continue his conspiracy. Now he had shown these ignorant people a miracle, and I was trembling with anger.

Gathering myself, I asked, "How do you think he did that? Obviously, the servants and the steward were in on the deception. How many of the people that were there heard what had happened? How many thought it was a miracle?"

Philip looked back at me and said, "I suppose that maybe the servants and steward could have been in on it. Probably everyone that was at the wedding, and now everyone around Cana has heard about it and thinks it was a miracle.

"Saul, it looked like it was real."

This conspiracy was more deeply rooted than we had thought. I asked Philip to leave and then went out to tell Gamaliel. He didn't take the news very well, either. He seethed with anger as he heard one of my best students being tricked into being baptized and told me, "That fellow must be the biggest idiot in Israel."

Gamaliel must have forgotten that I had been baptized by John as well. When I told him about the supposed miracle of turning water into wine at a wedding feast, Gamaliel couldn't even speak. After a few minutes, he looked over at me and told me that he had put me in charge of breaking up this conspiracy and now it was spiraling out of control. He ordered me to take care of it, or he would get someone who could.

"Don't forget, though, to be discreet, or all of the rabble will revolt, and then the Romans will step in to do what we couldn't," Gamaliel said. "We don't need that interference."

I left my meeting with Gamaliel dejected but more determined. Then again, I didn't have much choice but to increase my efforts. I was getting tired of this Jesus deceiving everyone.

The one thing I had done was to focus on John for continuing to criticize Herod. Once Herod got tired of John criticizing him, I thought he would throw John in jail. That would stop one of the leaders of the conspiracy and hopefully put an end to all of this. After Herod had John captured, we would need to catch John talking about the conspiracy or saying something blasphemous so he could be permanently silenced.

Thankfully, a few days later, I heard Herod had sent out his guards and picked up John for John's criticizing and judging

Herod and Herodias. I also heard that John's disciples had dispersed. This calmed me down a little. I didn't think that Herod would let John out of prison until John apologized for his comments about his marriage. Remembering John and his message, I didn't think John would ever do that. Well, at least one of the co-conspirators was out of the way.

37

After Gamaliel heard that Herod had put John in prison, he came over to where I was teaching and congratulated me on a "job well done." He then turned to my students and told them that they were learning from the brightest and best and, above that, a true patriot of Israel. That was quite an endorsement: I stood there breathing in his compliments. Across Solomon's Porch, I could see a couple of my fellow teachers looking at one another and saying quietly, "The Hebrew of Hebrews" and then chuckling. I wasn't amused.

The following morning, while meditating, I realized how completely I needed God's help to reveal Jesus as a fraud. Jesus, with the help of co-conspirators, had shown amazing knowledge and forethought to position him as the Messiah. Certainly, Satan was helping them with their plan.

I now knew I needed God's insight because I was having trouble stopping this conspiracy. I couldn't do it alone, but I was unable to see where I should be stationing our men to stop this threat. One thing I now had going for me, though, was that Gamaliel as well as the teachers of the law and the Pharisees saw the same threat I did. While I knew God was with me and was helping me root out the conspirators, I also realized that I needed to pray and meditate more, that I needed to give even more gifts, and that it was incumbent of me to focus on this task I was born to do. Jesus and his gang were too good for anyone else to handle.

With John now out of the way, I focused my men on Jesus and his followers. I told them to report not only on anything that Jesus said or did but also anything that his followers were saying. It dawned on me that Jesus would continue gathering followers, and, once he had enough, he would lead them in a revolt, which is something the Sanhedrin didn't want to happen. They didn't want to have anything disturb the Romans or Herod. We all liked everything the way it was.

As the weekly reports came in, I started believing that by just arresting John and not killing him, these conspirators weren't taking us seriously. As I thought about how to get Herod to kill John, I remembered that Herod liked John and enjoyed listening to him. But I remembered that Herodias hated everything about John, so I decided to set up a meeting with her.

Although Herodias thought it was odd when I contacted her about meeting, she remembered that I was the one who had set up John to get arrested. So, she agreed to meet with me. I spoke to her about John.

"Herodias, John not only was insulting both Herod and you, but he also is one of the leaders of a conspiracy to upset the government," I told her.

"OK, Saul, but what do you have in mind?" she said.

"I do not want to insult you or your family with what I am about to suggest, but we need to make certain we get John in a situation where Herod cannot stop from killing him," I said.

"Well, tell me your plan, and, if it's something I agree on, then I will help you execute it," Herodias said.

"We all know Herod is having his birthday party here in Jerusalem this week, and we all know he likes to have a great time. We also know that he likes to drink quite a bit at his birthday parties and, with a little help, will drink way too much."

"You are right," Herodias said, "but where are you going with this?"

"Once he has had a few too many, we know he likes to have ladies come and dance for him. We need to have someone dance so well or so naughtily that while Herod is drunk, he will promise to give her something."

Herodias, slightly blushing, looked at me and then started laughing. She was amazed that I, a distorted, confirmed bachelor, understood her husband so well. As she sat there a few more moments, she looked up and said that she would agree to what I had suggested. Very pleased with myself, I told her to send for me if she needed anything. She told me that she wouldn't have any trouble carrying out her part of the plot.

I left praising God that he had helped me develop a scheme to stamp out one of the conspirators even if it was a bit underhanded. On top of that, I couldn't wait to hear how Herodias would implement my plan.

Four mornings later, following my meeting with her, I heard that Herod had beheaded John in prison the night before. Herodias could execute a plot quickly. I called for one of my servants and told him to go ask if Herodias would see me again. She immediately agreed and asked that I come over right away.

As I entered, I bowed and congratulated her on a job well done.

"It was just like we had planned," Herodias said "During his birthday party, Herod started drinking, and it was easy to encourage him to have another drink or two. After I knew he was ready, I asked some girls to come in and dance for him. He would do anything for a lovely dancing girl.

"Well, he acted just like we thought he would. Herod finally was getting so lustful that he whispered to me that he wanted to give a gift to the next girl that danced for him. Once I heard that, I motioned toward the door and signaled my daughter, Salome—we also call her Herodias—to come in and dance. Even though she is my daughter, I still think she is by far the most sensual dancer in the kingdom.

"As Herod watched her dance, he was overcome with desire and shouted out that she had pleased him so much that he would offer her up to half of his kingdom. I was delighted since now I could influence Salome on what to ask for. I told her to ask for the head of John on a silver platter. I could see that Herod was surprised and disturbed about the request, and, even in his drunken stupor, he almost denied her request. If he hadn't sworn an oath, he would have turned her down. So, after a few moments, Herod ordered it done."

I looked at Herodias and decided two things then and there. First, Herodias and I made a great team; second, I would never cross her.

We had put one of the lead conspirators out of action for good, and no one saw that I had orchestrated the plot except Herodias and God. I thought Gamaliel and some of the priests would suspect I might have had something to do with it. I never told them, and they never asked.

Now I could focus on Jesus.

38

Leaving Herodias, I went straight home and told my servants to purchase three bulls on my behalf and have them delivered immediately to the temple for a special offering of thankfulness.

One of the older servants, Gabriel, who knew me well, casually mentioned that I was getting a lot like Jonathan with my extravagant offerings, and he was right. Another of the servants asked me what great thing had happened that I wanted to show the people my thankfulness. I just told him to get the bulls and meet me at the temple. Later on that day, Herodias heard of my offering and smiled at the thought, for she was the only one besides me who knew what the sacrifice was for.

After I had celebrated the Sabbath that week, I started planning how to trap Jesus. It would be difficult because all of the reports I had received told me that Jesus was very popular. I was going to have to discredit him in front of the people and show he wasn't the Messiah they all had made him out to be. I decided to spend the week fasting, praying, and mediating so that God would show me the right path.

During my week of worship, I also had each of my men who had been watching Jesus, his family, and followers come in to answer questions so that I could determine his weaknesses. After this week of focus, I came to the conclusion that the only way I was going to discredit Jesus was to keep my men out where they could listen to Jesus teach and catch him or his followers discussing their conspiracy or blaspheming God.

Also, I wanted my men to spend time with the crowd to see how they were reacting to his teaching as well. Maybe one of these followers would mention something about the conspiracy, and then we could question him and start arresting some of the leaders.

I met with Gamaliel about my plan, and he thought it would work. After our meeting, I called together all of my men who had been watching John to tell them to now focus only on Jesus, his family, and his followers.

One of the things I wanted them to watch and listen for was any reference to his being more than just a man or promising the people things that only a true ruler could deliver. I would have to indict him on either religious or political issues. The reason we were rid of John was completely political; with Jesus, I didn't care either way just as long as Jesus was removed.

Once I had explained the plan to my men, I told them to get started. I knew they were reliable and understood the law and the Scriptures well enough to know when Jesus or his followers were teaching according to the traditions of the elders or not.

I handpicked seven men—Stephen, Philip, Prochorus, Nicanor, Timon, Parmenas, and Nicholas—and then had Gamaliel come and speak to them about their mission. I prayed and laid my hands on the seven men and gave them their assignments. Each one was told to find someone to go with him. This second person would be needed to help them and to be a messenger for sending messages to me in Jerusalem or wherever I was so that I could quickly get to where I was needed when I was needed. I explained to them that if they heard that Jesus would be in an area for a while, I was to be told so I could come and ask Jesus some questions that would help us build evidence. Then we could arrest him and his followers.

While teaching at the temple, I had met several other men just a few years younger than the seven. I asked the seven to choose a companion from that group to help them with their mission. After they were chosen, I laid my hands on them and prayed for them to do God's will. After that, they all left Jerusalem to start their mission.

The twosomes left and scattered out across Israel to start listening and asking questions about Jesus and his disciples. Stephen and his companion, Aaron, had decided to go near the Sea of Galilee because they had heard Jesus was from Nazareth. As they traveled, they heard that Jesus had started recruiting disciples and was spending time near Capernaum. They decided to go there and celebrate the Sabbath. They knew that if Jesus was in the area, the synagogue leaders would ask him to read and speak. Once they got to Capernaum, they found a place to stay and prepared for the Sabbath service.

When they entered the synagogue that Sabbath, Stephen and Aaron heard that Jesus was coming to their synagogue to teach; the men that were there were excited. They sat down in the back and waited with their tablets on their laps so they could take notes. Neither of them had met Jesus before. They had seen him in Jerusalem over the years but hadn't had a chance to actually meet him. As Jesus and his disciples entered the room, the air seemed to change, and Stephen suddenly felt closer to God than he had ever felt before. As Jesus met and greeted the people, he came over to where they were sitting and introduced himself. His presence was overwhelming.

As Jesus walked away, Stephen saw Aaron writing on his tablet and looked over to see what he had written: "Met Jesus in Capernaum at the synagogue. Seemed to be a nice man. He did seem to be recruiting because he went around the room and introduced himself to everyone." Stephen found it odd that Aaron hadn't felt the way he did when he had met Jesus; he had felt something, sort of a cross between complete calm and strong adoration.

When the service started, Jesus was asked to read from the Scriptures. He read from the Psalms, explaining the Psalmist's words, and Stephen felt drawn to him as he spoke. He had never heard anyone teach with such authority—not even Saul or any of the other teachers of the law in Jerusalem. As he listened, Stephen thought that he also should be taking notes, but he just couldn't keep from listening to his beautiful voice.

As Jesus was finishing his message to the people, a man acting wildly, apparently filled with a demon, burst into the room and screamed, "What do you want with us, Jesus of Nazareth? Have you come to destroy us? I know who you are, the Holy One of God!"

Everyone looked at this crazy man and then back at Jesus to see what his reaction would be. From what I could tell, he went from being startled by the screaming to being angry to having pity for the man. Jesus looked at him and said, "Be quiet. Come out of him." The man shook violently, shrieked, and went silent. I was amazed that an unclean spirit would obey this man. All of the people of the synagogue were amazed, and word spread quickly throughout the city.

After they had gone back to where they were staying, Stephen asked Aaron to show him all his notes of what he had seen and heard during the service. From reading the notes, Stephen was amazed that Aaron hadn't heard or felt anything in the same way he had. It's like they had been in two different places at the same time.

Also, Aaron had written about the wild man who had come into the synagogue, suggesting that it had all been staged. He believed that the man had been hired or coerced into the role of acting like he had an unclean spirit and then being a part of staging the miracle. Stephen looked up and wondered if what Aaron had written could be true. The writing continued saying that this was done on the Sabbath and that it broke several of the thirty-nine laws regarding working on the Sabbath in the Talmud.

After Stephen finished reading the notes, he told Aaron that after the Sabbath he wanted him to ride back to Jerusalem and tell me what they had seen. Stephen contemplated the possibility that perhaps they, too, were guilty of working to trap Jesus.

Aaron departed for Jerusalem; Stephen searched out Jesus and started following him and his disciples as they walked down by the sea where two of his disciples' family lived. Stephen remembered it was home of the brothers Simon and Andrew.

Once they arrived, Stephen heard that the brothers' mother had a fever, but, when Jesus went into see her, the fever broke. As Stephen stood there, people from around the area started bringing their sick loved ones for Jesus to heal. Although Stephen and Aaron had heard rumors about Jesus performing miracles in Jerusalem, they had never had firsthand proof until now with Jesus healing the sick and driving out demons right before their eyes. After he went back to his room, Stephen took out his tablet and wrote down everything he had seen and heard.

Back in Jerusalem, I was getting reports daily from my seven teams. I reread the one that Stephen's team had sent. I concurred that Jesus had faked the miracle and that he had broken the Sabbath law to do it. Although I wanted to go and arrest him, this offense wasn't serious enough to get rid of him. I would need to find something else, something bigger.

When Aaron had returned to the Sea of Galilee from Jerusalem, he relayed to Stephen that I had told them to keep a close eye on Jesus and to now report in daily. To do this, I had sent some of the temple guards to help run the messages and tablets back and forth. Stephen then handed one of the guards the tablets he had recorded, and the guard left to come to me immediately.

The following day, as Jesus was walking down by the sea, a large crowd started gathering to hear him speak. As Jesus walked past a man named Levi, onlookers heard Jesus say, "Follow me." When they were told that the man was a tax collector, the onlookers were surprised. Stephen told Aaron to write this down and send it back to me.

As Jesus continued walking on the shore, he stopped and spoke for a while. After he finished speaking, he went to Levi's house and joined the tax collector for dinner. Aaron and I were shocked: not only were other tax collectors there but publicans and other sinners as well. Jesus even had his disciples eating with them. The following morning, another tablet was on its way back to me with more of this news.

39

It was evident Jesus was going to stay near the Sea of Galilee for a while, so after I received the message from Stephen, I decided to take a couple of my students and travel there. I asked one of the guards to go and find Philip and have him meet us there, too. I wanted to trap Jesus and see if we could start building our case against him.

Philip, our escorts, and I arrived in Capernaum around noon on Friday. We wanted to be there to see and hear what Jesus would do once he knew that I was there. I was so fixated on Jesus that I assumed he was just as fixated on me. He had to know by now that I was trying to stop his conspiracy.

Before I returned to my room, I walked to the synagogue to tell the synagogue leader that I was in Capernaum and would be there for the service. After that, I went to my room and started preparing for the service. I wanted to make sure that I had all the proper adornments on my robe so that Jesus and his followers would be able to see how learned I had become. I also planned what Scripture I would read and interpret.

Philip and Stephen decided to get to the synagogue early to get a seat. They assumed that with the two most distinguished speakers in Israel at the small synagogue at the same time, it would be standing room only. They were wondering what Jesus would do when the leader of the synagogue chose me instead of him to read from the Scriptures.

As the room started to fill, Stephen experienced the same feelings he had felt the first time he had been near Jesus. He started to explain this sensation to Philip when Jesus and his disciples came through the door, cutting him off. They came in smiling and greeting everyone.

You could tell Jesus enjoyed being with the people and worshipping God. As the room continued to fill, he and his group found seats in the back, and soon it was standing room only. Stephen, Philip, and the men with them started looking back at the door, anxiously awaiting me. It was almost sunset. Just as the doors were closing, I walked in. I paused there for a few minutes so everyone could see all of the adornments on my robe signifying all that I had achieved.

Everyone watched me enter, and I'm sure they all remembered who I was and that I had spoken to them before. Stephen, however, overheard some men saying they didn't realize I was going to be there. They had come to hear Jesus. As Stephen and Philip sat there, they heard these other men whisper that they hoped the synagogue leader would have Jesus speak and not the fellow from Jerusalem—me. The men that Stephen and Philip were listening to couldn't even remember my name, which seemed amusing to them for some reason. It wasn't amusing to me.

As I slowly and in a distinguished manner walked up the aisle to the front, I looked around and spotted Jesus. As I glared at him, Jesus responded with a warm smile. I frowned and turned back around as I continued to the front. The synagogue leader was asking a man seated in front to give up his seat so that I would be able to sit down. The man agreed, but I could tell he wasn't happy about it; he had gotten there early so he could be as close to Jesus as he could for when he spoke.

While the man who had relinquished his seat moved to the back, Jesus, who was sitting near the back, stood up and offered his chair to him although the man told him he would prefer to stand. Then Jesus whispered in his ear, and the man sat down. Later, after the service, the man told others that Jesus had asked the man to please accept his chair because he knew the man had a bad knee that was painful to stand on.

The leader of the synagogue was delighted that he had Israel's two most profound speakers in one of his services at the same time; now he had to choose which one would speak. Here was the leader's dilemma: I, Saul, was a member of the Sanhedrin and extremely influential; however, he thought he should let Jesus speak since he was who the people had come to hear. I hadn't realized that the synagogue leader was comparing me to Jesus. Didn't he know who I was? Didn't he know that I was the Roman Empire's most knowledgeable man of the law?

When I turned to look at Jesus, I could see he had a look of compassion for the leader. A moment later, he stood and spoke to the leader of the synagogue and said that he had listened to me on several occasions but had never heard me lead a Sabbath service. Jesus said that he had hoped upon seeing me enter the synagogue that I was there to lead the service. The leader of the synagogue nodded to him and then introduced me. I stood and walked up onto the podium, from where I read from the law.

I slowly opened the scroll and turned to Leviticus, chapter 24, verses 10-23:

> Now the son of an Israelite mother and an Egyptian father went out among the Israelites, and a fight broke out in the camp between him and an Israelite. The son of the Israelite woman blasphemed the Name with a curse; so they brought him to Moses. (His mother's name was Shelomith, the daughter of Dibri the Danite.) They put him in custody until the will of the Lord should be made clear to them.
>
> Then the Lord said to Moses: Take the blasphemer outside the camp. All those who heard him are to lay their hands on his head, and the entire assembly is to stone him. Say to the Israelites: "Anyone who curses their

God will be held responsible; anyone who blasphemes the name of the Lord is to be put to death. The entire assembly must stone them. Whether foreigner or native-born, when they blaspheme the Name they are to be put to death." Then Moses spoke to the Israelites, and they took the blasphemer outside the camp and stoned him. The Israelites did as the Lord commanded Moses.

After I read the passage, I put down the scroll and looked at the audience and said, "Do you all agree that if there were a blasphemer among us, we would carry out God's law and stone him?" All of the men in the room nodded in agreement.

After a few moments, I stepped off of the podium and sat down. The leader of the synagogue, standing next to the wall, looked at me for a moment, then walked back to the center of the room, and thanked me for the lesson. Next, he turned to Jesus and said, "Since Saul was so gracious to come speak to us on short notice and because we have some time left for the Sabbath celebration, would you come and read?"

Jesus accepted the invitation; he walked up to the podium and picked up the scroll to read. He always enjoyed reading about his loving Father, so he started with Psalms, chapter 103, verses 8-13:

> The Lord is compassionate and gracious, slow to anger, abounding in love. He will not always accuse, nor will he harbor his anger forever; he does not treat us as our sins deserve or repay us according to our iniquities. For as high as the heavens are above the earth, so great is his love for those who fear him; as far as the east is from the west, so far has he removed our transgressions from us. As a father has compassion on his children, so the Lord has compassion on those who fear him.

Jesus then turned to Deuteronomy, chapter 6, verses 4-9:

Hear, O Israel: The Lord our God, the Lord is one. Love the Lord your God with all your heart and with all your soul and with all your strength. These commandments that I give you today are to be on your hearts. Impress them on your children. Talk about them when you sit at home and when you walk along the road, when you lie down and when you get up. Tie them as symbols on your hands and bind them on your foreheads. Write them on the doorframes of your houses and on your gates.

Jesus rolled up the scroll, looked compassionately at the group, and then walked back to the doors and stood.

The synagogue leader again looked at Jesus for a moment or two and then came back to the center. He looked at both me and Jesus, and, after a prayer, he dismissed the group.

Everyone sat there for a few minutes talking quietly and wondering about the very different Sabbath celebration they had just witnessed.

40

As I left the synagogue, I noticed that most of the people were going up to talk to Jesus. They were laughing and talking with him like they were close friends. As I witnessed this, I felt a pang of loneliness. I started realizing what my mission was costing me. No one ever came up to me after a service to converse or discuss my reading. I left the synagogue and went back to my room.

On my way back, I shook off the sentimental nonsense and decided to focus on what questions I would ask Jesus so as to discredit him. I knew after watching people interact with him that I would need to show convincing evidence of Jesus's blasphemous and traitorous behavior. I also reviewed my part of the Sabbath celebration. I was confident that I had succeeded in demonstrating to the people my importance and knowledge. All I wanted to accomplish was to have the people remember what the penalty of a blasphemous traitor was. I knew that these backward, rural Jews were more forgiving than they should be; I wanted them to be alert to any behavior or words that were said by Jesus and his disciples that could be considered blasphemous. I also wanted them to be prepared to carry out the sentence of stoning Jesus when he blasphemed again.

I found it humorous recalling what Jesus had read when he came up after me in the synagogue. Any real scholar or leader would have either continued or countered my comments. But no, not Jesus: instead he had read a passage that everyone knew. *Love God with all your heart.* What sentimentality. No wonder the people loved him. He never challenged them to learn the law.

While sitting there, I decided to go back to Jerusalem and instruct the men I had hired to continue their surveillance on Jesus and his disciples. I decided to add one man per team so it would be easier for them to relay messages to me. I thought that keeping two teams where Jesus was and the other five teams scattered listening to what the people were saying about him worked well.

Whenever Jesus traveled to another area, one of my team members would follow and leave the other team member there. That way, there would always be some consistency. My role would be to stay in Jerusalem and build constituency among the Sanhedrin and other leaders regarding what evidence they needed and, once I had that evidence, to guide them on what they should do.

Without one of my cords available to summon servants, I banged on the wall, and one of my servants appeared. I told him to pack and get ready to leave to go back to Jerusalem. The servant bowed but then said, "Master, I will need to wait until the Sabbath is over to be able to pack." I had completely forgotten what day it was.

Once I returned to Jerusalem, I reported to Gamaliel and discussed the plans I had made for the surveillance of Jesus and his disciples. Gamaliel listened, added a few suggestions, and then prayed that God's will be done.

41

Finally, I felt I had the control I needed to keep Jesus and his disciples under close surveillance. Every day, I received reports from each team on what they were hearing and seeing. Sometimes, the reports were very short; others were long. Usually, the ones that came from the teams who were in close contact with Jesus were fairly long. They always had stories of Jesus's teachings, the crowds that followed him, and the miracles he was performing.

Because Jesus was staying near the Sea of Galilee, Stephen and Philip were the two men most often near Jesus. As the reports continued from the combination of Stephen's and Philip's teams, I started seeing some disturbing commentary. In the beginning, most of the reporting was matter of fact. The more current ones reported not only the facts but also started *praising* Jesus for the different miracles he was reported doing; then they would quote some of his teachings.

As this trend continued, I summoned one of the guards and asked him to have one of the men's junior companions, Aaron, send me a report on what was going on with Stephen and Philip; I now needed reports on the reporters. I wondered if their loyalty had been compromised: perhaps if you were around Jesus too much, you could be seduced by his wisdom and charm. I remembered just how charismatic John had been, and I knew Jesus was even more charming and knowledgeable than John had been. I was beginning to think I was the only human in Israel who could see through the fraud.

Two days later, the guard I had summoned brought me a report from Aaron. It was even worse than I had expected. Not only did the report say what I feared had occurred, but there also was another report for my eyes only from Stephen and Philip. Both men had decided to take time off from their service with me and spend time traveling and learning from Jesus. I was furious.

I threw the second tablet across the room and then cursed Jesus and the idiots that followed him. I paced back and forth for a full five minutes and then told the guard to go and get Prochorus and Nicanor, along with their companions, and take them to where Jesus was. Then he was to retrieve the two men left from the Stephen/Philip team and haul them away from Jesus before Jesus bewitched them as well.

Once the men had been reassigned, I sent a tablet to Prochorus and told him to accuse Jesus of using satanic power after he performed one of his miracles. I needed to initiate my campaign of discrediting him. I wanted the people to think as I did, that he was possessed by at least one powerful demon. Once Prochorus saw what I wanted them to do, he told Nicanor. They looked at each other for a minute and then reluctantly agreed. Neither of them felt that way about Jesus, and they were concerned that Jesus's followers might harm them.

Prochorus and Nicanor followed Jesus to the home of one of the synagogue's leaders, Jarius, who had gone to Jesus to tell him his daughter was dying. Jarius asked Jesus to come to his house and heal her. When they arrived at the house, though, they were told his daughter had died. Jarius looked at Jesus with tears in his eyes but thanked him and said he wasn't needed after all; it was too late to do anything. Jesus said something to him no one else could hear, and Jesus entered the house.

Suddenly, one of Jesus's disciples came out and said that Jesus had raised the girl from the dead. While everyone else was rejoicing, Prochorus yelled, "He is possessed by Satan. By the prince of demons, he is driving out demons." The people all looked at Prochorus and shook their heads. How ridiculous.

When Jesus came out of the house and heard the accusation, he called Prochorus over and began to speak to him in parables:

> "How can Satan drive out Satan? If a kingdom is divided against itself, that kingdom cannot stand. If a house is divided against itself, that house cannot stand. And if Satan opposes himself and is divided, he cannot stand; his end has come. In fact, no one can enter a strong man's house without first tying him up. Then he can plunder the strong man's house. Truly I tell you, people can be forgiven all their sins and every slander they utter, but whoever blasphemes against the Holy Spirit will never be forgiven; they are guilty of an eternal sin."

Both Prochorus and Nicanor stood there and wished they hadn't said anything.

When I received this report, I again became angry. "Those idiots couldn't do anything right."

The guard who had given the report to me was the same one who had been there when I heard the news that Stephen and Philip had defected. The guard thought I had been angry then, but he now saw me at a whole new level. I was screaming that I couldn't believe that his two men had let Jesus get credit for a complete sham of raising a girl from the dead. Then when they accused him, Jesus had turned it around and accused them. The accusation essentially included me since I was the one who had come up with the trap. How dare Jesus accuse me of blasphemy!

Now there was no doubt that Satan and a horde of demons were in control of Jesus; I had to stop him at all costs. I was getting annoyed that Jesus continued to evade my traps and get the better of me.

Not knowing what else I could do at that moment, I went to the roof to pray and meditate. As I walked by some servants, I told them that the whole household was to fast, pray, and meditate until I told them otherwise. The servants looked at me like I had gone insane.

I spent the rest of the day, night, and following morning on the roof. I came down only when I heard that another report had come in from Prochorus and Nicanor. After I read it, I looked up and thanked God. The report said that Jesus and his group were heading to Jerusalem for Passover. I would be able to question him myself.

As I received more reports over the next few days, I was informed by them that en route to Jerusalem, Jesus was continuing his hoax on the people. The report said that he had healed a leper, calmed a storm, and walked on water. This was too much. When I had asked Prochorus and Nicanor if they had seen any of these miracles, they said that they had seen the leper healed, but only a few disciples had seen him calm the storm and walk on the water. I knew they must have fabricated those things.

As Jesus continued toward Jerusalem, I instructed my men and their teams to return to Jerusalem so they could continue listening and reporting during the Passover. Once they were all back, I had them come to my house for a meeting.

After they were all seated, I thanked them for their service. I said, "With God's assistance, we will soon have evidence needed to stop Jesus from teaching anywhere."

I wanted the sham stopped. After I finished, I asked them what they were generally hearing about Jesus. It was much of the same about miracles and large crowds, and, they said, at one point it seemed that the people were going to crown him king. I smiled about the last comment. Herod, Herodias, and I had already stopped one of these traitors. Maybe we could team up again.

I told the men that I had come up with another way of trapping Jesus but I would need the help of the Roman guards. I asked one of the men to go to one of the Roman guards and ask him where we could find a prostitute. The men all looked around at each other wondering where I was headed with this.

"I want to find a prostitute and catch her in the act of adultery for a trap I have set up for Jesus. I figured that they would know where some of these women are and could get one for us."

The men looked at each other and thought it was a bit unorthodox, but they would do as they were told.

The next day, they came back and told me the mission was accomplished. I pulled a cord, and when a servant appeared, I told him to get one of the temple guards to come over. The servant nodded and left. I looked at the men seated with me and explained the trap I wanted to set for Jesus. In response, they told me how clever I was to think of such a great trap.

When the guard arrived, I asked him to go and arrest one of the prostitutes that evening and have her here at the house very early the next morning. I told the guard that she needed to be caught in the act of adultery. When the guard asked if I also wanted the man who had engaged in sexual activity with the prostitute, I said no, it wouldn't be necessary for my needs.

I couldn't help but think that Jerusalem was getting lax about the law if it was that easy to find a prostitute. Because the Romans who were running the city didn't prosecute prostitutes, Jerusalem had more prostitutes than ever before. The guard said that he would be there the following morning with the whore.

Early the next morning, I waited for the guard to arrive. I had also asked some other teachers of the law and some Pharisees to meet us there so they could witness my entrapment of Jesus. Eventually, there was a knock on my door. The servant answered, and I saw everyone I had invited standing outside. The guard and the prostitute were there as well. Of course, the teachers and Pharisees were keeping their distance from the harlot.

I came out and greeted my co-conspirators and then looked at who the guard had brought us. He held the lamp up to her, and I saw it was a young and beautiful girl. As I looked at her, I thought that in a few minutes she would be stoned to death. For a short moment, I felt a pang of what used to be pity but quickly dismissed it. I had to trap Jesus.

42

We all left my house and headed over to the temple, where we had been told Jesus would be. Jesus's disciples had told several people, who in turn had tipped us off, that he would be coming to teach at a certain area of Solomon's Porch at dawn.

As my group approached the area where we heard Jesus would be teaching, we saw that he was already there. He had arrived in the temple courts that morning before dawn. When the crowd had gathered around to hear him, Jesus sat down to teach them. As he taught, my group of teachers of the law and the Pharisees interrupted him as we dragged up the prostitute that we had caught in adultery. We shoved her toward Jesus so he, his disciples, and the people who were listening to Jesus could easily see her.

"Teacher," I said to Jesus, "this woman was caught in the act of adultery. In the law, Moses commanded us to stone such women. Now what do you say?"

Jesus saw that we were using this question as a trap in order to have a basis for accusing him. Instead of answering my question, though, Jesus bent down and started to write on the ground with his finger. As he did this, what annoyed me was that he wasn't looking at me. It's as if he were ignoring me, and so I continued questioning him. When Jesus finally straightened up, he said to us, "Let any one of you who is without sin be the first to throw a stone at her." Then he stooped down and started writing on the ground again.

At this, I watched as those who heard what he said begin to turn and go away one at a time. The older ones left first, and then the rest of the group filtered slowly away. I couldn't believe what had just happened. I was so upset that I almost threw the stone I carried at the whore, but I knew that no one else would have seen it anyway; they had all gone. After I left, only Jesus was there with her. Then Jesus asked her, "Woman, where are they? Has no one condemned you?"

"No one, sir," she said.

"Then neither do I condemn you," Jesus declared. "Go now and leave your life of sin."

After the woman left, Jesus walked out of the temple to the Mount of Olives to spend time with his Father. He stayed there the remainder of the day before going to celebrate Passover with Lazarus and his sisters. The following morning, we heard that he had left Jerusalem with his followers to teach about his Father back near the Sea of Galilee.

I didn't realize it for a couple of days, but Prochorus and Nicanor had by then joined the followers of Jesus after witnessing his show of God's mercy with the prostitute. They had seen Stephen and Philip with Jesus, and, as they left, they followed Stephen and Philip. Once they had gone a distance, the four men discussed the differences between my teachings, the teachers of the law, and the Pharisees versus what Jesus was teaching and showing about God.

43

couldn't believe Satan had won again. That Jesus sure was a slippery fellow. When I went over to where I usually spent time in the temple with my other teachers, I noticed none of them were there. I stayed around until noon thinking they would show up, but they never did. Oh well, I needed to go and get prepared for the Passover anyway.

After I completed the Passover ritual, I felt the need to spend a full day fasting, meditating, and praying for guidance. Once again, I needed to have God help me come up with a way to trap and discredit Jesus in front of the people. I was disturbed that I wasn't getting God's help in the manner I needed to trap Jesus. I told my servants not to disturb me no matter what and no matter who might come to see me.

The following morning, after my daily private time on the roof, one of my servants came to me and said that a couple of the men who had been watching Jesus and his followers had come to see me the day before. They needed to talk to me, he said. The servant had told them to come back this morning, and now they were waiting in my study. When I walked in, I saw three of my men; I had expected five. When I had greeted them, I asked where Prochorus and Nicanor were. I assumed they might be out spying on Jesus, and it turns out I was partially correct.

Timon, the oldest of the three men present, told me that after the incident at the temple, Prochorus and Nicanor had connected with Stephen and Philip and joined Jesus as followers. I stood there in disbelief. Every single person I had sent to spy on Jesus and send back reports was becoming his follower. *It seemed if anyone spent any time getting to know Jesus, he or she became his disciple.* I looked up toward heaven and said, "God, how long will you let this usurper continue to bewitch your people?"

I would have to start a more hands-on approach to this situation.

I told the men to go out and find another team to add to their surveillance efforts. I still wanted to hear what people were saying throughout the country even during those times Jesus and his followers weren't there.

"Sir, I might suggest that the three of us with our assistants and messengers just stay with Jesus and use your younger students to be runners reporting to you if they hear anything out of the ordinary," Timon said.

I thought it over and told Timon I agreed with his strategy.

"May I also suggest that you, or another Sanhedrin member, or a teacher of the law debate Jesus instead of one of us?" Timon added. "Jesus always comes out looking great, while the rest of us come out looking foolish and petty."

Even though I didn't like Timon's comment, I had to agree. I then laid out the plan we would follow going forward.

The three men packed their provisions and had their men meet them the following morning. We had gotten a report that Jesus had gone back north toward the Sea of Galilee. He was getting very easy to find. There was always someone either coming back from seeing and hearing him or heading to where they had heard he was.

As our men traveled, much like detectives, they asked their fellow travelers what they thought about Jesus and who they thought he was. Some said he was the Messiah, some said he might be Elisha or one of the prophets, while one of the travelers thought he was John the baptizer. Obviously, that last fellow had not yet heard that Herod had chopped John's head off.

Nothing about what they heard about Jesus surprised them anymore. Because of his miracles, his teaching, and even his disciples being able to do miracles as well, everyone wanted to be near him. The men heard from a traveler who had just been with Jesus say that he was next going to be in Bethsaida for a few days. The men were headed that way, but they stopped and had one of the messengers return to Jerusalem and asked me if I wanted to come question Jesus. They hoped that I would come or at least send someone who would be able to trap Jesus.

The next day, the three men arrived in Bethsaida and waited there to hear what message the messenger would bring back. I arrived a day later along with the messenger who had summoned me. I was told I looked tired from the travel, but I felt fine. I stepped down from my horse, went into the room where they were staying, and put on my finest robe, asking the other men with me to do the same. Once we were dressed, we followed the crowds to where Jesus was teaching.

I had prepared a good set of questions to trap Jesus. With so many people there, this would be a great opportunity for me to humiliate Jesus in front of enough people to convince all of them to stop following him. As we approached Jesus, Timon said that he saw Stephen, Philip, and the other two deserters and pointed them out for the rest of the group. I didn't bother looking; my focus was on finding and trapping Jesus. As we walked through the crowd, people stepped back to let us pass, knowing who we were, teachers of the law. As we were getting close, we could hear Jesus saying that he needed to have some lunch and would be teaching about God and his love after they finished eating.

As we gathered around Jesus, we saw some of Jesus's disciples eating food with their hands defiled, that is, unwashed. (We do not eat unless we give our hands a ceremonial washing, holding to the tradition of the elders. When we come from the marketplace, we do not eat unless we wash. We observe many other traditions, such as the washing of cups, pitchers, and kettles.)

While I was having to step around a couple of children darting around while playing with Jesus, Nicholas (a Pharisee and teacher of the law with me) asked Jesus, "Why don't your disciples live according to the tradition of the elders instead of eating their food with defiled hands?" I looked over at Nicholas and couldn't believe he had asked that question. That's what I was there for, to do all the questioning.

Jesus replied, "Isaiah was right when he prophesied about you hypocrites; as it is written, these people honor me with their lips, but their hearts are far from me. They worship me in vain; their teachings are merely human rules. You have let go of the commands of God and are holding on to human traditions.

"You have a fine way of setting aside the commands of God in order to observe your own traditions! For Moses said, 'Honor your father and mother,' and, 'Anyone who curses their father or mother is to be put to death.' But you say that if anyone declares that what might have been used to help their father or mother is Corban (that is, devoted to God) then you no longer let them do anything for their father or mother. Thus you nullify the Word of God by your tradition that you have handed down. And you do many things like that."

Again Jesus called the crowd to him and said, "Listen to me, everyone, and understand this. Nothing outside a person can defile them by going into them. Rather, it is what comes out of a person that defiles them."

I was so furious that Nicholas had interrupted that I didn't notice a group of people coming up to Jesus while leading a blind man. As they approached, they pushed me out of the way. When they got close to Jesus, they begged him to just touch the blind man. Jesus took the man by the hand, spit on his eyes, and then laid his hands on him, asking the man, "Do you see anything?"

"I see people," the man said. "They look like trees walking around."

Once more, Jesus put his hands on the man's eyes. Then his eyes were opened, his sight was restored, and he saw everything clearly. Jesus sent him home, saying, "Don't even go into the village."

I watched the man and his friends rejoicing as they departed. This was the first miracle I had witnessed. Even though I was sure it had been staged, I could see how everyone else would probably believe that Jesus truly did restore the man's sight.

As the man and his friends were leaving, a lot of children came around Jesus. I still wanted to question him, but I could tell the time wasn't right for the type of questions I had prepared. I told Nicholas to come with me but left the other two men to listen to Jesus.

When I had Nicholas alone, I sternly told him to never ever question anyone when I was along without clearing it with me beforehand. I told Nicholas that we had missed an opportunity to trap Jesus because Nicholas had reacted to the disciples not washing their hands.

The next morning, I heard that Jesus had moved on. I followed and caught up to him, listening to him while trying to plan another trap for him. After spending a few days traveling with Jesus and the crowd, I decided to go back to Jerusalem for a week to check in with the priests. I would then go back out where Jesus was teaching.

While I had been with the crowds following Jesus, I was amazed how gullible the people were. I started thinking of the possibility that there would be no way to discredit him enough for these people not to love and adore him. I soon heard that Jesus would be coming to Jerusalem for the Feast of the Dedication. I decided then to just wait for him there.

44

Jesus had in fact decided to go back to Jerusalem to see Lazarus and spend some time in the Garden on the Mount of Olives. Jesus truly felt close to his Father when he was there. While he loved teaching God's love to everyone who wanted to listen, he felt compelled to go to Jerusalem.

As he and his followers headed to Jerusalem, they realized they would be there during the Feast of the Dedication. Jesus and his followers were going to arrive right on the twenty-fifth of Kislev (November or December).

As Jesus was walking in the temple in the portico of Solomon, some other Jews and I gathered around him.

"How long will you keep us in suspense?" I asked. "If you are the Messiah, tell us plainly."

Jesus answered, "I told you, and you do not believe, the works that I do in my Father's name, these testify of me, but you do not believe because you are not of my sheep. My sheep hear my voice, and I know them, and they follow me, and I give eternal life to them, and they will never perish, and no one will snatch them out of my hand. My Father, who has given them to me, is greater than all, and no one is able to snatch them out of the Father's hand. I and the Father are one."

We had what we needed: Jesus had blasphemed in front of all of us. At that, we picked up stones to stone him.

"I showed you many good works from the Father. For which of them are you stoning me?" Jesus asked.

"We aren't stoning you for good work, but for blasphemy and because you, being a man, make yourself out to be God," I said.

Jesus answered: "Has it not been written in your Law, 'I said, you are gods'? If he called them gods, to whom the word of God came (and the Scripture cannot be broken), do you say of him, whom the Father sanctified and sent into the world, 'You are blaspheming,' because I said, 'I am the Son of God'?

"If I do not do the works of my Father, do not believe me; but if I do them, though you do not believe me, believe the works, so that you may know and understand that the Father is in me, and I in the Father."

When I motioned to the guards to seize him, his disciples and followers surged around him, and I quickly told the guards to stop. I was concerned that we would cause a riot and the Romans would get involved and arrest the wrong group.

The following day, I received a message that he had left and gone away beyond the Jordan to the place where John was first baptizing and that he was staying there. We heard many came to him and were saying, "While John performed no sign, yet everything John said about this man was true." Many believed in him there.

I may have made a mistake in not continuing to seize him. I am surprised that the rabble that was following Jesus would risk their lives to stop us from arresting him.

45

One day, I sent Timon a message asking him to ask Jesus about the subject of divorce. Timon got his chance the next morning after the crowd had gathered to hear Jesus.

Timon went up to Jesus with some others from the group of Pharisees.

"Is it lawful for a man to divorce his wife?" Timon asked Jesus.

"What did Moses command you?" Jesus answered.

"Moses allowed a man to write a certificate of divorce and to send her away," Timon said.

"Because of your hardness of heart, he wrote you this commandment," Jesus said. "But from the beginning of creation, 'God made them male and female. Therefore a man shall leave his father and mother and hold fast to his wife, and the two shall become one flesh.' So they are no longer two but one flesh. What therefore God has joined together, let not man separate."

Once the people had gone away, his disciples asked Jesus again about this matter. And Jesus said to them, "Whoever divorces his wife and marries another commits adultery against her, and if she divorces her husband and marries another, she commits adultery."

I kept getting reports from my team as Jesus taught. In one of the reports, I saw that Jesus and his disciples were going to start heading back to Jerusalem for Passover.

Jesus had decided that he wanted to stay with Lazarus and his family during the feast. As Jesus started making his way to Jerusalem, he received word that Lazarus was sick. When Jesus heard this, his disciples thought that he would rush to Bethany to be with Lazarus. He mentioned to them that "the sickness Lazarus had wouldn't be fatal, but would be for the glory of God." It would be to show that he was the Son of God and that God would glorify him.

Although Jesus loved Lazarus's whole family, he didn't leave where he was staying for another two days. After that, he said to the disciples, "Let us go to Judea and Jerusalem again."

His disciples and followers said to him, "Teacher, the Jews in Jerusalem were just now seeking to stone you, and are you going there again?"

"Are there not twelve hours in the day?" Jesus answered. "If anyone walks in the day, he does not stumble, because he sees with the daylight. But if anyone walks in the night, he stumbles, because the light is not in him."

After this, he told them that Lazarus had fallen asleep and that they were going to wake him. The disciples thought he had meant that Lazarus was just asleep, but Jesus meant he had passed away. Jesus then said, "I am glad for your sakes that I was not there, so that you may believe; but let us go to him."

Thomas, one of Jesus's disciples, then said to his fellow disciples, "Let us also go, so that we may die with him."

When Jesus and his disciples arrived at Bethany, they found that Lazarus had already been in the tomb for four days. Since Bethany was near Jerusalem, many of the family's friends had come from Jerusalem to be with Martha and Mary, to comfort them about Lazarus their brother.

When Martha heard that Jesus was coming, she went to meet him, but Mary stayed at the house. Once Martha got to where Jesus was, she said, "Lord, if you had been here, my brother would not have died.

"Even now I know that whatever you ask of God, God will give you," Jesus said to her, "Your brother will rise again."

Martha said to him, "I know that he will rise again in the resurrection on the last day."

"I am the resurrection and the life, he who believes in me will live even if he dies, and everyone who lives and believes in me will never die," Jesus said to her. "Do you believe this?"

"Yes, Lord," Martha answered. "I have believed that you are the Christ, the Son of God, even he who comes into the world."

After she said this, Martha left and called Mary her sister, whispering, "The Teacher is here and is calling for you."

When Mary heard this, she got up quickly and went to Jesus.

Mary's friends, who were consoling her, followed her, assuming she was going to the tomb to weep. When Mary got to where Jesus was and saw him, she fell at his feet.

"Lord," Mary said, "if you had been here, my brother would not have died."

When Jesus saw her and her friends weeping, he was deeply moved in spirit and troubled, saying, "Where have you laid him?"

"Lord, come and see."

As Jesus wept at the death of his close friend, one of Mary's friends said, "See how he loved him."

However, another said, "Why couldn't this man, who opened the eyes of the blind man, have kept Lazarus from dying?"

Jesus, still deeply moved, approached the tomb, which was a cave that had a large stone propped against it.

"Remove the stone," Jesus said.

"Lord, by this time there will be a stench, for he has been dead four days," Martha said.

"Did I not say to you that if you believe, you will see the glory of God?" he said.

So they removed the stone. Then Jesus raised his eyes and said, "Father, I thank you that you have heard me. I knew that you always hear me; but because of the people standing around I said it, so that they may believe that you sent me."

At this point, Jesus cried out with a loud voice, "Lazarus, come forth!"

Lazarus, who had died, came forth, bound in wrappings and his face wrapped around with a cloth.

"Unbind him, and let him go," Jesus ordered them.

Many of the Jews who had come with Mary and had seen what he had done believed in him.

Not me, though. This sounded just like one another of his so-called miracles. After some of them came and told me and other Pharisees what Jesus had just done with Lazarus, I decided to go to Bethany to see what Jesus would do or say this time. It would be impossible to try to arrest or discredit him after he had raised a man from the dead. I was probably the only person who knew he had arranged the entire ruse.

When I started out for Bethany, Nicholas came to me to say that Jesus had gone to the Mount of Olives to teach. By the time we got there, though, Jesus had finished speaking. So one of my friends who lived in Bethany invited Jesus and a few of us to eat with him; we accepted the invitation, going in and reclining at the table. But my friend, Abner the Pharisee, was surprised when he noticed that Jesus did not first wash before the meal. Abner moved close to Jesus and whispered something in his ear.

Then Jesus said to him, "Now then, you Pharisees clean the outside of the cup and dish, but inside you are full of greed and wickedness. You foolish people! Did not the one who made the outside make the inside also? But now as for what is inside you, be generous to the poor, and everything will be clean for you. Woe to you Pharisees, because you give God a tenth of your mint, rue, and all other kinds of garden herbs, but you neglect justice and the love of God. You should have practiced the latter without leaving the former undone. Woe to you Pharisees, because you love the most important seats in the synagogues and respectful greetings in the marketplaces.Woe to you, because you are like unmarked graves, which people walk over without knowing it."

"Teacher," I said, looking right at Jesus, "when you say these things, you insult us also."

Jesus replied, "And you experts in the law, woe to you, because you load people down with burdens they can hardly carry, and you yourselves will not lift one finger to help them. Woe to you, because you build tombs for the prophets, and it was your ancestors who killed them. So you testify that you approve of what your ancestors did; they killed the prophets, and you build their tombs. Because of this, God in his wisdom said, 'I will send them prophets and apostles, some of whom they will kill and others they will persecute.' Therefore this generation will be held responsible for the blood of all the prophets that has been shed since the beginning of the world, from the blood of Abel to the blood of Zechariah, who was killed between the altar and the sanctuary. Yes, I tell you, this generation will be held responsible for it all. Woe to you experts in the law, because you have taken away the key to knowledge. You yourselves have not entered, and you have hindered those who were entering."

When Jesus finished and went outside, we followed him and began to oppose him fiercely and to besiege him with questions, waiting to catch him in something he might say.

When we saw that a few of the Roman guards were moving toward us because we were shouting and it was looking like there was going to be a clash of two different groups in the crowd, I motioned for everyone to back off. I didn't want the Romans to attack us and throw all of us in prison. The Romans were touchy when it came to crowds, especially unruly ones gathering around the time of the Passover.

46

When everything had settled down in Jerusalem after the Passover, I wanted to get my men together to discuss what they had seen and heard. I sent out one of my servants to gather the men, but he only came back with Nicholas and two of his companions. When I asked Nicholas where Timon and Parmenas were, he told me that after Jesus had raised Lazarus from the dead, they had left and started following Jesus. I now had lost six of the seven men I had been using to try and trap Jesus.

Nicholas and his men were surprised when I didn't begin a tirade and threaten to kill somebody. I just walked over to a chair and sat down. After all of the attempts to trap Jesus over that Passover had failed, I was emotionally burned out. I asked them to have a seat and discuss the plan for the following year. I told the men that I just wanted Jesus watched and for them to report in as we had been doing the previous two years. I had given up on trying to discredit Jesus at someplace other than Jerusalem. We would need all of the resources at our disposal in Jerusalem to trap Jesus.

As the year progressed, I kept getting reports of what Jesus was doing. Most reports came back with stories about Jesus teaching to larger and larger crowds, casting out demons, and healing the sick. As I then reported to the Sanhedrin, they started asking me questions about how much influence Jesus and his followers could exert. They were concerned that at any moment, this group could start a revolt or that the people would start questioning the oral laws already being continually challenged by Jesus and his disciples.

One member mentioned that one of his Roman acquaintances had said that these gatherings of Jesus and his followers were also being watched carefully by the Romans. They apparently didn't believe there was anything to concern themselves about yet, but some of their reports mentioned some interesting teachings concerning how Jesus's followers were saying that he was the Messiah and was going to rule all of Israel. The Romans warned that if anything happened, it would be dealt with swiftly and that the governing body, the Sanhedrin, would be dealt with as well.

After that, Gamaliel stood up and told the Sanhedrin that this had gone on long enough. He looked at me and reminded me that I was supposed to keep this issue under control. He told me that if I couldn't handle it, they would get someone else to lead the effort to put Jesus in his place.

I stood and apologized for allowing the situation to get so far out of hand. However, I reminded them that I had warned them about Jesus two decades earlier and they hadn't dealt with it then. Now Satan had charmed the people and given Jesus unbelievable powers of understanding and the ability to perform miracles. I reminded them that I had tried everything that was legal to discredit him in front of the people but had been unable to do so.

"Every time I send someone to listen and watch Jesus and his disciples, they become his followers." I said.

Then Caiaphas, who was high priest that year, spoke up, "You know nothing at all. Don't you realize that it is better for us that one man die for the people than that the whole nation perish?"

I looked at Caiaphas for a few moments and then asked him, "Should I use any means, then, to put an end to this Jesus and his followers?"

"Yes," Caiaphas replied.

I excused myself and left.

Back at home, I told one of my servants to have Nicholas and the men brought back here. I knew I would never catch Jesus or his followers breaking any laws punishable by death away from Jerusalem. Since we were having no luck trying to trap Jesus with questions, I decided that we should try to get to him from inside his group.

Once Nicholas and the men returned, I had them come into my study. I wanted them to help me think of a way to have one of Jesus's followers turn Jesus over to us. At first, Nicholas and the men couldn't think of anyone who would betray Jesus in such a way. All of his followers loved Jesus too much and thought of him as their Messiah. As they continued thinking, I said, "The only issue that I know the followers don't agree on is that some say he is an earthly Messiah and others say he is a spiritual leader and will save all of us spiritually and not reign on the earth.

"I wonder if we can stir up one side or the other and get them arguing internally."

Nicholas said he thought that was a great idea. He told us about a report he had seen where the people who thought he was supposed to be an earthly king had tried to crown him, and Jesus had left before they could. It might be that if they could find one of Jesus's followers who is a Zealot and have him get a few of the other disciples and then the crowd to try and make him king again, they could trap him like the followers tried to crown him king.

Saul leaned back, looked at Nicholas, and said, "That is a great idea. Do you know which one of his followers is a Zealot and close enough to Jesus to get this started?"

Nicholas nodded and said, "I think there is one disciple that is frustrated that Jesus hasn't already declared himself king and attacked the Romans. I heard him talking to some of the other followers, and this disciple was saying, "How could any army defeat an army led by Jesus? He can feed thousands of people with a single fish and a few loaves of bread, raise the dead, and heal the sick."

"Who is this man?" I asked, smiling.

"Judas," Nicholas said.

"Judas who they call Iscariot?"

"Yes," Nicholas said. "Do you know him?"

"I do," I said. "His family and mine have some business connections. I think I will reach out to him when he is in Jerusalem and see what he thinks. Nicholas, is there anything else you can tell me about him?"

"He is the group treasurer as well," Nicholas said.

I was happy to hear that: I knew I would have a chance to succeed if dealing with Judas.

As the meeting ended, I asked Nicholas to find out where Jesus and his disciples were. Once I knew that, I could figure out the best way to meet with Judas.

I summoned a servant and told him to bring me Ezekiel, my business manager. He arrived about an hour later, and I took him into my study.

"I think I remember our family doing business with the Iscariot family; the man I remember was called Simon, right?" I asked the manager.

"Yes, that's right," he said. "The Iscariot family has supplied a lot of the different dyes for the tents we make."

"Now I remember," I said. "Do we still do business with them?"

"Yes, we do."

"Do we need any more dye at this time?" I asked.

"As a matter of fact, we are about to order some more," Ezekiel said.

"That's great," I said. "Another thing; do you know Judas, Simon's son?"

"Yes to that, too," he said. "We did some business with him once, but we did have some issues with the dyes he sold us. It seemed that Judas tried to dilute them and the colors weren't right. We had to get in contact with Simon to get it straightened out. We heard that they had a disagreement and then Judas ended up leaving to follow around that Jesus you don't like."

I leaned back in the chair, thinking that since Simon and Judas had had a disagreement, it wouldn't do any good to make a double order of dye from Simon. I would have to think of another way to use Judas to get to Jesus. I then remembered that Nicholas had said that Judas was the treasurer of Jesus's group and also that Ezekiel said Judas had tried to cheat us. Maybe there was a good idea there that I could exploit.

47

After finding out where Jesus was and where he would be returning a week later, Nicholas came to my house to meet with me. When I entered the study and sat down with him, he started his report.

"I found Jesus and his disciples, and I heard from one of the followers that Jesus was planning to come to Jerusalem for Passover," Nicholas said.

"Did you hear if any of the disciples or followers were going to come in early?" I asked. "Since their group is getting so large, they usually send a few in to make arrangements for lodging."

"Yes, there will be some coming in early to have everything ready for Passover."

I then asked Nicholas, "Did you hear if Judas Iscariot was one of the disciples planning to come in early?"

"I'm sure he is since he keeps the money for the group and would have to purchase some items for the group for Passover," he said.

I smiled and then said to Nicholas, "Get word to Judas that I want to meet with him when he comes."

Nicholas was a bit confused and wanted to know why.

"We have been trying to trap Jesus by spying on him and his followers, but it hasn't worked for us," I said. "I think I have found one of the disciples that might help us if he is approached properly.

Nicholas nodded and left to set up the meeting. At the same time that Nicholas was leaving my house, a Roman soldier approached. Nicholas was curious about what the soldier was coming there for, but he decided to go ahead and leave to find Judas. He knew I would be angry with him if he missed this opportunity.

When he got to my front door, the Roman soldier told the servant that he had a message for me, which he handed to the servant before turning around and leaving. After the servant brought the message to me, I read it for a couple of minutes, slammed my hands on the desk, looked up to heaven, and shouted, "Thank you, God, for delivering the killers of my father to justice. We have been praying to you for this since he was killed by that gang." I finished reading the message and then pulled a cord for a servant. Once the servant arrived, I told him to bring me a robe because I was going down to the prison to speak to the jailer.

Once I reached the garrison, I was ushered in to meet with the commander of the Roman guard.

"You finally caught the band of thieves that killed Jonathan." I said, eliciting a nod from the commander. "What do you think the legal process would be for these murderers and thieves? Also, what type of sentence do you think they would get?"

"Usually, we have a quick trial," the commander said, "and then we send men like these to the slave galleys or some other heavy labor jobs. I think the last group was sent to one of the mines."

I thought about that for a moment and then asked, "Is there any way I could ask to have two or three of these men crucified? This is the group that killed my father, and I would like to have them executed."

"I knew your father," the commander said; "You won't remember, but I was one of the guards that escorted you and your family to Jerusalem after your mother died. I will speak to the governor and see what he says. I don't think it will be an issue to have some of these hung on a cross as a reminder to everyone of the penalty for robbing and killing men like Jonathan."

I looked at him and said, "You're right; I don't remember you, but I do remember my father telling me how noble all of you were that escorted us here. He was right."

The commander and I shook hands, and I left to go set up a sacrifice of thanksgiving. What a great day God was giving me; all of my hard work was finally paying off. I would have Barabbas and Jesus where I wanted them by Passover.

48

I was getting irritated that I hadn't heard from Nicholas. I had hoped for a quick return so I could schedule a meeting with Judas as soon as possible. Passover was approaching, and I wanted to get everything set up and finished before the feast so I could plan a grand celebration with a great show of sacrifices to show the people my love for God.

Foremost, I wanted everyone to know that I had finally dealt with the men who had wronged Israel. The day before I had scheduled to send another man out to find Nicholas, I received a message from him saying that Judas would meet with me at my house the following day at noon. That's more like it.

The following day, right at noon, Judas knocked on my front door, was let into the house by a servant, and was shown into my study, where I motioned for him to have a seat.

After Judas sat down, we exchanged niceties, and then I told him that I had been studying Jesus and his message over the past few years.

"In my humble [but knowledgeable] opinion," I said to Judas, "the message about the Messiah's coming is great, but it is worrisome to the Sanhedrin because the message might have the people take action, and then the Romans might step in."

"There have been a few times where the people tried to make him king," Judas said, looking at me while nodding his head in agreement. "I don't understand why Jesus keeps stopping them. He says he is the Messiah, and, if he is, the Romans couldn't beat his people and his army."

"That is true," I replied. "I hear that he can feed the people starting with almost nothing and that he can heal the sick and even raise people from the dead. How could any army ever beat a leader with those powers? I wonder if there is a way to force Jesus into recognizing his responsibilities. All of us are looking for the Messiah."

Judas thought for a minute and said, "Maybe there would be a way during the Passover. Jesus keeps talking about being betrayed and then his Kingdom would begin. Maybe he is looking to have himself brought to trial for some reason, be condemned, rally the people, and then start his Kingdom. That way, he would be able to show all of Israel that he is the Messiah and King. That way, the people and all of the rulers would know he was the chosen one."

"Judas, I think you are right," I said. "That must be what God wants. I have been studying and praying, and I know that there should be a Messiah. If we can get Jesus before the Sanhedrin and then before Herod and have Jesus show them all the proof, no one can deny Jesus is the Messiah we have been waiting for.

"Judas, you mentioned he was to be betrayed, right? It sounds like he needs someone to turn him in so that this trial can get started, wouldn't you say?"

"I might be the only one of his close disciples that understands this the way we do," Judas said. "I might have to find one of the followers to do this, or I may have to do it myself. Let me think on this."

"Judas, you are probably right that you are the only one of Jesus's followers who understands what he is saying," I said. "I am in the same circumstances with everyone around me. None of them feel the way I do about Jesus. Since Passover is coming up soon, we will need to get a plan in place. I want to make sure the trial goes the way we want so that Jesus is proclaimed the Messiah during Passover."

As Judas and I finished our meeting, I called for a servant, who, as I had earlier instructed, brought two bags of money, which he handed to me. I took them, handed one to Judas, and told him to take it for the use of the group to prepare for the Passover. When I handed him the other bag, I said it was for him to use as he saw fit. Judas took the money and thanked me as he left. He told me he would get back with a plan the following day.

As Judas left, he lifted the sacks and calculated how much each one held. With his trained calculation, he decided that each sack contained about half of a year's wages. He could now set up Passover for the group and have plenty of money left over to support the group during their stay in Jerusalem until Jesus was named King and then had all of the resources of the Kingdom of Israel.

The following day, as Judas was walking over to my house to work with me to finish our plans, he praised God that he was being used as part of his plan. Judas thought it was great that God was using me as well since it would help put the plan in place with the right people and thus guarantee its success.

After an hour in my study with me, he left with the plan in place and another bag of money.

49

Since I knew that Jesus and his disciples and followers were coming to Passover, I had men stationed to bring me word of which way and when Jesus was coming into Jerusalem. I wanted to know where he was at all times.

One morning, as I was finishing praying and meditating on my roof, my servant came up and handed me the first message of the day. I read it and chuckled. It said that Jesus and his followers had started into Jerusalem and they had put Jesus on an ass covered with robes. They then lined the road, throwing their extra robes and small branches on the ground in front of him and singing and shouting: "Hosanna to the son of David, Blessed is he that cometh in the name of the Lord; Hosanna in the highest!"

Jesus and his conspiracy group never missed an opportunity to show that Jesus was fulfilling another prophecy. I thought of the one in Zechariah that said, "Rejoice greatly, O daughter of Zion! Shout, O daughter of Jerusalem! Behold, thy King cometh unto thee! He is just and having salvation, lowly, and riding upon an ass and upon a colt, the foal of an ass."

The next message from my men said that Jesus had gone to the temple. When he got to Solomon's Porch, he started knocking over the money tables and running people away with a whip, shouting, "It is written, 'My house shall be called a house of prayer,' but you make it a den of robbers.'" I smiled again; Jesus had found another prophecy to fulfill.

Then a message came from Gamaliel asking how long the Sanhedrin would have to endure Jesus and his mob running around Jerusalem. Gamaliel was worried that the Romans might step in and stop Jesus before Judas had turned him over to us. I sent a message back and said that I had discussed Jesus and his mob with the Roman commander and that they had agreed to let me take care of Jesus during the Passover unless it escalated. I also told him that Judas was attempting to deliver Jesus into our hands later that day.

I sent another message to the commander of the prison asking if he had any information on Barabbas's sentence. I told the servant to wait for the commander to provide an answer before he returned. After waiting for an hour, the servant came back and told him that the commander had replied that Barabbas and a couple of his gang had been sentenced to be crucified that coming Thursday or Friday The others would be put on a ship as slaves to row and serve that ship the rest of their lives. This pleased me greatly.

Around midafternoon, the servant brought me a message from Judas telling me that Jesus had sent a couple of men to set up where they would have supper that night. It also told me where the supper would be and how many men would be there.

Upon reading this, I started gathering my forces and preparing to arrest Jesus. I pondered how many men it would take to arrest only Jesus; another consideration was what it would take to also arrest the twelve men closest to Jesus. According to Nicholas, these twelve men were planning to help Jesus rule his new Kingdom. Also, I wondered if he would put up a fight or come peacefully.

After a few moments, I decided that a group of around twenty soldiers should be able to control the rabble that Jesus had around him, knowing that none of them were fighting men. The message also said that Judas would come to meet me at my house when everything was set. Judas said he would lead us to where Jesus would be, presumably on the Mount of Olives somewhere close to the Garden called Gethsemane.

I sent one message to Gamaliel asking for twenty of the best temple guards and almost simultaneously sent another to the commander of the Roman guard explaining what we were doing. Both Gamaliel and the commander quickly replied, concurring with my plan and requests.

Toward dusk, there was a knock at my door: the soldiers Gamaliel had sent were outside. I told my servant to tell them to wait there until I could find out where and when they would be needed.

By now, I was getting very excited, as everything was falling into place, to include the men of the Sanhedrin being prepared to take Jesus to trial as soon as he was captured. Although the Sanhedrin wasn't supposed to try anyone at any place other than their regular meeting place, I had gotten a waiver to meet them at the high priestly villa. I had convinced them that although it wasn't exactly legal, it would make the trial less of a public spectacle. This would keep the crowds calmer with fewer of Jesus's followers or other people around to cause the kinds of problems that would draw the interest of the Romans.

As we waited for Judas, I went into a room and prayed to God that my plans would be carried out just the way I had planned them; then everyone would know I was doing God's will. While I prayed, the servant came in and told me that Judas had arrived. I got up and went to the front of the house where everyone had gathered. Judas came up to me and told me that Jesus had finished dinner and had gone to the garden on the Mount of Olives. I grabbed his shoulder and told him he had done a great deed for the Jewish people.

As the soldiers gathered, Judas asked, "Why are there so many soldiers needed to arrest Jesus?"

"Judas, it needs to look right. Having more soldiers makes it appear impromptu and not staged," I said.

He understood.

"Since you are familiar with the garden and since it is dark, where would be the best place to arrest Jesus?" I asked. "Also, would you mind finding him and identifying him with some sort of greeting?"

Judas said that would be fine. As the group continued to where Jesus was, everyone started to quiet down and light a few more torches. There was concern that Jesus's followers might come to his aid. I had told them that I didn't think Jesus and his men would fight but to be ready just in case. I didn't want Jesus to escape again.

As we entered the garden, we could see a small group of men standing in a clearing. After Judas walked up to them, we heard him talking, and then, after a moment, we saw Judas greet Jesus with a kiss. Immediately, I motioned to my soldiers to move in. When we had Jesus and his men surrounded, Jesus said, "Whom do you seek?"

"Jesus of Nazareth," I said.

"I am he."

When Jesus spoke, my men and I stepped back and fell to the ground. After we got up, I told them to arrest Jesus and his disciples. Jesus said, "I have told you that I am he, and since you seek me, let these go on their way."

When the soldiers looked at me for instruction, I nodded in agreement to what Jesus had requested. However, as the soldiers started to apprehend Jesus, one of his followers grabbed a sword, swung it, and cut off the ear of one of the men with me. At that, all of the soldiers drew their swords and waited on my word to attack. Quickly, Jesus stepped in the way and went to the man who had been cut and healed him. Jesus then looked at the man who had attacked with the sword and said, "Peter, put your sword in your sheath; I will drink the cup my Father has given me to drink." As soon as Jesus said that, the soldiers bound Jesus and started taking him to Annas.

As we started walking away with Jesus in our custody, I watched all of Jesus's followers run off in different directions. I chuckled quietly, as it confirmed to me that I had been right all along about Jesus's followers; they were just a group of rabble. Looking around, though, I suddenly noticed that Judas was nowhere to be seen, and that worried me because my hope was to have Judas testify at Jesus's trial.

Regardless, I was overwhelmed with joy and with great satisfaction. God, I thought, had finally allowed me to arrest Jesus, the man I had hated, hunted, and sworn to kill twenty years earlier. In a few minutes, I was going to get to try and convict Jesus, the blasphemous bastard from Nazareth. As we escorted Jesus out of the garden, I looked closely at him, hoping to see panic in his eyes, which would confirm for me that I had sprung the perfect trap on him. However, when I looked, I saw a perfectly calm and serene expression on his face.

Once we had Jesus at the villa, I took charge of the trial and started questioning him. I brought in many different witnesses to tell the judges of the different times Jesus had blasphemed. As these witnesses testified and were asked questions about their testimony, none of the different stories added up. Every time we seemed to have enough evidence to convict him, someone else would tell the same story but with a different outcome. After a few hours of this, we moved everyone out and reconvened at the Sanhedrin, where they started questioning him again.

While we were moving to the Sanhedrin, I found several of the witnesses who hadn't testified yet and coached them on the best way to get the conviction I wanted. The men said they would do as I asked. Once the trial started again, a couple of these men testified, "We heard him say, 'I am going to tear down this Temple, built by hard labor, and in three days build another without lifting a hand.'"

Still, even these men I had coached couldn't agree with all parts of their testimony. In the middle of this, the chief priest stood up and asked Jesus, "What do you have to say to this accusation?"

Jesus was silent. He said nothing.

The chief priest tried again, this time asking, "Are you the Messiah, the Son of God?"

"Yes, I am, and you'll see it yourself," Jesus answered, "The Son of Man seated at the right hand of the Mighty One, arriving on the clouds of heaven."

Hearing this, the chief priest lost his temper and, ripping his clothes, yelled, "Did you hear that? After that do we need witnesses? You heard the blasphemy. Are you going to stand for it?"

We condemned him one and all. The sentence was death.

After the Sanhedrin was dismissed, I motioned to some of the guards, who grabbed Jesus and spit in his face. They covered his face and then hit him, while others, mocking him, would ask him who had hit him. As they did this, others came up and told of other blasphemy he had spoken.

After we had abused Jesus for some time, he was taken to be tried by the Romans. The Sanhedrin could pronounce the death sentence on Jesus, but they needed the Romans to carry out the sentence. At the time, Pilate was in Jerusalem. Once Pilate made himself available, he asked what the charges were against Jesus. I stepped forward and said, "Pilate, we found this fellow perverting the nation and forbidding to give tribute to Caesar, saying that he himself is Christ the King."

Pilate looked at Jesus and asked, "Are you the King of the Jews?"

Jesus answered, "You have said it."

So Pilate turned to me and said, "I find no fault in this man."

"This man went about stirring up all of the people, teaching throughout all Israel starting in Galilee all the way to Jerusalem," I said, sternly.

When Pilate heard me say, "Galilee," he asked whether the man was a Galilean. I answered that he was from Nazareth.

When Pilate heard this, he knew that Jesus belonged in Herod's jurisdiction, and so he sent him to Herod, who himself was in Jerusalem. I was disappointed because I had hoped Pilate would listen and then proclaim sentence on Jesus to be crucified. Now I had to move Jesus over to Herod's court and start over. Besides, you never knew what Herod would do.

When Herod saw Jesus, he was thrilled because he had wanted to see him for a long time. He had heard a lot of things about

Jesus, and he hoped to have Jesus perform some miracles for him. After he had asked me why they had brought him, which I explained, Herod turned to Jesus and asked him many questions, but Jesus didn't speak a word.

At that point, the chief priests, teachers of the law, scribes, and I stood and vehemently accused Jesus of blasphemy. When Jesus wouldn't answer any of our accusations, Herod and his soldiers started mocking and beating him. They put Jesus in a beautiful robe and placed a staff in his hand. To make it complete, I made a crown of thorns and forced it onto his head until it started bleeding. Then we all mocked him, beat him some more, and sarcastically called him the King of the Jews. Once we had finished abusing Jesus, Herod told us to take him back to Pilate.

Judas watched while all of this was going on, waiting for Jesus to stop them, call everyone to him, and start the revolt that would begin the earthly kingdom he thought Jesus was going to build. Once he saw Jesus being led back to Pilate without lifting a finger to protect himself, Judas knew he had sinned and had helped me and the Pharisees set up Jesus to be crucified.

What a fool I have been, Judas thought. *Jesus and his Father will never forgive me.* He went to the Sanhedrin and said that he had betrayed innocent blood and threw the coins on the floor that I had given him. After that, he went outside the city and hanged himself.

After Jesus had been taken back to Pilate, Pilate called together all of the chief priests and the rulers of the Jewish people and said to them, "You brought this man to me called Jesus and told me that he had blasphemed and taught the people false teachings. I have questioned him and found no fault in this man of anything you have accused him of. Also, I sent him with you to Herod, and he didn't send any evidence back that this man did anything to deserve death. Therefore, I will beat him and release him."

Pilate waved me over and reminded me that he was required to release a Jewish criminal from prison at the feast. I said I would check with the high priest and see what he wanted to do.

Before I walked away, I turned and asked who else we could have released. Pilate waved over one of the guards and asked him. The guard looked at his tablet and said the other prisoner that could be released was named Barabbas.

I turned and walked out of Pilate's view, and then I fell on my knees in anguish. I couldn't believe the choice I was having to make. I had to recommend releasing Jesus, God's and my sworn enemy, or the man Barabbas, who had killed my father Jonathan. I knew I had to do God's will and went to speak to the high priest. I told him that we should release Barabbas and crucify Jesus. He looked at me knowing what kind of sacrifice I was making. After we spoke, I waved Nicholas over and gave him instructions of what to say to incite the crowd when Pilate asked them who they wanted released. I told him to get a group of men and shout, "Away with Jesus. Release Barabbas to us."

After I had told Pilate that I had spoken to Caiaphas, Pilate turned to the crowd and said, "I have found no fault in this man and will release him to you for the feast." When I heard this, I motioned to Nicholas, and Nicholas and several of the men around him started shouting, "Away with Jesus! Release Barabbas to us!" Even though I was the one who told him to start the crowd chanting to release Barabbas, I was sick that Barabbas was going free.

Pilate quieted the crowd and said he would recommend releasing Jesus. Before he got the last word out, the crowd started screaming again to release Barabbas.

Pilate again motioned to the crowd, but they cried, "Crucify him! Crucify him!"

After Pilate listened to this for a few minutes, he authorized the sentence that would allow us to take Jesus and crucify him.

50

While the Romans finished the paperwork on the three men they were to crucify, I still felt sick about the decision I had been forced to make, choosing between Jesus and Barabbas for release. It had been an excruciatingly painful decision, but I knew I had passed the test God had given me. I had let my father's murderer go to give God justice on Jesus the blasphemer. The only thing that could have been better was to have the Romans let the crowd take Jesus out and stone him according to the punishment God wanted for a blasphemer. At least Jesus would finally be stopped from deceiving the people any further.

As Jesus and the two other men, Jabari and Gabe, who were a part of Barabbas's gang, started the walk to where they would be crucified, I went and found Nicholas and the men who had joined with him in starting the chant to have Jesus crucified. I thanked them for a job well done. I then asked them to follow the criminals and make sure nothing happened that would stop the sentence for Jesus from being carried out. I told them I would meet them at Golgotha, where they would crucify Jesus and the two other men.

I went back to see Pilate to thank him for his decision and to ask if he would be able to have guards posted around the cross.

They would then need to escort the corpse of Jesus as well as the people who came to bury him. Finally, I asked Pilate to keep those guards stationed at the tomb where Jesus would be buried.

Pilate looked at me with a strange look on his face and asked, "Saul, you are known as one of the leaders of your people and as the most knowledgeable man in the kingdom. It seems that you are taking the execution of this Jesus to a ridiculous level. Why would I post guards around the cross, have them escort the corpse, and then guard a tomb?"

In response, I told Pilate the complete story of Jesus, not leaving anything out. I told him of my mission and how I had faithfully fulfilled it despite having to allow Barabbas to go free.

"The reason it is necessary to guard the men and then the corpse," I said, "is that there have been rumors that Jesus said that if he were killed, he would be raised from the dead in three days. I just want to make sure his followers and disciples don't steal the body and then tell the people he was raised from the dead."

After hearing this from me, Pilate quickly told his guards what he wanted them to do. The last thing he needed was a supposed corpse running around Israel. After Pilate gave orders to his captain of the guard, several Roman guards followed me to Golgotha, where I planned to stay as Jesus died.

As the guards and I approached the place where the men were to be crucified, we saw that they had already been hung on their crosses. I stopped for a moment to take in the sight of a blasphemer and two of the men who had killed my father being crucified at the same time. Once the guards I brought got to the base of the crosses, they moved everyone back several paces so no one could get close enough to touch any of the men. I looked around and saw that Nicholas and my men were there, and I asked Nicholas how the trip to Golgotha had gone. He said it was uneventful except Jesus kept falling because of the weight of the cross he had to carry. "Finally, one of the soldiers grabbed a fellow out of the crowd and made him carry it so we could all get up here," Nicholas added.

As a dying Jesus suffered on the cross to which he had been nailed, passersby hurled insults at him, shaking their heads and saying, "You who are going to destroy the temple and build it in three days, save yourself! Come down from the cross, if you are the Son of God!"

The chief priests, the teachers of the law, and the elders also mocked him, saying, "He saved others, but he can't save himself! If he's the king of Israel, let him come down now from the cross, and we will believe in him. He trusts in God. Let God rescue him now if he wants him, for he said, 'I am the Son of God.'"

Likewise, Gabe, one of the two thieves being crucified with Jesus, started mocking him and asking him to tell his Father to get them off of the crosses. The other criminal, Jabari, told Gabe to shut up and said, "Don't you fear God? We are in the same condemnation. We deserve what they are doing to us, but there is no reason they are crucifying this man." He then turned to Jesus and said, "Lord, remember me when you start your kingdom."

Jesus said to him, "Today you will be with me in paradise."

About that time, it started getting dark, and it stayed that way for about three hours. During those hours, Jesus quietly spoke to some of his followers while the soldiers split up all three of the men's belongings. At the third hour, we heard Jesus say something, but we couldn't understand him. One of the men thought he was calling Elijah. We waited to see if Elijah would come and save him.

A few more minutes passed by before Jesus looked directly at me, smiled, and gave a quick wink just before he let out his last breath. As soon as that happened, there was an intense earthquake and I heard one of the soldiers who was standing near me when he died say, "Surely, this was the Son of God."

We later heard reports that during and right after the earthquake, onlookers started seeing people who had died, raised from the dead, coming out of their tombs and going into the city. Also, one of the priests said that the curtain that blocked anyone from looking into the Holy of Holies was torn in two from top to bottom.

I stayed there with the guards to be sure no one touched Jesus's body. Since it was getting late and the bodies needed to be taken off of the crosses before the Sabbath, a soldier came to be sure Jesus was dead. Sometimes, when the guards needed to speed up the execution process, they would break the legs so that the person on the cross would suffocate faster. When they came to Jesus, they saw he was already dead. To be absolutely sure, though, one of the guards jammed a spear into his side; blood and water poured down the spear and onto the ground as we watched. There was no doubt that Jesus of Nazareth, the bastard blasphemer, was dead.

After a few minutes, I told Nicholas to stay and make sure all of the orders in regard to the guards and the tomb were properly carried out. Finally, I went back home. It had been a long and tiring but rewarding day.

51

Wait a minute; no, I guess that was just something falling somewhere. It sounded like a key turning a lock. I thought the jailers were coming in to get me for my final earthly walk.

Now you should be thinking, "How did Saul the hater and murderer of Jesus become Paul, Jesus's apostle?" I might have time to finish my story before they come for me.

The Sunday morning following Jesus's execution, after my normal prayer and meditation session, I bounced downstairs, went into my study, and pulled a couple of servants' cords. I wanted to get the day going and find out what had happened over the Sabbath. I assumed that all of the followers and disciples of Jesus had run or were in hiding. I knew that I would have been if my leader got hung on a cross like a common criminal.

As the servants came into my study, they handed me several messages from different people. I scanned through them looking for the one I would read first. Since there were a few from Nicholas, and because I wanted to hear what had happened to the corpse of Jesus, I opened the first one. It said that a man and several women had taken Jesus from the cross and had taken the body to the man's own tomb. It seems that he had loved Jesus and since Jesus didn't have a tomb, he let them use his. The man's name was Joseph from Arimathaea.

Once they had prepared the body as well as they could, as it was getting close to Sabbath, they rolled a large stone over the entrance. As a group of mourners was leaving, they saw the Roman guards who had been ordered to watch the tomb over the Sabbath go up to the stone and seal it. Before they left, he checked everything to make sure it was exactly like I had ordered.

The next message was from the chief of the Roman guard, Marcus. It said that everything was fine; nothing out of the ordinary had happened.

The next two were both from Marcus and had the same message.

I was feeling good about how I had orchestrated the past few days. I decided I needed to offer a few more sacrifices and give some more money to the temple for a thanksgiving sacrifice.

As I was sitting there basking in my glory, there was a knock at the door. *Who could it be at this early hour?* My servant went to the door. When the servant returned to my study, he handed me a few more messages.

I looked through them and saw a message from one of Gamaliel's servants. I opened it at once and started reading: "Saul, since you went home from Golgotha, you probably haven't heard some of the different stories that are circulating around Jerusalem about some things people say they saw as Jesus died. There seem to be quite a few people saying they saw people that they knew were dead walking around the streets of Jerusalem. They are saying that they were raised from the dead somehow by Jesus.

"Another item is that the tapestry that covers the Holy of Holies ripped in half from top to bottom about the time Jesus died. We checked this, and indeed it is torn in half; we are looking for the vandals that did this. We're not sure how it could have been done. Some of the followers of Jesus are saying that it tore because Jesus redeemed everyone when he died and was the sacrifice that God needed to pay for our sins once and for all. Of course, this is nonsense, but we need to figure out how it was done and by whom so we can silence these people."

I looked up and asked God how some people can be so stupid. It looked like we would have to make a few examples of Jesus's followers to get this situation quieted down.

Once again, I heard a knock on my front door. This one sounded more urgent. I heard some loud voices at the door that started coming down the hall toward my study. I stood up, not knowing what to expect. I hoped it wasn't any of Jesus's followers coming to hurt me. I needed to get some guards out there. As they rounded the corner, I could see that it was one of the guards that was supposed to be guarding the tomb and two of my servants trying to stop him from coming into the study without announcing me. The guard was Marcus; he was red faced and out of breath.

"Saul," Marcus huffed, "I have some very unusual news for you." He finally caught his breath, and I asked him to sit down; I told the servant to get him some water.

"I was with the original group that had followed the corpse and the people who had taken Jesus off of the cross," he said. "Once they left, we sealed the tomb and set up the watch. Everything went as it should … until early this morning."

I sat up taller in my chair with the expectation I was about to hear another stupid story that Jesus's followers were telling everyone.

The guard continued: "This morning, right at dawn, two of my fellow guards and I were talking about cooking up some breakfast when all of a sudden we were surrounded by a brilliant bright light. We could barely see what was happening.

"As we stood there, two figures that looked like men or angels, or something, appeared out of the light, and the stone we had sealed on the tomb rolled away. Both of the men or angels or whatever went into the tomb. When they came back out, there were three, and I saw the middle one grow taller and taller and end up being as tall as the heavens while the other two grew taller as well but not as tall as the middle one. We tried to move toward them and stop them, but we were frozen where we were. We couldn't move. I tried to say something to them but couldn't get my mouth to work. After a few moments of this, the beings went away, and then the light slowly turned back to normal."

I looked at the guard for a minute trying to comprehend what he was telling me. Then I screamed at him, "So, you are telling me that someone, or something, has stolen Jesus's body? Are you telling me that they stole the body while you were supposed to be on duty? Do you know what the penalty is for abandoning your post?"

The guard insisted that the story he had told me was the truth and there was still more to it. He said that after everything had gotten back to normal, he and the other guards cautiously went over and looked inside the tomb to see what was in there.

"The body was gone from the tomb," he said, "and I saw the linen wrappings lying there. The face cloth that had been on his head wasn't lying with the linen wrappings, but it had been rolled up and put in a place by itself."

I was dumbfounded. Of all of the ridiculous things I had ever heard, this was the most preposterous. I told the guard to just sit there until I figured out how to deal with this.

I thought about all of the dreadful things that could happen, and this was the worst. If the disciples and followers of Jesus believed that he had risen from the dead like he said he would, I would never be able to shut them up. I looked over at the guard and told him to inform my servant where the other guards on duty were. I wanted them all brought to me immediately. I didn't want them spreading this story to anyone else, which is why I needed to talk to them.

The guard told the servant where they were, and he then assured me that they wouldn't tell anyone because by letting the body escape or dematerialize or get stolen or whatever happened to it, they could be tried and executed. When the servant was leaving to go get the other two guards, I asked him to also bring the commander of the guards with whom I had spoken about Barabbas and his gang. He said he remembered him and would bring him as well.

The guard watched as I stood up and started pacing the floor. After a few rounds, I summoned another servant and told him to get me some bags of coins. I told him to get four bags—three with thirty pieces of silver each and the fourth with sixty.

I didn't have to wait too long for the other two guards to arrive. When they came in, I asked them to tell me their version of what had happened at the tomb, wanting to see if their story would match the first guard's account of events. The story they told was exactly the same. About the time they finished, my servant came in with the commander. The three guards hadn't heard that I had sent for him, and they were extremely frightened when they saw him enter. They thought I was going to turn them in.

After the commander took a seat, I asked the guards to repeat their story. However, they wouldn't say anything until I promised them that I wouldn't press charges. I only wanted the commander to hear their story so he and I could figure out what to do about it. The leader of the three guards again told their story, leaving nothing out. The commander listened to the whole story intently, and then he looked at me and asked, "What do you want to do about this? I know that you had the tomb guarded so that this wouldn't happen, but I don't think anyone on earth could have kept Jesus in that tomb when angels or whatever came and got him."

"If that is how that happened," I said, "we still need to tell everyone that it didn't happen. The only reason I could think that anything like this could occur is that Satan, Jesus's partner, wants to continue deceiving the people and try to have everyone think that he was resurrected like he said he would be.

"Here is my proposition. I am willing to make it worth your while to keep this quiet. I do not want these men tried because I do not want them to tell their story where anyone else can hear it. Commander, I am asking you to transfer these guards out of Israel. I will give you sixty pieces of silver for this and your silence, and I will give the three guards thirty pieces of silver apiece for their taking this transfer and their silence."

The commander looked at me and then looked at the guards, and they all nodded their heads. I motioned to the servant, and he handed out the purses to each man. After they had their purses, I had the servant escort them out of the house.

I then told the servant to go find Nicholas and bring him to the house. I needed him and the other men who had helped watch Jesus and his followers to start looking for Jesus's corpse and the followers of Jesus. I wanted to see if I could coerce another one like I had Judas to help me find out what had happened.

52

Once I finished dressing, I went to find Gamaliel. I needed to tell him what had happened and what I had done about it

As I walked to the temple, I felt the old rage rising up inside of me. I couldn't believe after my great triumph that Satan had pulled this trick. I looked up and told God that it was putting me at wit's end to understand what he was doing. Didn't he want to show Israel that I was his chosen one?

By the time I met up with Gamaliel, I had calmed down. The walk had done me good. As I approached him, I could see that he was in close discussions with several other Sanhedrin members. They saw me and went silent just looking at me. I then asked Gamaliel if I could speak to him in private. He reluctantly agreed. I knew then that he had already heard some of the rumors circulating around about the different events that may (or may not) have occurred.

As we walked, I told Gamaliel about the events as I had heard them and what I had done in response. He told me that the Sanhedrin had heard about the tapestry and people being seen risen from the dead, but they hadn't heard the story about Jesus being carried off by angels or whatever they were. After thinking for a minute or so about what I had told him, he agreed with what I had done in regard to the guards and commander. He didn't want them in court telling that crazy story, either.

After we walked in silence a few minutes, I looked over at him and said, "Gamaliel, I have called the men back in that were watching Jesus and his followers. I want to get them out looking for the corpse or to see if I can use one of Jesus's followers or disciples like we did Judas. We need to find out what happened. We need to be very careful because if the people hear we are looking for Jesus, it will make them think he has risen." Gamaliel agreed.

The plan we decided on was to keep the in-the-know group as small as possible. The men watching Jesus and his followers had proven themselves loyal, and there were enough of them to listen and see what could be learned. Once we found out what had happened, we could then hunt down and prosecute the perpetrators of this deception.

I returned to the house to see how many of the men the servant had found. Five of them were there, although Nicholas hadn't arrived yet. As I sat down in my study, I motioned for the servant to bring the men in. Once they had seated themselves, I asked if they knew where Nicholas was. After a pause, one of them finally said he had seen him that morning with Stephen and Philip.

"I went up to Nicholas and asked what he had been doing, and he said that he had decided to become a follower of Jesus after all the things that he had seen," the man said.

I was stunned. The final man among my seven best students had become a follower of Jesus. I sat there for a moment seething in anger. I wanted to kill every single one of his followers. They were making a mockery of me. I told the men to go out and listen to what the people were saying about Jesus and his followers and report back to me daily.

Once they had left, I wrote a message to Gamaliel asking him to give me the authority and some guards to arrest any of the disciples or followers that my men found, to see if they knew anything. When I received a return note from Gamaliel, I opened it and read that he wanted the men to just continue listening and watching the followers. He told me to send him a message or come see him if we learned anything, and then we would decide what was the best thing to do. He wrote, "Now that we have the head of the snake cut off, the rest will slowly die off as well."

I thought about that for a few minutes and hoped he was right. This Jesus and his disciples were always surprising me.

53

For the next month and a half, my men sent messages about what they were hearing. They would hear that someone would say they had seen Jesus, but then he would disappear. Others said they would be in a room with the doors locked, fearing they were going to be thrown in jail and killed for being Jesus's followers, and Jesus would suddenly appear, say a few things, and then disappear.

There were a few stories about Jesus asking his followers to touch him to prove he wasn't a ghost. Another account said that he made lunch and ate with them. The men couldn't substantiate any of the stories and couldn't get close to anyone who had any idea where they had hidden the corpse.

It seemed Gamaliel was right. This group was losing steam and had dispersed.

I also was hearing that the Sanhedrin and chief priests believed I had overstepped my authority in having Jesus killed. They thought it would have been just as effective if we had merely beaten him and let him go like Pilate had wanted to do. There also was talk that a few of them were thinking of indicting me because of the illegal things I had perpetrated to get Jesus to trial and executed, although Gamaliel put a stop to that.

As the messages got fewer in number and shorter in content, I told the men to just send me one when there was anything worthwhile to report.

I started looking forward to our next feast, called Pentecost, coming up in about a week. I had always enjoyed it. I did get one message about that time that said that one of the men had overheard a group of people talking about a speech that Jesus had given, and then he ascended to heaven. They didn't hear it well enough to report all of the facts, but it still sounded odd.

54

A few days before Pentecost, I sent a message to the men that they could stop watching and listening for any of Jesus's followers. I told them to return to Jerusalem and resume their studies.

Because we had hushed up the theft of Jesus's body and he hadn't shown up or been heard of for quite a while, his group had completely been stopped. I also decided to give extra money and additional sacrifices to show the people and God how thankful I was that God had finally used me to stop the blasphemous Jesus and his followers. After I had put the money in the temple treasury and sacrificed several bulls, I started walking back out of the temple and out onto Solomon's Porch, when I heard the sound of a violent, strong wind blowing. But I didn't see or feel anything.

Upon hearing this sound, I joined a crowd that had congregated in bewilderment. We all were hearing men speaking in several languages; each person was hearing his or her own language being spoken. Utterly amazed, I heard one of the men ask, "Aren't all these who are speaking Galileans? Then how is it that each of us hears them in our native language? Parthians, Medes, and Elamites; residents of Mesopotamia, Judea and Cappadocia, Pontus and Asia, Phrygia and Pamphylia, Egypt and the parts of

Libya near Cyrene; visitors from Rome (both Jews and converts to Judaism); Cretans and Arabs; we hear them declaring the wonders of God in our own tongues!"

Amazed and perplexed, they asked one another, "What does this mean?"

I also heard some people making fun of the speakers, saying, "They have had too much wine."

Then I saw Peter stand up, raise his hands for silence, and in a loud voice he said to all of us:

"Fellow Jews and all of you who live in Jerusalem, let me explain this to you; listen carefully to what I say. These people are not drunk, as you suppose. It's only nine in the morning! No, this is what was spoken by the prophet Joel:

"'In the last days, God says, I will pour out my Spirit on all people. Your sons and daughters will prophesy, your young men will see visions, your old men will dream dreams. Even on my servants, both men and women, I will pour out my Spirit in those days, and they will prophesy. I will show wonders in the heavens above and signs on the earth below, blood and fire and billows of smoke. The sun will be turned to darkness and the moon to blood before the coming of the great and glorious day of the Lord. And everyone who calls on the name of the Lord will be saved.'

"Fellow Israelites, listen to this: Jesus of Nazareth was a man accredited by God to you by miracles, wonders, and signs, which God did among you through him, as you yourselves know. This man was handed over to you by God's deliberate plan and foreknowledge; and you, with the help of wicked men, put him to death by nailing him to the cross. But God raised him from the dead, freeing him from the agony of death, because it was impossible for death to keep its hold on him.

"I can tell you confidently that the patriarch David died and was buried, and his tomb is here to this day. But he was a prophet and knew that God had promised him an oath that he would place one of his descendants on his throne. Seeing what was to come, he spoke of the resurrection of the Messiah, that he was not abandoned to the realm of the dead, nor did his body see decay. God has raised this Jesus to life, and we are all witnesses of it. Exalted to the right hand of God, he has received from the Father the promised Holy Spirit and has poured out what you now see and hear. For David did not ascend to heaven, and yet he said,

"'The Lord said to my Lord: "Sit at my right hand until I make your enemies a footstool for your feet."' Therefore let all Israel be assured of this: God has made this Jesus, whom you crucified, both Lord and Messiah."

When the people heard this, they were cut to the heart. I heard them ask Peter and the other apostles, "Brothers, what shall we do?"

Peter replied, "Repent and be baptized, every one of you, in the name of Jesus Christ for the forgiveness of your sins, and you will receive the gift of the Holy Spirit. The promise is for you and your children and for all who are far off, for all whom the Lord our God will call."

I stood there dumbfounded by what I had just seen and heard. Peter and the other apostles continued to warn the people with many other words, and Peter pleaded with them, "Save yourselves from this corrupt generation."

As I watched, it looked like about three thousand accepted his message and were baptized.

I walked back to the house in a daze. What had I just seen? The men who were speaking were the disciples who had followed Jesus around the past few years. I couldn't figure out why they were so bold. Hadn't we just killed Jesus? Now they were telling the people that God had wanted that to happen so he could raise him from the dead. Weren't they afraid by uttering the same blasphemy that they would be accused, judged, and stoned?

Once I got home and sat down in my study, I tried to figure out the best way to attack these men. They seem to have been infested with the same spirit as Jesus.

55

The following morning, I knocked on the door at Gamaliel's house. I had prayed all night for God to show me his will. I wasn't completely sure, but I did have a plan I wanted to discuss with Gamaliel.

Once the servant answered the door, he told me that his master was still asleep but he would wake Gamaliel if I thought it absolutely necessary. I hadn't noticed the time, but since I was already there, I told the servant to wake him. After a while, Gamaliel came in and greeted me, looking very sleepy, and it occurred to me I should have waited longer to discuss plans for Jesus's followers.

"Gamaliel," I said, "I was in the temple yesterday when one of Jesus's followers named Peter stood up and told the crowd that Jesus was raised by God from the dead and that God had used us to crucify him. I think the term Peter used for us was 'wicked men.'"

"I didn't think the crowd was listening to the message, but, as he continued, more than three thousand who had listened got baptized and became followers of Jesus even though he is dead. It is ridiculous. How can the people be so stupid to be a disciple of a dead man?"

Gamaliel looked at me and said, "I remember you wanted to go and kill the closest of the followers and a few others like Lazarus who are living proof of one of Jesus's miracles, but I decided that Jesus's group, after he died, would stop testifying that he came back to life. It looks like I have made a mistake."

He and I sat there for several minutes thinking about what our next move would be. Gamaliel looked at me and said, "Saul, I assume you have thought about this and have something in mind. I don't need to tell you that some of the Sanhedrin members such as Nicodemus think we shouldn't have had Jesus killed. I don't think the Sanhedrin will let you start arresting these men."

I responded: "I know there is opposition to any persecution of these men, but Jesus's disciples were boldly preaching that we, the chief priests and teachers of the law, were to blame for an innocent man's death and that Jesus was God's Son. As much as it galls me to suggest this plan, Gamaliel, I believe we should let these men preach to the people again, and then we can have them brought to the Sanhedrin to tell them to quit preaching and stop telling the people a lie. We all know that Jesus was crucified. That would let them know that we want it stopped. It will show the people that we know they are lying about Jesus being alive."

Gamaliel thought a few minutes and said, "Saul, I think that will work. We aren't arresting them, but we are allowing them to tell the Sanhedrin what they are doing, and then we can tell them to stop without anyone being arrested or punished. Hopefully, that will stop this."

As I walked home, I recalled the faces and the message of Jesus's disciples and was concerned that our plan wouldn't even slow them down. Having three thousand converts in one day and witnessing them all be baptized was incredible. Even when John was performing baptisms in the Jordan, there were never anywhere near that many baptized in a day.

A few days later, I was in the temple when I heard a disturbance and walked over to see what had happened. On my way to where the crowd had gathered, I asked one of the male bystanders what had happened. He told me that Peter and John, two of the followers of Jesus, had just healed a lame man in the name of Jesus.

Once I heard that, I went into the crowd to see what would happen next. As I was getting close, Peter raised his hands for silence and said:

"Fellow Israelites, why does this surprise you? Why do you stare at us as if by our own power or godliness we had made this man walk? The God of Abraham, Isaac, and Jacob, the God of our fathers, has glorified his servant Jesus. You handed him over to be killed, and you disowned him before Pilate, though he had decided to let him go. You disowned the Holy and Righteous One and asked that a murderer, Barabbas, be released to you. You killed the Author of Life, but God raised him from the dead. We are witnesses of this. By faith in the name of Jesus, this man whom you see and know was made strong. It is Jesus's name and the faith that comes through him that has completely healed him, as you can all see."

After hearing this, I motioned to the guards, and they took Peter and John so we could tell them to quit preaching about Jesus. When we got to the Sanhedrin, we saw that it had already adjourned for the day, so we decided to put Peter and John in jail for the night.

The next day, the rulers, the elders, and the teachers of the law and I met at the Sanhedrin. Annas, Caiaphas, John, Alexander, and others of the high priest's family were there as well. We had Peter and John brought before us and began to question them: "By what power or what name did you do this?"

As Peter stood to address us, it seemed that a spirit was coming over him. His face appeared different, almost holy, and it seemed he was very content, maybe joyous. He said to us: "Rulers and elders of the people! If we are being called to account for an act of kindness shown to a man who was lame and are being asked how he was healed, then know this, you and all the people of Israel: It is by the name of Jesus Christ of Nazareth, whom you crucified but whom God raised from the dead, that this man stands before you healed. Jesus is 'the stone you builders rejected, which has become the cornerstone.' Salvation is found in no one else, for there is no other name under heaven given to mankind by which we must be saved."

When we saw the courage of Peter and John and realized that they were unschooled, ordinary men, we were astonished, and we took note that these men had been with Jesus. But since the man they had healed was standing there with them, there was nothing we could say. We ordered them to withdraw from the Sanhedrin. Then we conferred together.

"What are we going to do with these men?" we Sanhedrin leaders asked ourselves. "Everyone living in Jerusalem knows that they have performed a notable sign, and we cannot deny it. But to stop this thing from spreading any further among the people, we must warn them to speak no longer to anyone in this name."

Then we called them in again and commanded them not to speak or teach at all in the name of Jesus. But Peter replied, "Which is right in God's eyes: to listen to you, or to him? You be the judges! As for us, we cannot help speaking about what we have seen and heard."

We threatened them some more and then let them go. We couldn't punish them because all the people were praising God for what had happened. The man who was miraculously healed was more than forty years old.

After the Sanhedrin had adjourned for the day, I found Gamaliel and walked with him. I told him that we were acting on the plan but I was getting concerned that these followers seemed more bold and determined than Jesus had been. I told him that one of the men who was watching them had said that the numbers of converts had expanded to more than five thousand. Gamaliel told me to stay focused. As he was leaving, he turned to me and said, "Saul, if they continue, we will need to punish the next offense. I think a good beating would get their attention. I don't think we're ready for a martyr."

56

I told the men who were watching Jesus's apostles to make sure and report anything to me that was unusual. For a few days, I didn't get much in the way of reports, but all of a sudden, I started receiving many reports that the apostles were preaching again that Jesus was risen and was God's Son, and they were blaming us for having him crucified. On top of this, they told of large numbers of miracles the apostles were performing; all types of diseases and illnesses were being healed.

After I relayed this to the members of the Sanhedrin, they told me to have them all jailed. We were jealous that these people were following the apostles. I motioned to the guards, and we went out and found the apostles and put them in jail. We planned to have them back in the Sanhedrin the following morning.

When we had assembled the next morning, the high priest called for the guard to bring the prisoners to us. The guard returned in a few minutes and told us the prisoners had somehow escaped even though all of the locks and bars were still in place. Just as we were about to question the guard, a man came in and said that the men we had arrested were at the temple preaching to the people about Jesus. We sent the guards to get them.

We brought the apostles in to be questioned by the high priest.

"We gave you strict orders not to teach in this name," Caiaphas said. "Yet you have filled Jerusalem with your teaching and are determined to make us guilty of this man's blood."

Peter, on behalf of the other apostles, replied: "We must obey God rather than men! The God of our ancestors raised Jesus from the dead, whom you killed by hanging him on a cross. God exalted him to his own right hand as Prince and Savior that he might bring Israel to repentance and forgive their sins. We are witnesses of these things, and so is the Holy Spirit, whom God has given to those who obey him."

When we heard this, we were furious and wanted to put them to death. But Gamaliel, who was honored by all the people, stood up and ordered the men be moved outside of our meeting room and into another room where they would be watched by guards. Then he addressed the Sanhedrin: "Men of Israel, consider carefully what you intend to do to these men. Some time ago Theudas appeared, claiming to be the Messiah, and about four hundred men rallied to him. He was killed, all his followers were dispersed, and it all came to nothing. After him, Judas the Galilean appeared in the days of the census and led a band of people in revolt. He, too, was killed, and all his followers were scattered. Therefore, in the present case I advise you: Leave these men alone! Let them go! For if their purpose or activity is of human origin, it will fail. But if it is from God, you will not be able to stop these men; you will only find yourselves fighting against God."

His speech persuaded us. They called the apostles in and had them flogged. Then they ordered them not to speak in the name of Jesus and let them go.

Even though we had flogged them and told them to quit teaching, my men reported that they never stopped teaching and proclaiming the good news that Jesus is the Messiah.

57

Only about a week after we had flogged the apostles, one of my men reported that Jesus's closest followers were now calling themselves "the Church."

"The Church" certainly sounded better than "the rabble." It seems the apostles had recruited seven men to help serve the Church. The seven men just happened to be my old students who I had made to watch Jesus before they all started following him.

I can't tell you how angry that made me. We had killed one man, and that man wouldn't stay dead.

A week later, I was at the temple when I heard some men arguing. It was a few rabbis arguing with Stephen, one of my old students, which of course made him a tough argument opponent. In one way, I was proud of him; in another, I wanted to shut him up. As I walked up to these men, I decided to get involved. I would take on the task of showing that Stephen and his Messiah were a fake. As I argued with him, I was astounded. The pupil had become the teacher. Every comment I had he countered with expertise I couldn't fathom. He obviously had that satanic spirit in him just like Jesus had.

Consumed with jealousy and hate, I told some of the students that were there to say, "We have heard Stephen speak blasphemous words against Moses and against God." So these students and I stirred up the people, the elders, and the teachers of the law. We seized Stephen and brought him before the Sanhedrin.

We produced false witnesses who testified, "This fellow never stops speaking against this holy place and against the law. For we have heard him say that this Jesus of Nazareth will destroy this place and change the customs Moses handed down to us."

All who were sitting in the Sanhedrin looked intently at Stephen, and they saw that his face was completely placid like the face of an angel.

Then the high priest asked Stephen, "Are these charges true?"

"Brothers and fathers, listen to me!" Stephen said.

"Our ancestors had the tabernacle of the covenant law with them in the wilderness. It had been made as God directed Moses, according to the pattern he had seen. After receiving the tabernacle, our ancestors under Joshua brought it with them when they took the land from the nations God drove out before them. It remained in the land until the time of David, who enjoyed God's favor and asked that he might provide a dwelling place for the God of Jacob. But it was Solomon who built a house for him.

"However, the Most High does not live in houses made by human hands. As the prophet says: 'Heaven is my throne, and the earth is my footstool. What kind of house will you build for me? Says the Lord. Or where will my resting place be? Has not my hand made all these things?'

"You stiff-necked people! Your hearts and ears are still un-circumcised. You are just like your ancestors: You always resist the Holy Spirit! Was there ever a prophet your ancestors did not persecute? They even killed those who predicted the coming of the Righteous One. And now you have betrayed and murdered him, you who have received the law that was given through angels but have not obeyed it."

When we had heard this, we were furious and gnashed our teeth. But Stephen, while he was standing there, looked up at heaven and said, "Look, I see heaven open and the Son of Man standing at the right hand of God."

At this, we all covered our ears and started yelling at the top of our lungs. We rushed at him and then dragged him out of the city and began to stone him. I went around picking up and holding the coats of the men while they stoned him.

While I watched them stone him, Stephen prayed, "Lord Jesus, receive my spirit." Then as he fell on his knees, he cried out, "Lord, do not hold this sin against them." After that, he fell over, dead.

58

A s we were walking back into the city, Gamaliel and a few other leaders told me to meet with them the following morning. They told me to get my strategy in place to capture these blasphemous rebels and either have them disavow the name of Jesus as God's Son or suffer the fate of Stephen.

Finally, I had what I had always wanted. The authority to obliterate the name of Jesus and all of his followers.

The next morning, I went to Gamaliel's house, where he had told us to meet, and I was led into the study. I had assumed there would be several priests and leaders there, but the only man in the room was Gamaliel. Once I was seated, he asked me how I was going to stop this.

"Saul, I know you have been in favor of a more aggressive solution to this problem, and, looking back, you were right," Gamaliel said." The Sanhedrin has told me to allow you free rein with any resources you need to shut these people up. They are making a mockery of us and our laws."

I told him I would take the men I had left, five solid men, and give them several guards each to go from house to house if necessary to arrest any of the people who believed Jesus was alive and God's Son. I told him that we would throw these people in jail and the Sanhedrin could do as they pleased with them.

"I think it would be good to give them a chance to publicly recant their oath when they openly proclaimed Jesus as their Messiah and Savior," I said. "If they don't, then I would stone them all."

"Do it," Gamaliel said.

I quickly left and went home, where I told the servant to get the men together immediately.

Once the men arrived, I explained the plan and told them that we would all go to the Sanhedrin, where the guards we needed were standing ready.

That was the very day my men and I started a great persecution against the Church in Jerusalem. We arrested and jailed Jesus's followers all day around the temple and other parts of Jerusalem. These followers weren't too worried about being arrested; they all kept saying that they thought it was great to be arrested for believing in Jesus.

After the Sanhedrin started having Christians stoned, they scattered everywhere. We began going house to house and dragging out entire families to take to jail. We would arrest them all morning then have them in front of the Sanhedrin and out of the city for a mass stoning in the afternoon. After a week or two of this, it was getting harder to find any of Jesus's followers anywhere in Jerusalem. We had gone to every house where we had heard there was a member of this Church and taken them to be tried. It looked like we had run this rabble out of Jerusalem.

Because we had accomplished our mission of "clearing" Jerusalem, I thought my men and I should travel to different towns and capture the ones who had escaped. I had received a report that these followers were running all over Israel converting more people to believe in Jesus. In scattering the followers, we had inadvertently helped the Church to grow.

I went to the high priest and asked him for letters to the synagogues in Damascus so that if I found any there who belonged to the Church, no matter if they were men or women, I could bring them back as prisoners to Jerusalem. The high priest asked me why Damascus. I told him that several of my old students had escaped to there and I wanted to get all of them for having converted and then embarrassing us.

The following morning, my guards and I mounted our horses and started out to Damascus with my letters and two wagons with a cage built on top of each for transporting prisoners. We expected it would take three days to get to Damascus.

Getting closer and closer, I started feeling excited, knowing we were doing God's will and stopping this "church" established around this blasphemous, fake Jesus. What a pity that he had been used by Satan. I wondered how someone so sincere who obviously thought he was doing God's will could get so confused.

As we approached Damascus, there suddenly was a brilliant light that engulfed me, and I fell off of my horse. When I tried to get up, I couldn't see anything and fell back and lay still. I could hear my men asking me what had happened, but then those voices faded out, and I heard a voice I had heard before ask, "Saul, Saul, why do you persecute me?"

"Who are you, Lord?" I asked.

"I am Jesus, whom you are persecuting," the voice replied. "Now get up and go into the city, and you will be told what you must do."

I continued laying there trying to comprehend what I had just heard. As I looked into the light, I saw Jesus of Nazareth in his glory. My heart seemed to turn in my chest when I realized that I had been the mistaken one and that it was *my* knowledge and drive and everything about me that was satanic, not Jesus. I couldn't shake the dread I was feeling that I had persecuted the Holy One, God's Son, the Messiah, and now my Savior. I couldn't believe my sacred pride had taken me to where I was killing God's people in his name. I was so ashamed.

The men traveling with me stood there speechless; they had heard the voice but could not see anyone. I got up from the ground, but I couldn't see anything; I was blind.

As I groped for my horse, one of the guards helped me onto it, and they led me into Damascus. For three days, I was blind, and I did not eat or drink anything. I prayed and begged for forgiveness and for someone to come and baptize me into my Savior's Church. I needed to be saved, and I needed to try to undo all of the wrongs I had done.

As I prayed, a man named Ananias came to me and told me that he was from the Lord. He laid his hands on me and said, "Brother Saul, the Lord Jesus, who appeared to you on the road as you were coming here, has sent me so that you may see again and be filled with the Holy Spirit." Immediately, something like scales fell from my eyes, and I could see again. I got up and was baptized, and after taking some food, I regained my strength.

59

Well, that was definitely a key turning in the lock to my cell door. It looks like I finished my story just in time. I hope you can see how gravely mistaken I have been most of my life. I let pride become my god. Mine might be the ultimate cautionary tale for all mankind.

As they take me to where they execute Roman citizens, I am reminded of how my father made sure I was a Roman citizen for several reasons. However, I assume this wasn't one of those reasons. On the other hand, it is probably better than being fed to the lions or getting crucified like what the Romans are doing to other believers.

While we ride the cart out of Rome to the section of the Ostian Road where they carry out the punishment, I want to finish telling you my story and give you some thoughts to help you on your journey. My son in the faith, Timothy, is here with me and will finish writing down my words as we travel, as I am prepared for my execution.

As I look back to the time I was trying to kill Jesus and his followers, I realize that pride, which had caused the archangel to sin and become Satan, is the most treacherous sin of all. It uses the good in us and then distorts it into the nastiest of all sins. I see that having pride in something like your family can be a good thing, but we need to be careful that we don't cross the line of making that too important to us.

I wrote a letter to the church here at Rome. Here is a small part of it:

"But God shows his anger from heaven against all sinful, wicked people who suppress the truth by their wickedness. They know the truth about God because He has made it obvious to them. For ever since the world was created, people have seen the earth and sky. Through everything God made, they can clearly see his invisible qualities, his eternal power, and his divine nature. So they have no excuse for not knowing God.

"Yes, they knew God, but they wouldn't worship him as God or even give him thanks. And they began to think up foolish ideas of what God was like. As a result, their minds became dark and confused. Claiming to be wise, they instead became utter fools. And instead of worshiping the glorious, ever-living God, they worshiped idols made to look like mere people and birds and animals and reptiles.

"So God abandoned them to do whatever shameful things their hearts desired. As a result, they did vile and degrading things with each other's bodies. They traded the truth about God for a lie. So they worshiped and served the things God created instead of the Creator himself, who is worthy of eternal praise. Amen. That is why God abandoned them to their shameful desires. Even the women turned against the natural way to have sex and instead indulged in sex with each other. And the men, instead of having normal sexual relations with women, burned with lust for one other. Men did shameful things with other men, and, as a result of this sin, they suffered within themselves the penalty they deserved.

"Since they thought it foolish to acknowledge God, he abandoned them to their foolish thinking and let them do things that should never be done. Their lives became full of every kind of wickedness, sin, greed, hate, envy, murder, quarreling, deception, malicious behavior, and gossip. They are backstabbers, haters of God, insolent, proud, and boastful. They invent new ways of sinning, and they disobey their parents. They refuse to understand, break their promises, are heartless, and have no mercy. They know God's justice requires that those who do these things deserve to die, yet they do them anyway. Worse yet, they encourage others to do them, too."

You can see how Satan can twist and turn you without you even realizing you are sinning. He surely did it to me.

He lets you take one of your great traits and turns it against you. Satan let me take the pride of knowledge and family and then distort it into a sacred pride that let me justify killing people who didn't believe in God exactly the way I did. Additionally, my pride also made me convince others to do the same.

There were several times in my life, as I looked back telling you this story, that I should have known I was going down the wrong path, but my jealousy and pride got the best of me. Satan had a strong hold of me starting at an early age.

One of the times that I should have known was when Jesus and I met at the temple while we were young. His message and presence caused unbelievable jealousy in me. While everyone else was listening to our Savior discuss his Word, a few others and I were trying to show everyone how smart *we* were.

Another time was when I heard the message from John that I needed to repent, but I thought that was for other "normal" people that weren't called by God. My pride in my knowledge of God's Word and my legalistic ways prevented me from seeing myself as a sinner. The signs that I was on the wrong path did get stronger, but by then, I was helplessly a victim of my sin. Instead of listening to my students and watching them embrace the Lord, I was angry that they had abandoned me.

Looking back, God even gave me a great excuse to not continue trying to kill his Son. He let Barabbas be captured and gave me a choice of whom to redeem. I chose wrong again.

I now understand that by my jealousy and pride, I caused others with the same issue to follow my lead. I am devastated that I had something to do with perverting their pride and making it like mine. I suppose Satan used me to inflame their pride into a killing rage as well.

When my pride became a sacred pride, and let this be a warning to you, it turned me into a sinner. I actually was responsible for killing God and a multitude of his Church. But now, through my newfound faith in Jesus Christ, I have been redeemed! I had been a part of God's plan after all!

The Romans are now taking me from the cart with several other prisoners and standing us all in a line. Timothy is off to the side watching me and taking it all in so he can finish writing my story. I am in the middle of the group of seven prisoners, and while the other prisoners are begging for their lives or being dragged to the block, I, Paul, am more than ever resigned to my fate and actually feel a sense of peace as I continue to move up in line.

Now it is finally my turn. I kneel in front of the block, and before I lay my head down to expose my neck, I say, "Father, forgive them, for they know not what they do." And then I whisper, "Into your loving arms I commit my spirit!"

It is finished.

ABOUT THE AUTHOR

Jack Minter has been interested in and a student of the Bible and the history surrounding the Bible for as long as he can remember. A graduate of Abilene Christian University in 1981, he currently lives in Dallas with his wife. He has three grown children who also live in the Dallas area.

Jack's career has been in the commercial real estate business, and he has been an investments sales broker and manager for over twenty-five years. A certified public accountant and a licensed real estate broker, Jack has distinguished himself in many parts of the real estate industry. He has developed a website to market commercial real estate named MYRETA. Jack has also authored another book titled *Careers: Be Savvy, Be True to Yourself and Don't Be a Moron.*

Made in the USA
Middletown, DE
17 March 2019